"Tee Morris walks you through the basics of twitter with hum   you
want to be a member of the Twitterverse. *All A Twitter* is one   rom
Twitter whether you are using it for a nonprofit, business, P.   )cial
community. Tee knows this community. He doesn't present the information as an expert speaking about a community of which they don't belong; he is a Twitter member."

—Shireen Mitchell
Social Media Strategist and Technology Advocate Washington D.C.
Social Media Women of Color (http://socialmediawoc.com)

All A Twitter is the essential reading for anyone wishing to employ Twitter as part of a Social Media initiative. Tee Morris guides you through the basics with Twitter with his recurring refrain: *Once you've built a network, you participate in the conversation.* Tee Morris knows his stuff—it shines through in *All A Twitter*.

—Coach Ian Scott
Professional Speaker, Author & Life Coach
Lancashire, UK
www.coachianscott.com

Tee Morris is the proverbial Swiss Army Knife of social networking. He is razor sharp in his analysis of what twitter isn't and shown it for what it is: simple.

—Catherine White
Professional Speaker & Jazz Singer
Syndey, Australia
www.catherinewhite.com.au

Tee Morris has created a perfect guide for both personal and business users into Twitter's world of microblogging and network building. Even advanced users will find new and useful nuggets in this entertaining read and will catch themselves nodding along while thinking, "Yes, exactly!" "Welcome to the local coffee house that never closes." Yes, exactly!

—Craig Fisher
Co-Founder of A-List Solutions, Recruiter, Career Branding & Social Media Authority
Dallas, Texas
www.fishdogs.com

"*All a Twitter* is the go-to guide for anyone interested in the fast changing world of Twitter and Social Media. Weather you are looking at Twitter to promote your business or just to play and talk to friends *All a Twitter* is a must have resource."

—Megan Enloe
Professional Community and New Media Liaison Orange County, California
http://meganenloe.com

"The 'A Little Birdie Told Me...' tips throughout the book were especially helpful and featured clever advice or fun hints and information on tools to make the most of Twitter. This book is a useful reference guide I can turn to again and again as I build my Twitter community and become more familiar with all of Twitter's many benefits."

—Becky Moore, APR

All a Twitter: A Personal and Professional Guide to Social Networking with Twitter

Tee Morris

800 East 96th Street,
Indianapolis, Indiana 46240 USA

All a Twitter: A Personal and Professional Guide to Social Networking with Twitter

Copyright © 2010 by Pearson Education, Inc.

All rights reserved. No part of this book shall be reproduced, stored in a retrieval system, or transmitted by any means, electronic, mechanical, photo-copying, recording, or otherwise, without written permission from the pub-lisher. No patent liability is assumed with respect to the use of the information contained herein. Although every precaution has been taken in the preparation of this book, the publisher and author assume no responsibil-ity for errors or omissions. Nor is any liability assumed for damages resulting from the use of the information contained herein.

ISBN-13: 978-0-7897-4228-5
ISBN-10: 0-7897-428-4

Library of Congress Cataloging-in-Publication Data:

Morris, Tee.
  All a twitter : a personal and professional guide to social networking with Twitter / Tee Morris.
    p. cm.
  Includes index.
  ISBN-13: 978-0-7897-4228-5
  ISBN-10: 0-7897-4228-4
  1. Twitter. 2. Online social networks. 3. Blogs. I. Title.
  HM742.M675 2010
  302.30285—dc22

2009021096

Printed in the United States of America

First Printing: July 2009

Trademarks

Warning and Disclaimer

Bulk Sales

Que Publishing offers excellent discounts on this book when ordered in quan-tity for bulk purchases or special sales. For more information, please contact

> **U.S. Corporate and Government Sales**
> **1-800-382-3419**
> corpsales@pearsontechgroup.com

For sales outside of the U.S., please contact

> **International Sales**
> international@pearson.com

Associate Publisher
Greg Wiegand

Acquisitions Editor
Michelle Newcomb

Development Editor
Kevin Howard

Managing Editor
Patrick Kanouse

Project Editor
Mandie Frank

Copy Editor
Apostrophe Editing Services

Indexer
Ken Johnson

Proofreader
Williams Woods Publishing Services

Technical Editor
Philippa Ballantine

Publishing Coordinator
Cindy Teeters

Designer
Anne Jones

Compositor
Bronkella Publishing LLC

Contents at a Glance

	Introduction	1
1	What Is Twitter (and What It Is Not)	7
2	Setting Up Twitter	25
3	Talking on Twitter	49
4	Working Beyond the Website	63
5	Terrific Twitter Tools	93
6	Tracking Twitter	111
7	Twitter to Go	127
8	iPhone, Therefore iTweet	149
9	The Trouble with Twitter	169
10	Getting Personal	185
11	Taking Care of Business	201
12	ANTI-Social Media: The Dark Side of Twitter	227
13	Why I Am on Twitter	253
A	Tools for Twitter	259
B	Twitterspeak	265
	Index	269

Table of Contents

Introduction 1

Welcome to All a Twitter 1

This Book Is Written by a User 1

This Book Focuses on Building a Community 2

This Book Is for Users of All Levels 2

This Book Follows a Logical Progression with Twitter 3

This Book Is Written in More Than 140 Characters 4

What to Expect from Here 4

Going Beyond the Book 5

We'll Always Have Twitter... 5

Imagine That! Studios 6

Bird House Rules 6

1 What Is Twitter (and What It Is Not) 7

A Brief History of Social Media 9

First Forums, Which Begat Blogging 9

Proceeding with Podcasting 11

The Rise of Social Networking 13

What Is Twitter? 16

Twitter's Role in Social Media 16

What It Does 17

What You Should Do to Make It Work 17

What Twitter Isn't 19

Twitter Is Not a Chat Application 19

Twitter Is Not a Blog 20

Twitter Is Not Like Facebook, MySpace, or
Other Social Networks 22

2 Setting Up Twitter 25

Registering on Twitter 25

Setting Up your Twitter Profile 29

What's in a Name? (Quite a Bit, Actually!) 30

The Importance of a Good Avatar 32

Protecting Updates: The Good and the Bad 41

Making Twitter Your Own 42

Changing Your Password 43

Receiving Tweets on Your Mobile Phone 43

Staying in the Loop 44

Giving Your Twitter Home a Redesign 44

Building the Network 46

Following Someone at Random on Twitter 47

Following Someone You Know on Twitter 47

Following Someone That's Following You on Twitter ... 48

3   Talking on Twitter **49**

Writing a "Tweet" 49

Editing Your Tweet 50

Posting Your Tweet 51

Following Followers 53

Following @Mentions 54

Replying to a Tweet 55

Replying to a Direct Message 57

Your Twitter Archives 59

Your Favorites 59

4   Working Beyond the Website **63**

Twitterific 64

Installation and Setup of Twitterific 64

What I Like About Twitterific 67

What I Don't Like About Twitterific 67

DestroyTwitter 69

Installation and Setup of DestroyTwitter 70

What I Like About DestroyTwitter 74

What I Don't Like About DestroyTwitter 74

Twhirl 76

Installation and Setup of Twhirl 77

What I Like About Twhirl 80

What I Don't Like About Twhirl 82

TweetDeck 83

Installation and Initial Setup of TweetDeck 84

Setting Up Groups in TweetDeck 85

What I Like About TweetDeck 88

What I Don't Like About TweetDeck 90

5 Terrific Twitter Tools **93**

Mr. Tweet 93

Starting with Mr. Tweet 94

Shorten URL Services 98

Is.gd 98

SnipURL 100

Twitter Tools for WordPress 102

Installing Twitter Tools 102

Configuring Twitter Tools 103

TwitPic 107

Uploading Pictures on TwitPic 108

Using TwitPic with Twitter Clients 108

6 Tracking Twitter **111**

Twitter Search 112

Bit.ly 115

TweetStats 116

Twitalyzer 120

Hashtags 123

7 Twitter to Go **127**

Twitter for the BlackBerry 128

Blackbird 129

Twibble 130

Tiny Twitter 132

TwitterBerry 136

Twitter for the G1 140

Twidroid 141

TwitterRide 145

8   iPhone, Therefore iTweet **149**

Tweetie 151

What I Like About Tweetie 153

What I Don't Like About Tweetie 154

Twittelator 155

What I Like About Twittelator 160

What I Don't Like About Twittelator 161

TwitterFon 163

What I Like About TwitterFon 165

What I Don't Like About TwitterFon 166

9   The Trouble with Twitter **169**

The Double-Edged Sword of Success 170

The Fail Whale 170

Lost Tweets 172

Followers Dropped Without Consent or Knowledge .. 173

Twitter Abuse 174

When Twitter Is Used as an IM 174

When Things Get Too Personal 176

Hi…My Name is Tee and I Have a Twitter Addiction .. 177

Remedying the Noise in Your Signal 179

The Outsider's Perspective 182

10   Getting Personal **185**

Staying in Touch with Friends 185

Call Me When You Get Home 186

What Are You Doing This Weekend? 187

Sharing with the Community 188

TwitFic 188

Tweet-by-Tweet Commentary and TwitReviews
(No Spoilers Please!) 191

Trademark Tweets 194

Solidarity (J.C. Hutchins) 195

11:11—Make a Wish (Heather Welliver) 196

News from New Zealand (Philippa Ballantine) 196

Follow Friday (All of Twitter) 197

Rick Rolling 198

Becoming Part of the Community 199

11 Taking Care of Business **201**

Identity Crisis 202

Using Twitter to Market Your Business 205

Build Your Network 205

Observe 208

Engage 209

Twitter for Nonprofits 212

Using Twitter to Market Yourself 217

Using Twitter Tools to Promote Your Blog or Podcast ..217

Using Twitter to Market a Product or Event 218

Becoming Part of the Community: Revisited 225

12 ANTI-Social Media: The Dark Side of Twitter **227**

To Follow, or Not to Follow? 227

Why Would I Want to Block Someone? 230

Guaranteed Drops and Blocks 232

Spammers and Twitterbots 232

Tweeting in L33t 232

Automated Direct Messaging 233

Incomplete Profiles 234

Few To No Updates 234

Selling Your Twitter Self 234

Automated Twittering 236

A Broad Definition of Participation 237

Retweeting Isn't Participation 237

Tweeting Famous Quotes Isn't Participation 238

Circulating Links (Especially if the Only One You're Circulating Is Your Own) Isn't Participation 239

Concerning Weblebrities, Celebrities, and Gurus 240

Weblebrities: Life on the A-Listserve 241

Celebrities: A Peek at the Life of a Hollywood Star 243

Fast Times at Twitter High: How CNN, Ashton Kutcher, and Oprah Completely Missed the Point 246

Gurus: Snake Oil Salesmen 2.0 248

13   Why I Am on Twitter **253**

Professional and Personal Connections 253

A Deeper Appreciation for the Real World 254

I Believe in Twitter 256

A   Tools for Twitter **259**

Adding Media to Your Tweets 260

Adding Organization to Your Tweets 261

Tracking Your Tweets 261

Network Maintenance 262

Simply for the Fun of It 263

B   Twitterspeak **265**

Twitterspeak That's Just Plain Fun... 266

Twitterspeak That's Just Plain Annoying... 266

Twitterspeak That I Hope Never to Hear Uttered Again... 267

Index **269**

Foreword

Postcards from Five Years Forward

Living in the future must be frustrating, especially when you are forced to live among those in the present. You see what's already here, clear and obvious, and everyone else stares at you like you're crazy. I get glimpses of the future and formulate plans from them. Tee Morris *lives* there.

This is the man who wrote a book about podcasting before most anyone actually even knew there was such a word. You see, that's another super power that Tee Morris has: Not only does he see the future, he comes back and trains us on it for when we're ready. And now, it's time again.

Twitter. Let's be honest: It just *sounds* stupid. The first impression most people have when they hear about Twitter is that it's a website for a bunch of people to talk about what they ate, their cats, and other information we could all live without. Some folks stick around for about 30 days, and then they *get it*. Heck, they don't get it; they switch from being haters to viral evangelists. It happens. Over, and over, and over.

I believe Twitter is as important as the telephone, email, and several other (sometimes used for) business tools that were first misunderstood, then maligned, then adopted as a very important part of business. It might not be *this* Twitter, but I feel Twitter is the testing grounds that will bring us the next communications tool we consider imperative.

Tee Morris is thoughtful, thorough, insightful, and lacks pretension. He is, thusly, the best kind of teacher. Learning from Tee Morris means learning at a pace that matches your comfort level. But then, you've already bought this book (or borrowed it, or stolen it). You'll see this soon.

My personal hope, the hope of someone writing the Foreword to someone else's book, is that you don't shelve this when you're done. Give it to someone else. Spread what Tee Morris shares with you to those who need it. If you need another copy, buy it later. But share this one with someone who needs to be on top of the biggest communications shift in recent years.

And if you glimpse Tee Morris at an event, shake the man's hand before he escapes back to the future. Ask him for a postcard. It seems only fair.

Chris Brogan

President, New Marketing Labs

chrisbrogan.com

About the Author

Tee Morris has been an active member of the Twitter community since 2007 and part of the Web 2.0 movement even longer. He established himself as a pioneer of podcasting by being the first to podcast a novel in its entirety. His fantasy epic, *MOREVI,* went on to be a finalist for the 2006 Parsec Award for Best Podcast Novel. That production also led to the founding of Podiobooks.com, the writing of *Podcasting for Dummies* (with Chuck Tomasi and Evo Terra), and the writing of *Expert Podcasting Practices for Dummies* (with Evo Terra and Ryan Williams). Tee continues to explore the application of blogging, podcasting, and Twitter at Imagine That! Studios (online at imaginethatstudios.com), and has spoken across the country and around the world on Social Media for Book Expo America, NOAA, Te Papa Tongarewa: The Museum of New Zealand, and LIANZA.

Photo by Kreg Steppe (@steppek) of spyndle.com

Along with being a Social Media specialist, Tee is a columnist and critic for AppleiPhoneApps.com and writes Science Fiction and Fantasy found in print at Dragon Moon Press and in audio at TeeMorris.com. His fantasy-detective novel, *The Case of The Singing Sword: A Billibub Baddings Mystery*, received an Honorable Mention for *ForeWord* Magazine's 2004 Book of the Year award, Finalist for the 2005 Independent Publisher's Best Science Fiction and Fantasy, and Best Audio Drama: Long Form at the 2008 Parsec Awards.

Find out more about Tee Morris at imaginethatstudios.com and teemorris.com on the Internet.

Dedication

The book is dedicated to The Daily Show's Jon Stewart (and others not so sure about Twitter). This book holds the answers to your questions.

Acknowledgments

What. A. Ride.

I've been on Twitter since the Spring of 2007, and in the two years I have been amassing updates, connecting with friends old and new, and reaching out to listeners of my podcasts. I have watched Twitter go through its growing pains, reinvent itself (several times), and evolve through its members of various cultures, agendas, and backgrounds. I've seen a lot of things in that time that have been inspirational and endured a few things that have made me screw my eyes shut and ask, "Why am I here again?" Throughout it all, there has been a constant that reminds me of why this social networking site won me over after one week of using it. This is the constant that you discover as you reach out to your community and connect with them. No matter how long or how often you update, this constant continues to tap you on the shoulder and grant you a daily dose of "A-ha."

The constant: No matter how much you think you know, you will always learn something new.

No truer words have been spoken concerning Twitter.

I started where you are; and had I known I was going to be here, working on what is your one-stop-shop on all things Twitter, I would have tagged my first tweet in 2007 as a Favorite so that I could consider how far I've come. I remember my friend and Social Media cohort Evo Terra (@evo_terra) walked me through that first day, immediately hooking me up with my first desktop client. I remember Chris Brogan (@chrisbrogan) steering me to some terrific Twitter resources, two of them being his blog and the desktop client, TweetDeck. And in this book, I have Social Media specialist Megan Enole (@MeganEnole) sending me resources that only made this book better; Gennifer Snowfield (@acclimedia) and Craig Fisher (@fishdogs) offering their professional perspectives on Twitter and Social Media; and Annette Holland (@daNanner), Heather Welliver (@HeatherWelliver), and Ben Wassink (@bwassink) helping me with Twitter on platforms alien to me. These Twitter users are part of two amazing communities where I have the pleasure of being an active participant. Without these communities, *All a Twitter* would have been incomplete. My communities pointed me in the right direction through exchanged links, quick replies, and unending support. I was kept in the loop on the many innovations and recent updates for Twitter and appearances of Twitter in the news. If I had a question, all I had to do was ask. Twitter, appearances of the Fail Whale aside, never let me down.

I thought I knew a lot about Twitter. Seven new applications, several account registrations, and many, many tweets later, I discovered that I still share a lot in common with that (devilishly handsome) guy who started tweeting two years ago. We are both discovering new and exciting possibilities, and we are learning so much from those in our networks that continue to grow, mature, and evolve.

To you, the people, the corporations, and organizations represented on the cover and to all of you across my Twitter networks, thank you for being there. This book is your testament to the power of a community, to the potential of an idea, and to just how incredibly cool this social network is. At Twitter's core is you, as it is with this book. Thank you for being there and giving this book the personal touch that we practice every day, 140-characters at a time.

We Want to Hear from You!

As the reader of this book, *you* are our most important critic and commentator. We value your opinion and want to know what we're doing right, what we could do better, what areas you'd like to see us publish in, and any other words of wisdom you're willing to pass our way.

As an associate publisher for Que Publishing, I welcome your comments. You can email or write me directly to let me know what you did or didn't like about this book—as well as what we can do to make our books better.

Please note that I cannot help you with technical problems related to the topic of this book. We do have a User Services group, however, where I will forward specific technical questions related to the book.

When you write, please be sure to include this book's title and author as well as your name, email address, and phone number. I will carefully review your comments and share them with the author and editors who worked on the book.

Email: feedback@quepublishing.com

Mail: Greg Wiegand
         Associate Publisher
         Que Publishing
         800 East 96th Street
         Indianapolis, IN 46240 USA

Reader Services

Visit our website and register this book at www.informit.com/title/9780789742285 for convenient access to any updates, downloads, or errata that might be available for this book.

Introduction

Welcome to All a Twitter

Hey there! Thanks for picking up my book on Twitter. With all the hype you have heard and with all the books out there, both in bookstores and online, you have stopped to consider my book over the others grouped alongside it. Because you're giving me a moment here, allow me to give you a quick rundown on what makes this book different and why this book is for you:

- This book is written by a user.
- This book focuses on building a community.
- This book is for users of all levels.
- This book follows a logical progression with Twitter.
- This book is written in more than 140 characters.

That is just a sampling of what you can expect with *All a Twitter*. If you're still reading, this means you saw something in that glimpse. So let's expand on these points, and I'll give you a more detailed look at what you can learn and who you can get to know in this book.

This Book Is Written by a User

Many of the books produced on Twitter are written by folks who specialize in making money off the Internet, by marketing experts determined to show you how to make a fast buck by "monetizing" your Twitter experience. These authors also have tens of *thousands* of people following them.

What makes me different from them is two-fold:

- I have only a few thousand follows (between two accounts), far from the colossal numbers of these other authors.
- My updates number well into the tens of thousands.

What does that mean? That means I have worked to build a community, to make connections with people around the world. My feed ranges from updates to link exchanges to direct conversations. I don't focus on regurgitating the thoughts of others, and I stand against the automation of anything in Twitter. I use Twitter to promote on occasion, but I focus more on communication, on sharing a thought with a group of people and seeing how it might make a difference.

I am not an Internet Marketer, a Social Media guru, or an SEO expert. I am a user. Have been for years. And I connect with my community.

This Book Focuses on Building a Community

If you are new to Social Media, that is what makes this innovative approach to the Internet so very cool: the community you nurture around your likes and interest. *All a Twitter* not only gives you a primer on exactly what Social Media is, this book also gives you a variety of tips on how to engage that community. Whether this engagement is for personal or professional purposes is completely up to you. Yes, there is some talk about how you can use Twitter as a means for promotion and public relations, but that isn't going to happen without a community to connect with. This is the intent of *All a Twitter*: helping you create a community and connect with its members.

This Book Is for Users of All Levels

Twitter continues to change, continues to grow; and whether you are completely new to Twitter or have been "tweeting" for a time, you can learn something from this book. *All a Twitter* begins with the simplest of steps and then ends with true stories, real time applications, and philosophies behind Twitter where anyone at any level can pick up a new idea or refreshing perspective on this social networking initiative.

During the writing of this book, I introduced absolute beginners to the language and the culture of Twitter and also introduced someone who had been tweeting since 2006 to a new application that has become a favorite on his iPhone. In this book, whether it is Twitter from beginning to end or looking for a new service or client to help make Twitter more efficient, there is something for you in *All a Twitter*.

This Book Follows a Logical Progression with Twitter

All a Twitter is designed to guide you through the process of setting up a profile to sending out your first tweet. With each chapter, you discover there is more to Twitter than just messages composed of 140 letters, numbers, and symbols.

- **What is Social Media?**—Chapter 1, "What Is Twitter (and What It Is Not)," is the primer for Social Media, also known as Web 2.0. It is a simple summary of different initiatives that work together to compose this *next step* of the Internet. This chapter gives you a background that helps you understand more about building communities and using the Internet to connect.

- **Working with Twitter**—Chapter 2, "Setting Up Twitter," Chapter 3, "Talking on Twitter," and Chapter 4, "Working Beyond the Website," can get you on Twitter and get you talking, or *tweeting*. Covered in this section of the book is the process of completing a profile and why that is so important. You also get an idea of how to tweet, or how to communicate effectively under the limitations of 140-characters. Finally, you are introduced to several applications available online that work independent of Twitter.com and automatically deliver you the most recent tweets from members of your network.

- **Expanding Twitter's capabilities**—Chapter 5, "Terrific Twitter Tools," and Chapter 6, "Tracking Twitter," offer a sampling of the many websites that offer services for Twitter users. Some of these services help you build your network and suggest people of various backgrounds that might be good matches for you and your network. A few of these services help you track your impression on Followers reference links you can circulate among your network, and tell you what you can do to improve your application of Twitter. Here, you improve your performance and unlock more potential from your community.

- **Taking Twitter on the road**—For owners of smartphones like the Blackberry, the Android G1, and the iPhone, Twitter is readily available through a variety of applications that offer many of the options found in the desktop clients featured in Chapter 4. Chapter 7, "Twitter to Go," and Chapter 8, "iPhone, Therefore iTweet," go into the pros, cons, benefits, and challenges of making your experience on Twitter a portable one.

- **So I have the basics, now what?** Chapter 9, "The Trouble with Twitter," Chapter 10, "Getting Personal," Chapter 11, "Taking Care of Business," and Chapter 12, "ANTI-Social Media," are different from the rest of the book because I go into the Zen of Twitter. Exactly what is that? I cover the times when Twitter falls short of its expectations. I explore where people are comfortable and lines drawn concerning what they do (and don't) share on Twitter. For the professional wanting to use Twitter for business, I cover success stories of corporations and nonprofits all successfully implementing social networking. Chapter 12 is a tough, hard look at people tending to dismiss their communities and implement Twitter more for self-satisfying purposes.

Whether you hop from chapter to chapter or if you read from beginning to end, *All a Twitter* is an all-purpose book that takes you through the process of getting onto Twitter, getting the most out of Twitter, and most important, how to approach Twitter and the network.

This Book Is Written in More Than 140 Characters

Yes, I've heard that joke. I've heard it often. If you are at a book signing and are thinking of asking me, "So is this book written in more than 140 characters?", please reconsider. The fact that this book is as thick as it is and has thirteen chapters should be the hint that there is a bit more to Twitter than you might expect.

And just tonight, as I was writing this, someone cracked that joke. So, please, don't make that joke. It's just not working for me anymore. Thank you in advance.

What to Expect from Here

As you can guess, there is a lot to this book, just as there is a lot to Twitter. Throughout the book you can also find a few gems to help you in your own experience on Twitter.

A Little Birdie Told Me...

You have a lot to learn about Twitter, and now and then I throw into the mix some tidbits and tips that are helpful to make Twitter that much better. These bits of advice range from interesting background trivia to truly cool options you might miss in desktop clients and applications if you blink at the wrong time. These are the Easter Eggs of Twitter that you need to know.

Fail Whale Says...

The Fail Whale (discussed in more detail in Chapter 9) is synonymous with Twitter. You will hear users talk about Fail Whale sightings, and on your own third sighting, you will just sigh and shake your head. With *All a Twitter*, the Fail Whale sightings are the cautionary tales and networking faux pas you will want to take to heart and make sure you avoid before jumping in feet first with Twitter. Tempting as it is to start tweeting and figure things out as you go, the Fail Whale Says... segments are your safety nets to make sure Prime Directives are intact, protocols are protected, and etiquette is upheld.

Going Beyond the Book

Keeping books on anything involving your computer up-to-date is a Herculean task. Just in the time of writing *All a Twitter*, a lot of things have happened and there are promises of new changes and developments coming. So how do I compete with the books that are about to hit the shelves or compare to the books currently on the shelves?

I don't stop. The book may conclude at the closing of its cover, but the lessons, the assistance, and the insight continues online through a variety of outlets.

We'll Always Have Twitter...

Of course you can find me on Twitter, and of course, I would be more than happy to answer your questions concerning Twitter. If you find yourself stuck or curious as to what to try next, go on and drop me a tweet at @ITStudios (for Imagine That! Studios) and I will reply when the tweet arrives. Feel free to also share with me feedback, both the congratulatory and the critical, on this book. Twitter is all about reaching out and connecting, and I'm out there if you have a question for me.

Imagine That! Studios

Imagine That! Studios (http://imaginethatstudios.com) is my online home where I discuss creative solutions in the workplace. Through Social Media, audio and video production, and clever thinking, solutions are discovered. That's my mantra there, and on occasion, my blogposts will turn to Twitter. If you are looking for additional resources or commentary concerning the subjects addressed in this book, you might find what you need at Imagine That! Studios. Come on by, take a look around, and enjoy what my blog has to offer.

Bird House Rules

Finally, there is the official podcast of *All a Twitter*, found at http://allatwitterbook.com. This ten minute podcast picks up where the book leaves off, keeping the content you'll find here current and up-to-date. It is a handy audio addendum to this book and your chance to put a voice with the tweets. The podcast will also feature interviews, clips from Twitter seminars I host, and topics generated by you, the new and experienced Twitter user. Have a listen through the podcast's blog or subscribe through iTunes or your podcatching client of choice.

Now that you know what to expect, it's time to take a closer look at the most popular social networking initiative. It's all about the community, the connections, and the camaraderie. It's all about the people you reach out to and get to know. It's all about speaking your mind in 140-characters or less.

Forge ahead, and soon you'll find out what has the world *All a Twitter*.

1

What Is Twitter (and What It Is Not)

Limitations are in place to help us. "No more than ten items" in the grocery store's Express Lane. "Maximum Capacity" of a meeting suite, so you have room to network and socialize. "You're carry-on bag must fit in this space…" for the airlines, to accommodate everyone's luggage. (If only more people paid attention to that one!) These limitations, although we might not always like them or abide by them, are there to help us out. I still remember how angry I was as a kid when a ride operator would break out the "great stick of judgment" (You know the one—most of it painted red while the rest was topped off in green?) after spending hours in line. Of course, when I would feel myself achieve zero gravity on the roller coaster's first drop, I understood the reasoning behind this limitation: For my own good.

Limitations tend to become unpopular when it comes to communications, though. When you have something to say, it can be a little aggravating to be told you have only so many words and so much time to get your point across.

So when people ask me about Twitter and say, "I only have 140 *characters* to make a point? Doesn't really give me a lot to do or say, now does it?" Let me give a few examples of what you can say with 140 characters…or less:

> *We have nothing to fear but fear itself.* (41 characters)

> *Imagination is more important than knowledge.* (46 characters)

> *Remember no one can make you feel inferior without your consent.* (65 characters)

> *People with clenched fists can not shake hands.* (48 characters)

And finally there is this:

> *Twitter is changing the way we talk to one another and the way businesses relate with clients, all within 140 characters or less.* (130 characters)

FIGURE 1.1

Twitter takes the world's thoughts and whittles them down to quick, 140-character-sized blog posts.

Welcome to Twitter, the fastest growing Social Media initiative since Facebook and MySpace. In 2006, the "microblogging" website went online and between 2007 and 2008 its popularity exploded, along with other websites and online developers creating a variety of services (good and bad) for this unassuming yet innovative communications tool.

Still, Twitter is far from mainstream, and a lot of people have questions about it. A *lot* of questions, it seems. The ones I hear the most often are

- Is Twitter like an Instant Messenger?
- Why would I care what you are doing?
- Isn't following someone kind of stalker-ish?
- What exactly is Social Media?

How about along with these four, we take a moment to understand exactly what Social Media (a term often associated with Twitter) means.

With the background and foundation in place, we can then continue working on what Twitter is and how you can get the most out of it.

A Brief History of Social Media

To understand and appreciate what Twitter is, we have to step back to the early nineties when the Internet was very one-sided. When I say "one-sided" I mean that information was presented in a stationary, static format. Hypertext Markup Language (HTML) after all was just that: plain old text. Granted, you could format it, add pictures to it, and hop from page to page and place to place; but that was about it as far as interactivity went.

To become an active participant in a webpage's message and chiming in on a topic discussed, some websites might offer a contact page where your comment, feedback, or criticism might reach someone and maybe, if timed right, would be implemented into a website's development when the content would be updated, provided it *was* updated. (Updating content in the early days of the Internet was a labor-intensive process.) For many years, the Internet worked this way and was regarded as a wonderful resource of information, the digital library that never closed and where an answer remained a mouse-click away. Still, the information remained static and constant, rarely offering visitors the chance to participate.

First Forums, Which Begat Blogging

With the development of more powerful scripting languages such as ASP and PHP, web developers began experimenting with more interactive websites where visitors could interact with one another and even leave comments pertaining to topics started by the host website's subscribers. These dynamic websites were called *Forums* and are still in use, most popular at fan sites for various entertainment outlets, and also on tech-related websites such as Apple, Adobe, and Digital Juice.

Visitors to a forum subscribe, giving themselves a username, profile, and any other personal details they wish to share into the site's database. Members then surf from topic to topic, finding one that piques interest and, if interested, chime in with a reply to the main topic. These discussions are also called *threads*, and the replies within replies can sometimes become threads of their own. If you are a member of a forum, you can start up a topic, and within the replies you can offer other resources for forum members to review. Members subscribed to a specific thread can receive email notification that someone had replied to them, and then forum members can click on the link provided, log into the forum, and reply.

FIGURE 1.2

To encourage interaction and build communities, forums (like this one found at DigitalJuice.com) would be offered at host sites.

Around 2000, *RSS* was beginning to take shape as a language that people would need to know and adopt. RSS (which stood for *Really Simple Syndication)* would serve as the foundation for "weblogs" or what people would commonly refer to as *blogs*. The difference between a blog and a forum is that a blog is usually written by one writer, or a core group of writers. Subscribers can interact with the authors via comments, but they themselves cannot start up a new topic as they can in a forum. Another major difference between blogs and forums is that unlike a forum where you have to go to the host website to interact, the blog's content on subscribing comes to you through an RSS reader like *Bloglines (http://blog-lines.com)* or *Google Reader (http://google.com/reader/)*. Now, topic by topic, subscribers and guests to the blog are given the chance to interact with its author, commenting with resources to share. Blog comments are an open invitation to both guests and subscribers, unless moderated by the blog's hosts. Another unique capability with RSS is that now the content can be *syndicated* through other blogs, increasing traffic for both the host blog and the blog referencing the original content. Now topics previously confined to a host forum could be distributed through a vast network commonly known as the *blogosphere*.

FIGURE 1.3

Weblogs, or more commonly referred to as blogs, changed the way Internet users interacted with websites.

This ability to interact with the creative minds behind the website's content and with other subscribers served as the foundations of *Web 2.0*, a more interactive form of the Internet where instead of information presented in a static manner, the content of a website was always changing, evolving through involvement of online communities built around the subject matter discussed.

Proceeding with Podcasting

In 2004, blogging ascended to a higher form of communication, thanks to one of RSS's pioneers and a former MTV VeeJay. Dave Winer and Adam Curry developed a new RSS tag—the <enclosure> tag—to allow RSS to syndicate more than just text and images. By adding an enclosure tag, the RSS feed was now able to distribute more robust media such as audio and video files.

And thus, *podcasting* came to be.

FIGURE 1.4

Podcasts (such as George Hrab's Geologic Podcast, pictured here) encouraged interaction between the shows and their listeners.

Podcasting (a subject I am intimate with as I first embraced it as a listener in October 2004, became a producer in January 2005, and released my first book on the topic in October of that same year) can be best described as "DVR meets the Internet". When you find a podcast that you like, be it audio, video, or enhanced, you subscribe to it. Much like a DVR, after you subscribe to a podcast, episodes are stored on your computer or portable media player until you view or listen to it. Unlike audio or video streaming that happens at a prescheduled time and is not stored locally on your computer, or *webisodes* (exclusive video content usually found only on the Internet) that are made available for a period of time and then taken offline, podcast media gives full control to subscribers. In other words, the media is yours to keep. Whether it is the video antics of *Tiki Bar TV* (http://tikibartv.com), the variety of free novels from Podiobooks.com (http://podiobooks.com), the mysterious and macabre from *Stranger Things* (http://strangerthings.tv) or the *SpyCast*™ presented by the International Spy Museum (http://spymuseum.org), podcasting offers a variety of programming for all.

Podcasting also encourages listeners to give feedback and, in many cases with services such as TalkShoe (a website that offers podcasters the ability to host a "call-in style" show, and found at http://talkshoe.com), become active participants in the podcast. Much like with blogging and forums, listeners and viewers are encouraged to write in or leave voice mail for the show, and in many cases their feedback and participation can drive the show. Regardless of whether producers are podcasting audio or video, many of the creative minds behind productions in the podosphere will attest that listener feedback, view mail, and the community feel of the podcast audience is what keeps everyone going to the next episode, and the next season.

The Rise of Social Networking

With the popularity of content being delivered to computers via RSS, another form of communication evolved. It, too, tapped into the capabilities of RSS and offered subscribers a way of networking with others, similar to actual networking opportunities you would have at a conference, an expo, or a formal business function. As this networking was happening online, though, there was an informal air about these "meet and greets," and although some participants regarded the ability to build these networks to build either on their business (regardless of the company's size), others regarded these online connections as a way to chat informally with people that "grokked" (for the fans of Robert A. Heinlein) with them. This became known as *social networking,* where how you connected and communicated with others in your virtual community was left up to you. Were you establishing a profile to make professional contacts, or were you there to enjoy the company? Social networking enables you to do both.

Social networking can include millions of members on one site with smaller, more concentrated communities forming within the host site. There are many social networking sites online, all of them offering various services and benefits to its members. A few of note include the following:

- Friendster (http://friendster.com)—Founded in 2002, this site holds the title as the first "socal networking site" as it offered to its members the ability to share photos and videos with those in its network, and helped complete strangers connect and nurture new friendships. The current membership of Friendster is more than 90 million registered users worldwide and is considered by many as the cornerstone of online social networking.

FIGURE 1.5

Social networking sites, such as Facebook, brought people of like interests, passions, and past experiences together for resource exchanges, reminiscing, and quick contact.

- **LinkedIn (http://linkedin.com)**—Following in the footsteps of Friendster is the less-fun, professionally polished networking site, LinkedIn. Although this site does not offer the same social aspects of Friendster, LinkedIn does offer a more corporate approach to social networking. On LinkedIn, it's less about "Did you see what happened on *Lost* the other night?" and more about "How do I get a job working at the studio behind *Lost*?". Here, users post their job experience, ask for references and endorsements, and interact with others in their profession through online discussion groups. When it comes to job hunting, particularly in tech-related fields, LinkedIn is an essential tool.

- **Flickr (http://flickr.com)**—Sometimes, Flickr is disregarded as a social networking site, but look at what it offers: a place for photographers both amateur and professional to display their work, the ability to comment on photographs, the option to build networks with individuals and groups, and RSS feeds granting others to subscribe to photography feeds. That is Flickr, and that is social networking. It is still one of the most popular websites online, hosting billions (that's *billions* with a "b") of photographs for your viewing pleasure.

- **Digg (http://digg.com)**—Often imitated, never duplicated, Digg grants its members the ability to share online content with one another. This is why for many blogposts, podcasts, YouTube videos, and other online media outlets, you can see "Digg This" at the end of the posting. Registered users vote whether they like it , and the more an item is "digged" (or would that be "dug"...I'll have to look into that...), the longer it is featured in certain sections of Digg's host site. Digg also encourages community by offering discussion platforms on why something is Digg-worthy.

- **MySpace (http://myspace.com) and Facebook (http://facebook.com)**—We now come to the 800-pound gorillas of social networking sites, MySpace and Facebook. The argument that both websites are different and should never be compared to one another still rages online, but I will argue that these two sites—both giving Friendster credit for their genesis—are kissing cousins of each other. MySpace and Facebook both offer users interfaces to build networks with old friends, make comments to one another, post photos, find others of like-interests, and even create discussion groups. Both are leaders in social networking sites. As reported by TechCrunch.com at the beginning of 2009 (http://bit.ly/MSvFB), MySpace supports an active membership of more than 125 million, while Facebook continues to grow in popularity with more than 200 million users. Both also have a love-hate relationship with their users. Both sites enable users to connect with old friends from college and high school. MySpace can slow down browser performance, though, with its liberal surrendering of design attributes and audio-video embedding options for users. Facebook's Achilles' Heel is the time needed to weed though the invitations to causes, games, "pokes" and various groups.

There are many others out there—Technorati, last.fm, uStream.tv, GoodReads, FriendFeed, Ning—and more social networking sites than I can sign up, set up a profile, and manage on a daily basis. It seems that since 2005, social networking has exploded on the Internet, changing the way information is exchanged; relationships are cultivated between corporations and clientele. With all this user-generated content available in text, audio, and video, *Social Media* has now become the new buzz word of business. Encompassing blogging, podcasting, and social networking, Social Media is the new wave of communications that both the casual user and the professional can find something they like. Social Media can be geared strictly as free entertainment for some, whereas others use it as a powerful marking tool reaching 100 percent of their target audience.

It was in the middle of this wave that on March 2006, Twitter came to be. Since 2007 and 2008, this unassuming communications tool experienced a membership boom of over 750 percent. People can now let their respective network know where they are, what they are doing in that moment, and even provide exact coordinates as to where they are doing what they are tweeting.

And now, the guy who wrote the definitive book on podcasting is writing the definitive book on Twitter. So you have questions? No problem. I have the answers. And yes, although I could answer your questions in 140 characters or less, I'm going to allow myself a bit more latitude.

What Is Twitter?

This has become, in the past year, a Question of the Ages: *What is Twitter?* The two comments I get the most often are "I tried Twitter and I don't get it." Or "Why do I care what I'm doing?" At first glance, it does seem a little confusing as to exactly what it is, and with the many third-party applications that are out there, it can easily be confusing as to exactly what it is and what it can do.

Twitter's Role in Social Media

Twitter, at first glance, might have seemed late to the party (going live in 2006); but with the earlier cited 750 percent growth, Twitter has become one of the essential tools in enjoying Social Media and implementing Social Media in business. The reason for its growth can be its initial ease of use.

Hold on a moment? If Twitter is so *easy to use*, why dedicate a *whole book* to it?

There is a lot to Twitter after you get past the initial introduction, but even when you get past the learning curve, you can see where Twitter fits in the grand scheme of Social Media. Twitter serves as a true union of Social Media with social networking. How it bridges the gap between networking and Media is in how you build your network and then chat about what you are doing. From a marketing perspective, this is a dialogue you have opened with an audience that—on making the decision to follow you—wants to know exactly what you are up to. This is a great time to share with your network your brand or product because your audience has made the decision to find out more—truly, a marriage of networking with creating media. Although it probably did not start out to do so, Twitter has raised the bar for other social networks online, and throughout the book we explore some of the applications of Twitter, both for a personal and professional use, and work on ways of building your online community, maximizing your time and investment online.

What It Does

If you have never blogged or even considered hosting a blog, Twitter is a bit like the test drive of blogging. Whether you call it *nanoblogging* or *microblogging*, Twitter is like a blog or your "status" in Facebook. You type your thoughts or actions at that particular moment into the offered interface at http://twitter.com. Unlike the Facebook status or a blog, though, you have a number starting at 140 and counting down with each character you type. This includes spaces. This limitation makes you pair down your posting (or a *tweet*) to the bare essentials. *"What are you doing?"* No room for (a lot of) pontification. You tweet and you are done. When you send out a tweet, those in your network (your *Followers,* which are listed by their avatars in a grid on the main page of your Twitter account) all see your tweet. That is how Twitter works. It's your quick response to the world outside.

What You Should Do to Make It Work

Right now, when you log into the website, Twitter directs you to a static web page displaying the tweets of your followers. You also have options to access the replies to your followers. You can also access from here *Direct Messages* that are tweets sent to you and only you, *Favorites* that are tweets that you just want to hang on to because they were that cool, and finally the *Everyone* option that enables you to take a look at all the tweets happening on the Twitter network.

Safe to say, that is a LOT of tweets.

Many people work with Twitter this way, refreshing their browser window when they feel the need to check Replies or if they want to keep track of those in their Twitter feed. Is this an efficient way to monitor Twitter? Not really. Part of the appeal of Twitter is catching people in the moment, of sharing an experience with other followers (or your community that sports a variety of colorful names like *Twitterverse* and *Twittersphere*), but a manual refresh is just one more thing you need to do to make Twitter go.

FIGURE 1.6
The popularity of Twitter has now encouraged developers to create better and badder third-party applications (like DestroyTwitter, featured here) to enhance your Twitter experience.

This is why incorporating a third-party application with Twitter is a real benefit. Instead of having to refresh and refresh your browser window, a third-party application fetches your tweet for you at intervals you set and will even alert you when people reply or directly message (or *DM*) you. Popular applications that bring the tweets to you include

- Twitterific
- Twhirl
- DestoryTwitter
- TweetDeck

These applications take care of the refreshing for you, can help you organize who is in your network, and in some cases filter out any unwanted noise in your feed. These applications also allow you to tweet, reply, and even *retweet* (repeat another's tweet under your own account without the need to copy and paste) from its interface. This does not mean you never need to visit your homepage on Twitter.com, but with these additions to your Twitter account (many of them offered for free), it does increase the efficiency of your Twitter experience.

What Twitter Isn't

Although I am touting all the wonderful things about Twitter in this introduction, that does not necessarily mean that Twitter is for everyone, or that it made the best first impression. I don't think it is a failure of Twitter, but more of a misconception of exactly what Twitter is. Twitter could be called the Swiss Army Knife of Social Media, considering all of its capabilities and possibilities; but where Twitter fails is when new users believe it is something that it is not.

Twitter Is Not a Chat Application

Some approach (and walk away disappointed) when they discover that Twitter is not an Instant Messenger (or *IM*), or try to use it as an IM application with one wicked delay!

Twitter does seem to resemble a chat application like *Skype, AIM (AOL Instant Messenger), iChat*, or the various chat add-ons you might find in MySpace or Facebook, but it is not meant to be a chat application nor was it ever built to be one. For one thing, while you are replying to another follower's tweet, this is not a private conversation you are having. You are sharing whatever you are discussing with this individual with your entire network. In other words, you are inviting everyone into the conversation. You can use DMs to have truly private conversations, but considering the third-party application (if the person you talk to is using one), there might be a long delay before you get an answer.

The most blaring reason not to use Twitter as an IM is simply because of the 140-character limitation. It's there to keep your communication to the basics, to keep Twitter and the conversation with the communication moving. If you cannot keep a single statement within one (or two) tweets, it's time to move the talk to Skype, iChat, or Facebook Chat.

The 140-character limitation is also Twitter's strongest attribute because it forces you to avoid going on tangents, long-winded replies, and other tendencies that happens with other IM applications. Hours of chatter on true IMs are gone, provided you are using Twitter correctly. Speak your peace in 140 characters or less, return to your previous work, and if you are alerted to a reply or a series of replies, it is your *option* to reply. In an IM Chat, whether it is you and another or a conference call, the conversation is driven by instantaneous, continuous communication. By design, Twitter is not meant to be a timesink. (It can be, but all in how you use it.) Stick to its restrictions, and if you feel the need, invite the follower to join you on a true instant messenger, provided you can afford the time.

FIGURE 1.7

The 140-character limitation built into Twitter keeps you on topic, avoiding tangents you might go on in true chat applications.

Twitter Is Not a Blog

You have seen me refer to Twitter as "the test drive of blogging," but let me be clear on something: Twitter is not a blog. True, Twitter does use RSS feeds to allow your tweets for the day to appear as a blogpost. True, Twitter is asking you what you are doing at that very moment. True, people do follow you much in the same way that people subscribe to your blog.

Twitter can do all this, just like a blog; but trust me—it's not a blog.

Blogs usually follow a theme, or if they are of a more personal nature they can follow a variety of subjects. Twitter covers everything including the kitchen sink and, depending on the person tweeting, things you would never want to do in, on, or anywhere *near* the kitchen sink! Following a single topic in Twitter can be a bit challenging. It's possible, but limited to how much you can say about the topic at hand. Additionally, you can reply and comment on a topic in Twitter; but if a week later, you want to return to that original tweet, you would find that a challenge because you would need to weed through a week's worth of tweets before finding it. Then you would have to bring others in your network up to speed on exactly what you are talking about. With blogs, you have posts catego-rized, organized, and always with a reference point that its comments continuously reference.

FIGURE 1.8

Blogposts like this one, although Twitter can provide links to them, would be impossible (or downright annoying) to display through a series of tweets.

Also, blogposts can be more than 140 characters. Some postings can be 140 words or even, if the blogger is particularly passionate, *1,400* words! There is also the ability to make images, audio, and video part of a blog-post whereas Twitter can only give reference links. Twitter, although it might behave like a blog in many ways, is far from a proper blog. Yes, you can use Twitter as a blog (and many users choose to do so), but in many cases Twitter is serving as the nanoblogging extension to a larger blog elsewhere on the Internet.

Twitter can serve, though, as a nice primer to how it is to blog. If you find Twitter a lot of fun, check out *WordPress* (http://wordpress.org) or a similar blog host. Within minutes, you can have a true weblog up and running, and with a few clicks you can even have a plug-in that automatically tweets for you when your latest blogpost goes live.

Twitter Is Not Like Facebook, MySpace, or Other Social Networks

"I really don't have the time for Twitter."

This is probably the biggest excuse I hear from people on why they are not giving Twitter a shot. Where is this coming from? Could it be the hours of productivity lost when going to MySpace and weeding through the variety of Friend Requests, trying to figure out which profiles are truly legitimate people and how many are simply *spambots* (automated programs that search out accounts, send requests to join your network, and serve as portals to other "unsavory" websites) posing as bikini-clad singles "ready to meet you"; or could this animosity to Twitter come from the several hundred "Li'l Green Patches," "Pillow Fights," and "Mob Wars" you needed to ignore on your Facebook page? Or how about, in the Ning Community you recently joined, there is a discussion you feel compelled to jump into; and an hour later you are still working on that discussion post? Whether it is approving others to join your Flickr feed (and trying to figure out if they are Friends, Friends & Family, or simply a "Contact") or if you find yourself drawn into a thread appearing on a forum you just joined, the perceived investment of time into Twitter seems to be a major barrier for others to clear.

Twitter took that into account, and it keeps it simple. You have only three options when you are notified that someone is following you on Twitter:

- Follow
- Not Follow
- Block

Simple as that.

So now you start following that person. Now what? Do you stare down your Twhirl or Twitterific until your new-found community member responds, or do you take more of a "Jack Torrance" approach to your web page on Twitter.com and continue to refresh...and refresh...and refresh...and as the snow continues to fall outside your office, you refresh your browser...and refresh...and refresh....

All work and no play makes Jack a dull boy.

No, of course you don't do that! (But if you do, I'd avoid the hedge mazes if I were you...) Once you decide to either follow, not follow, or block a follower, you return to work as usual. Twitter, by design, was meant to run in the background. You can cast a cursory glance at what is happening in your feed, and if something catches your interest, you reply. If someone sends you a direct message, maybe your attention is needed provided you want to reply to the DM. Twitter is the definition of low maintenance. Perhaps, if you want to delete previous tweets, or if you are searching out followers in your community, you no longer want to follow or feel uncomfortable in having them follow you, the interface does not lend itself to user-friendly actions. You cannot "Select All" of previous tweets and press a delete key, and you cannot search out Twitter users unless you remember their name or handle. However, building your network takes only a few minutes. How deep your involvement with your Twitter network falls back on you and the parameters you set. Twitter becomes high maintenance only if you allow it to be.

Now that we know enough about Social Media to be dangerous, what Twitter is, and what Twitter isn't, the time has come to stop talking about how cool Twitter is and discover it for yourself. It's time to set up an account and reach out to a group of friends and strangers, all with differences and commonalities. With me and my 35,000 (and some change) previous tweets as your guide, I'll help you get the most out of those 140-characters you're allowed. Welcome to the local coffeehouse that never closes, to the mixer that goes global, to the think tank of minds and hearts from places near and far.

Welcome to Twitter.

2

Setting Up Twitter

The appeal of Twitter, after you grasp the notion of what it is and what it can do, all boils down to ease. When it comes to a user-friendly interface, it rarely comes as easy as Twitter.

Our goals here are to set ourselves up with an account, and what I mean by "setting up an account" is more than just signing up. To attract followers and effectively begin building your network, we will be going deeper into establishing our presence in Twitter. We will complete our online profile, put some serious thought behind our avatar, and then start seeking out people online that we share common interest with. The first few steps are a breeze, but it is in the details where people tend to trip up. No need to worry about those details because when you get the lay of the land, the Twitterverse becomes an easy one to master.

So, fire up your browser of choice and let's begin this adventure into self-expression with 140-characters or less.

Registering on Twitter

Welcome to the first step in building your network. As you see in Figure 2.1, the developers at Twitter want to help you through this process, too. Along with this book, you can watch online, through Twitter.com's welcome page, a two-and-a-half-minute video from "Common Craft" that explains how Twitter works. If video isn't your thing, you also have the What?, Why?, and How? buttons that take you to Twitter Support, offering everything you want or need to know to start.

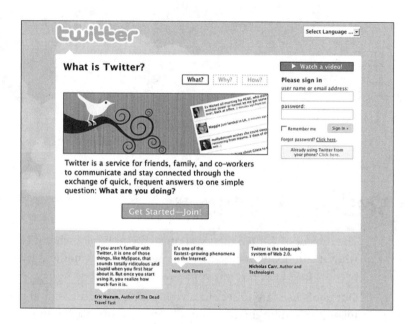

FIGURE 2.1

Twitter greets users old and new with a simple, easy-to-follow user interface.

Whether it is with me or with the website, we're all here to get you tweeting.

First, let's register.

1. Go to http://twitter.com on your Internet browser.

2. Just underneath the boldface phrase "What are you doing?" is a button reading "Get Started—Join!" Single-click that button.

3. In the field marked full name, type in your full name or your business' name, or both.

    Honesty is the best policy when building your profile, so don't be shy or elusive here. A real name or a company name here can better help you in establishing an identity on Twitter. Also, you can change this to fit your mood or intent at any time under Settings, which we discuss later in this chapter.

4. Set up a User Name for yourself, no longer than 15 characters (Twitter's built-in limit). This can be a nickname, clever moniker, or wordplay you create, or simply you or your organization's name or acronym.

A Little Birdie Told Me...

Keep in mind when creating usernames that others might be typing in your username when "tweeting" you. You can use underscores in lieu of spaces, but keep your monikers simple. Avoid using numbers in your usernames as these IDs immediately grab Twitter's security attention. Many spammers use auto-generated names like Darrin123 and Jessie654, for example. Also, for some third-party applications, the usernames are case-sensitive. Be aware of that, as well.

5. Create your password.

   Along with letting you know if a full name is "too big" or a username is available, Twitter also tells you if a password is *strong* (meaning it will be difficult to crack) or *weak* (meaning "Yeah, I can hack that...."). Strong passwords usually have uppercase letters in the middle of them and a number instead of a letter in some instances. When you come up with a password, make it something easy to remember but not easy for others to figure out.

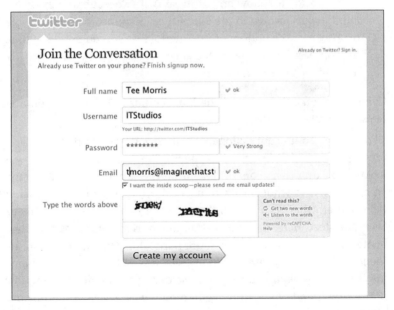

FIGURE 2.2
When creating your Twitter account, you start with the basics: who you are, where Twitter can contact you, and what your password will be.

6. If you want to be notified of new followers and when people send you direct messages, check the box for email updates.

7. In the final field, type the verification code provided by Twitter. If you cannot read the code, you can refresh the verification by single-clicking on the Get Two New Words option or hear an audio version of the verification code by single-clicking on the Listen to the Words link, both located to the right of the field.

8. Single-click Create My Account to finish registration.

9. Following the creation of your Twitter account, Twitter offers you the option to check for Twitter-registered friends on a variety of email services. If you choose any of these services, have your user details for your mail accounts ready to enter. You will be asked for them. If you do not want to check for friends, single-click on Skip This Step at the bottom of the interface.

10. Twitter then selects at random a variety of Twitter users for you to start following. This can include celebrities, organizations, frequent Twitters, or Twitter accounts often referenced or retweeted by others. If you decide to follow any of these Twitter accounts, click on the check boxes located to the left of their accounts, and then single-click on Finish at the bottom of the interface. If you do not want to follow any of these randomly selected accounts, single-click on Skip This Step under the Finish button.

Congratulations! If you have a desktop similar to Figure 2.3, you are now registered with Twitter!

Okay, okay...so it is a little lonely right now. If you skipped all the opportunities to add other Twitters, no one is following you. Your window is looking like an artist's canvas fresh from the supply store and mounted on an easel. And what is with that avatar of the O's and the underscore?! (Look closer...there is a face in there. Sort of.) This is merely the first step. Everyone starts here. If you are fortunate, a friend or a group of friends invited you to join Twitter. If you are particularly lucky, you might be friends or colleagues with a "power user" and can automatically tap into his or her network. If you start from scratch, you might be surprised at how many friends you can make in a matter of tweets. After all, you already have something in common: Twitter.

So, you are all set up and ready to build that network? Well, not quite. Although it is tempting (as many new Twitter users find) to start building up your network, connecting with others that share the same passions that you do, and embracing this hot new social networking initiative, let's stop a moment and consider that. *Social networking*. It's all about the first impression, and when making contacts and building a network—even the virtual ones—it is imperative to put your best foot forward.

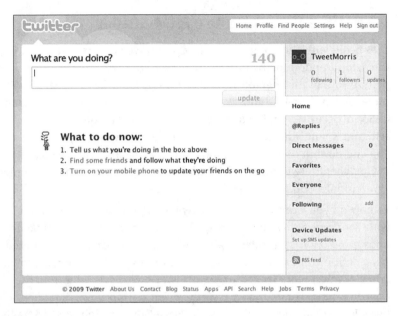

FIGURE 2.3

By default, Twitter accounts have a basic avatar in place along with a basic background, your username, and even quick tips on building your network.

Setting Up your Twitter Profile

It's a little alarming how many people new to Twitter skim over these details. Failing to set up your profile is a bit like heading out on a first date without making that last check in the mirror. Before making that first impression—you know, the *unforgettable* one—it is always a good idea to check the small details: breath check, teeth check, and wardrobe check. Skipping those precious few minutes of preflight puts you at risk of making your first night on the town your last night on the town, which is why we always run down the basics before heading out.

Twitter is no different. You are now registered and ready to make new friends and connect with current ones. To people who don't know you, what does your home page say about you? Does it say too much? Does it say enough? What kind of introduction are you making on the Twitterverse? This is what the profile is all about: your chance to introduce yourself and make a good first impression. You want to let people know as much as you can (in a short amount of characters), who you are, and what you will bring to Twitter. The more you let people know about who you are, the easier it will be for you to foster a strong community.

What's in a Name? (Quite a Bit, Actually!)

Let's begin with the name. Right now, you have your username displayed, the default option for Twitter. Many people stick with this as their identity, perhaps out of that nervousness in revealing too much online. A legitimate reason? Maybe, but it is not like you are giving out your credit card or Social Security number as your Twitter name. You are introducing yourself, and if you want to go with a nickname or a company brand name, you can do that as well. This moniker is how people will see you in their Twitter clients (Twitterific, Twhirl, and so on). (More on that in Chapter 4, "Working Beyond the Website")

So how do you want to be seen on Twitter? If you are not comfortable with your real name on Twitter, give a nickname a go. It could be an alias hung on you in college, which went on to become my username here, or you can use a character's name from your favorite role playing game or latest read. Or come up with your own clever spin from the last book you read. For example, if you're a fan of Dan Brown's riddle-solving hero, Robert Langdon, call yourself "PuzzleGuy" or "SolutionGirl". When you deduce how people will see you on Twitter, take a few moments to move beyond your username.

1. Log into Twitter (if you haven't already) and when your home page (found at http://twitter.com/home) loads, click on the Settings option, located at the top of the page.

2. In the Name field, you can set up your real name, nickname, company moniker, or your own moniker-of-the-day.

   For your name, you are allowed twenty characters. That includes spaces.

3. In the Username field, you see the identity you logged in with. Although you can change this, it is best to stay with the one you originally came up with, for simplicity's sake. Same goes for the email address, unless you decide to give your Twitter account a complete makeover, which you can do here.

4. In the Time Zone field, select what time zone you currently reside in or where you are in the world. These are for the time stamps appearing in your tweets and details that other clients report to their users.

5. More Info URL is where you can enter in a website that best represents you. If you have a personal site or are using Twitter for your day job, here is your chance to invite potential members of your network to see you beyond that 140th character.

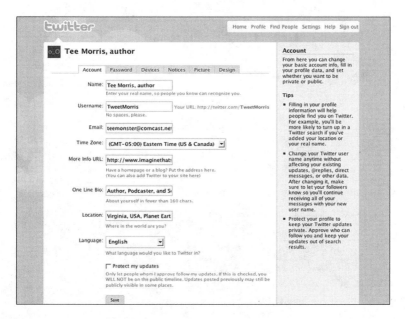

FIGURE 2.4

At the top of your Twitter homepage are options for your Twitter account. Settings is where you can customize and adjust your Twitter presence to fit your mood or intent.

6. In the One Line Bio field, enter in a message, a personal tagline, or a quote that best represents you. Twitter limits what you can say here to 160 characters or less.

7. In the Location field, enter in where you are hailing from. This can be a literal location, a state of mind, or (for some Twitter users) coordinates from Google Maps.

8. If you tweet in a different language, you can change your dialect in the Language drop-down menu.

   The final options under Language are security options: Protect My Updates and "Delete My Account." We cover those later in this chapter.

9. Single-click on Save to save your changes.

10. When your changes have been verified, click on the Profile option at the top of the screen to take a look at your profile in progress.

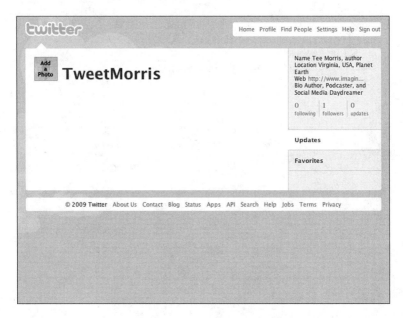

FIGURE 2.5

The Profile option in the Twitter menu gives you a look at how your page appears to others in Twitter and displays your public tweets and replies independent of other tweets in your network.

And so begins the building of your Twitter profile. You can see in Figure 2.5 by the small icon (also known as an avatar) to the left of your username that Twitter is making a suggestion: Add a photo. Why not? Anything (within reason) can serve as your avatar, but your avatar is much like your Name on Twitter. It can fit your mood for the day, week, or in general. Some images do make better avatars than others, but these are also easy to add to your Twitter account.

The Importance of a Good Avatar

It might seem like a tiny detail to concern yourself with, but in the same way a name, bio, and URL say a lot about you, so does your avatar. The icon you create for Twitter becomes (to coin a marketing term) your personal brand on Twitter. When using Twitter for business, it stands to reason that your company's logo (used with permission, of course) serves as your avatar. With your own personal account, your avatar can work as a "mood ring" and can be replaced within a few clicks to reflect what kind of a day, week, or life you are having. The avatar can take the "What are you doing?" aspect of Twitter to a visual level.

1. Click on the Settings option at the top of your Twitter interface, and then single-click on the Picture tab.

2. Currently displayed to the left of the blank data field is your current avatar. Single-click Browse to search through your computer for an avatar that best represents you, your business, or your current mood.

   Images you consider should be no larger than 700K in file size, no larger than 600 x 600 pixels in dimension, 72 pixels per inch in resolution, and saved as either JPEG or PNG formats in RGB mode.

3. When you find the image you want to use as an avatar, select it and then click OK.

4. Single-click on the Save button.

5. You receive confirmation that the avatar is in place when you see That's a Nice Picture along the top. (This message disappears after a few seconds.)

A Little Birdie Told Me...

If you have difficulty using an image for Twitter, or still are not sure what makes a good avatar, take a look at the suggestions from Twitter under the Picture bar along the right side of the page. You can get a few helpful hints on what to consider or what could be causing the problems with uploading the image.

6. Single-click on Profile and then click on the image. Twitter shows you the image at its full size with the Name you entered.

FIGURE 2.6

Once a new avatar is in place, Twitter renders it in your Profile full size for potential followers to see. (How's this picture for a first impression?)

When creating an avatar, you should consider that impression you want to make. The priority is, of course, to get away from the default image that Twitter has given you; but what do you want your avatar to say about you? Is this a professional impression you want to make or are you wanting to introduce yourself to your growing network with a sense of humor? And although you might find one picture to be a terrific picture representing you, does it work as an avatar? Camera phones and simple photo editors make avatar creation a breeze, but what should you use and what should you avoid?

Using your Own Likeness

Perhaps the simplest and best way to introduce yourself to people is to use the headshot, a photo of you preferably from the neck up. With this avatar people now have a face to put with a name. It is a more personal connection you are making with the people you're reaching out to and communicating with through Twitter; and depending on your creativity, the avatar of you can also work on reflecting your particular mood that day.

FIGURE 2.7

Here are a few examples of personal avatars from my TeeMonster account. They range from simple to candid.

One of the arguments against personal avatars is that you might not consider yourself photogenic or you don't want to make such a personal connection with your network, and that is your own choice. The personal avatar is just that: personal. If you are comfortable in sharing your likeness with your network, then feel free to do so. The important thing here is to represent yourself as accurately and as honestly as possible.

When selecting a photo of yourself, here are a few things you might want to consider:

- **Find images that are taken either from the waist or neck up—** Images that will become avatars are usually reduced in size. Any full body shots of you will be discernable on Twitter and third-party clients. The curious (such as myself) will probably follow the links to your profile picture (as shown in Figure 2.6), but if you are trying to give people at a glance who you are, the full-body shot may be lost. Try to keep the avatar tightly cropped and close up.

- **Use images that are square—**Although you can use images that are rectangular, Twitter—for your avatar—crops it for you and might crop out a detail you wanted to point out. Refer back to my suggested settings for your avatar featured in this chapter, and then consider your scanned image or digital photo from that perspective. Many inexpensive photo editors allow you to preview an image cropped before actually cropping it.

- **Avoid images with busy backgrounds—**If you take a closer look at Figure 2.7, you notice that what is behind me in the photos does not overpower or distract you from me. What is happening behind you is just as important as the picture of you because too much detail (or what some photographers refer to as "noise") in the background can make avatars on Twitter difficult to make out. Keep it simple.

- **Avoid offensive imagery—**No, this is not some sort of "Oppression of your Right to Expression," but this is Twitter laying down its law: If you use the site, you need to keep it clean. No nudity. Refrain from obscene gestures. Keep your gore level to the barest of minimums. Does everyone follow these rules? Not always; but on a whole, the community does a good job in policing themselves. Still, Twitter asks that your avatars remain within the boundaries of good taste. It's not asking a lot, and your network will appreciate it.

Using a Logo on Twitter

Branding has been a term associated with big business, public relations, and marketing strategies for years. Although there are many definitions and practices involved in building a brand, the simplified definition of branding is an approach to your business through association with a word, catch phrase, or an image. If you see two golden arches, you're probably pulling into a McDonald's. When you hear someone say "Are you in good hands?" then you might be working with Allstate Insurance. You can even brand with music. If you were to play the theme to *Star Trek*, it might surprise you how many people "can name that tune in four notes." (Another kind of branding as well with a reference to the game show *Name That Tune*.) If you have a product or a service that people associate with a phrase, name, or some other identifier, that is successful, effective branding.

With the rise of Social Media, this concept is no longer reserved for advertising agencies to pitch and charge corporate entities top dollar. Now, other Social Media enthusiasts, small businesses, and even the passionate Twitter-from-Home are taking the same principles of branding and applying them to their networking outlets. Outlets like Twitter.

When using a personal brand as an avatar, keep this in mind:

- **Using a logo lacks the personal touch**—One of the intimacies of using a picture of yourself is that your network feels as if it is getting to know you. That is a really nice feeling, but when your avatar is a company logo or podcast artwork, is your network getting to know you or getting to know the company's or media's communication outlet? Again, there is nothing wrong with using brands as avatars, but in making that all-important first-impression, keep in mind that those joining your network already have an expectation level in place. They know you are the voice of a business, group, or professional perspective.

- **With a brand as an avatar, you speak with the voice of that entity**—I admit, that does sound rather ominous, but there really is no way around that. If you are branding your Twitter account with a logo, be it for a podcast, a start-up, or the business you are working for, you are now speaking as the voice of this company. Maybe you knew that from the start and think, "So long as I stay in the parameters...." but with Social Media being as new as it is and so many businesses clamoring to become part of it, there are no guidelines in place. (Don't worry, I offer a few suggestions in Chapter 11, "Taking Care of Business.") What exactly are the parameters? What if there is a talk on my network about politics? About religion? How much interaction should you take with this network you have built up? When you are working Twitter from a professional status, you need to stop and think before you tweet, and ask yourself, "how will this reflect on me and my company?"

- **As with a personal avatar, avoid text-heavy or busy images**—Some Twitter accounts attempt to fit in tag lines and show slogans and key names or locations into an avatar that, at first glance, will appear in a space smaller than 50 x 50 pixels. How you create your professional avatar is up to you; but the busier you make it, the harder it will be to recognize it at a glance.

When using a professional brand for your Twitter account, this does not mean you cannot give it your own flair or personal touch. As seen in Figure 2.8, I use a photograph of me looking over my faithful PowerBook G4 at a rendering of the double koru, the logo I use for Imagine That! Studios. In the early days of Imagine That! on Twitter, I simply used the double koru image, but during the Christmas holidays, I used an image of myself with the computer and logo, a stocking cap clearly visible and setting a festive air. The response to it was so positive I went with a more personal avatar from that point on. Imagine That!'s end result is a professional brand with a personal touch.

A personal approach to the corporate brand can be highly effective if you have a number of employees of the same corporation on Twitter. What is important in creating the avatar for your professional Twitter account is that it represents you and your company or organization in the manner you are happiest with. Much in the same way you create an avatar for personal use, take a moment to consider your company's avatar. Are you going to keep it professional, or do you want to give your branding a personal touch?

FIGURE 2.8

When using a personal brand on Twitter, you can give it that personal touch to remind your community that there is a person on the other side of the username.

Using Interests, Hobbies, or Out-of-the-Ordinary for Your Avatar

Then you have the not-so-personal and I-really-hate-to-be-photographed avatars, and there are many online at Twitter. Some avatars I've seen on Twitter that make me tip my head to one side have included a zombified George Washington, a variety of characters from anime (Japanese animation), video game icons (both of the 8-bit days and the modern *Halo* resolutions), popular characters from television and film, and political posters during the 2008 Election.

You might think these nondescript images don't say a lot about a Twitter account, but they speak volumes.

Twitter users that choose not to use their own likeness are simply choosing to keep their visage to themselves, but the same precautions and considerations for the other avatars discussed here apply. You want to avoid the overly busy imagery, too much text (especially when you consider the 50 x 50 space you're filling on your Twitter home page), and the nature of the image you choose. Also, you need to consider what the avatar says about you. During the last race for the White House, it was clear by the Obama/Biden—McCain/Palin avatars where users were showing support.

If your avatar is an image of William Shatner being carried off by a group of Imperial Stormtroopers, you are a fan of *Star Trek, Star Wars,* or all of the above. If your avatar is your profile picture from *World of Warcraft,* then chances are you are a gamer. While you are protecting your identity by using a generic image, you are still telling the community something about yourself.

A Little Birdie Told Me...

Online you can find a variety of websites that help you create avatars in your likeness. Maybe they are not exact likenesses, but they can be a lot of fun to display in the stead of photographs. If you are a fan of Comedy Central's *South Park,* you can always create an avatar of yourself in that style at its site. Bitstrips (found at http://bitstrips.com) gives you the ability to not only create a caricature avatar of yourself, but also an interface to place yourself (and others) into your own comic strip! Whether it is "Face Your Manga" (at http://faceyour-manga.com) or seeing yourself as someone from the world of *The Simpsons,* the Internet can give you the best of both worlds when it comes to finding that avatar just right for you.

Most important, you are taking a moment to create or select an avatar for yourself. The default avatar from Twitter should be regarded as a placeholder, not a solution, temporary or otherwise.

Fitting Your Mood: Switching Your Avatar

As seen in this chapter, changing your avatar only takes a few minutes. Why would you want to swap out on image for another? After all, it's just a picture, right? Why would anyone really care?

The amount of people that do pay attention to your Twitter avatar might surprise you.

Picture those mornings when you wake up in a bad mood. No matter how good that morning shower feels or that morning's cup of java tastes, you can't shake that grumpy feeling. And what makes the day worse? It's Friday. Now comes the time to get dressed for work. Are you going to don cheerful colors or that wacky Tobasco necktie? Probably not. You're going to dress down and, if you can find it, head into the office with the giant travel mug that reads "Talk to Me if You Dare."

Taking a moment to swap out your avatar is your "shot across a ship's bow" for the community, letting folks know that the following tweets might be slightly punchy. On those days when I want my network to know that I'm not in the best of moods, I have two avatars on call: one of R. Lee Emery giving "good drill sergeant" from *Full Metal Jacket,* and another of me holding a cap gun with a perturbed look on my face. This is my nonaggressive way of telling friends "I'm in a state." They work pretty well.

Not all avatar swaps need to hinge on your mood. Sometimes the avatar can be a tribute, such as my "HAL 9000" and "Paul Newman as Henry Gondorff" avatars. Sometimes, it can be a theme such as my *Robocop* or *Star Trek* avatars for when the conversations turn particularly geeky. On holidays, avatars can be festive and lively, stocking caps are quite popular around the Christmas season. Avatars can also help you promote events, as seen in Figure 2.9. With every tweet, you can remind your network of an upcoming event where you are either making an appearance or promoting a cause. Again, hop ahead to Chapter 11 for more on using avatars to promote. You can even offer the avatar to others, making it viral in nature and spreading the word about your special date. Make sure, however, that you keep your avatar timely and swap it out for a more-current one when the date has passed.

FIGURE 2.9

Authors have used their avatars as reminders or countdowns to their respective networks of upcoming book releases and special promotions.

The problem you run into with swapping out avatars on professional Twitter accounts is that you are no longer branding yourself or your company. Part of what makes branding work is the repetition of a logo or image so that consumers associate you or your company with it. If you want to take advantage of establishing a personal brand or identity, consider keeping your avatar consistent. (Of course, there are exceptions to this advice, but consider the branding aspect of your avatar before swapping it out.)

Fail Whale Says...

A growing trend with Twitter has been incorporating animated avatars. They are cute. They are unique. They are also annoying with a capital A-N-N-O-Y-I-N-G. A throwback to chat room and forum artwork that, on the rare occasion, caused a problem with browsers, animated avatars are not only an eyesore on Twitter, they are also inconsistent as to where they work. Sure, they work on Twitter's web page and they might work on versions of Twitterific, but when it comes to TweetDeck, mobile devices, and Twhirl, only the first frame is visible. If your first frame is a blank space, that won't work out so well on these applications.

The long and short of what kind of animated avatar you should incorporate on Twitter is don't. They are eyesores in the long run and are inconsistent as to where they work in the Twitterverse.

Protecting Updates: The Good and the Bad

If you take a look under the Account tab of your Twitter settings, you see under Language the Protect My Updates option. This is explained in brief, but as seen in Figure 2.10, your home page looks a little different than the other Twitter pages that are not taking advantage of this security feature. Protecting updates not only keeps your tweets off the public timeline, but also anyone who comes across your profile—whether by random or following the email link that informs them you are following them on Twitter—must wait until you approve them, and only after approval is granted will your updates become visible.

A positive in protecting your updates is that no one enters your network or even becomes privy to your activities or whereabouts unless you grant access. For people who want to enjoy the benefits of Twitter without dealing with cyberstalkers or abrasive individuals, protecting updates gives users the best of both worlds, allowing for the social aspect of Twitter's network while providing security, if desired.

The only adverse effect of protecting updates, though, is how the action completely works against the whole intent of social networking. After all, you go onto Twitter for more than just connecting with friends. You are there to cultivate a community and make new contacts. Arriving to a page with protected updates can seem a touch defensive, especially after visiting other Twitter accounts requesting to follow you sans such security measures in place. Why request a follow from me if you are so protective of your own updates? It could be interpreted as a mixed signal, and some may not want to request a follow back.

FIGURE 2.10

Twitter accounts with protected updates can offer you the option to send a request to the user for approval. When granted, the user's updates are revealed, but only to those in their Twitter network.

Another deterrent for potential followers is that the protected updates limits them to only your name, bio, and any website you offer to serve as a reference to you. A lot can be found out about people based on their updates (which we find out more about in Chapter 3); but if these updates are protected, potential followers will either move on to other accounts or take a chance, watching you carefully as some phishers and spammers are using this security measure to get their numbers up.

Working with Protected Updates is a judgment call. There are pros and cons to having your updates protected, but remember where the option is located in your Settings. When you decide it is time to turn the measure on or off, you will know where this option is located.

Making Twitter Your Own

Right now, your Twitter profile is set, but there are still a few options offered under Settings that go beyond your avatar and preferred URL. How about that web page Twitter offers you? Did you want to reset the color scheme and overall look of the page? What if you want to change your password? Or what if you have an unlimited text messaging plan, how can you get Twitter to send updates to your phone?

All this you can do from the Settings window in Twitter.

Changing Your Password

Under Settings is the Password tab. If you have forgotten your password, you can have Twitter help you out and send you a reminder of what it was, provided you give them the email you opened the account with. The email is sent and you follow the steps through Twitter to set up a new password. You can also, after you enter in your old password, create a new password. These changes will not take effect until you single-click on Change and are given verification that the change has happened.

As with the avatar, Twitter also provides you with password tips on the right side of the page.

Receiving Tweets on Your Mobile Phone

Even if you are not using a "smart phone" along the lines of a Blackberry Storm or Apple's iPhone, you can still get your Twitter fix by going into the Settings of your Twitter account and clicking on the Devices tab. Provided you accept the permission for Twitter to send you SMS text messages, enter in your mobile phone number and click on Save. Twitter works with you and your carrier to keep you connected.

Heather (@HeatherWelliver) is a podcaster and singer who is an active member of the Twitter community. She is also one of the first people I know who took advantage of the SMS option. For a while, Heather's SMS Twitter experience was no different than anyone else's. "The way you reply to tweets with text messaging is to send your reply or DM to Twitter's phone number."

A downside of using SMS with Twitter is when you are charged on however many messages you are allowed in your plan. If you have unlimited messaging, though, you can follow everyone's tweets and reply without worry. It can become overwhelming when you have many followers, so Twitter offers an option to follow specific Twitters in your network instead of everyone. "The messages you receive can also take up a lot of memory on your phone," Heather adds, "but by filtering out whom you receive notifications from, you can manage that." Another advantage to receiving SMS tweets is you can assign "dark times" for when you don't want to receive tweets at all.

Staying in the Loop

The Notices tab is where you customize how Twitter is keeping you in touch with your network. Auto Nudge, if you feel the need, sends your phone a text message that reminds you that it has been 24 hours between tweets. With Replies, you can set up your Twitter account to show all replies from anyone and everyone, from only the people in your network, or no replies at all. It is also here where you control the amount of email you receive from Twitter. You can either receive an email on new follow-ers, the arrival of a Direct Message, and new developments at Twitter H.Q., or receive no extra email at all.

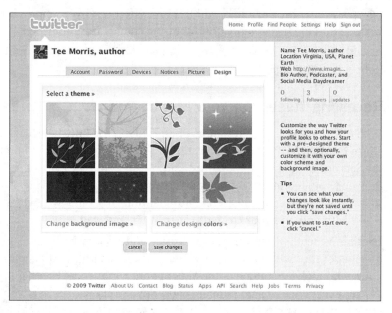

FIGURE 2.11

Want to give your Twitter home page a style that is truly you? Click on the Design tab and start creating!

Giving Your Twitter Home a Redesign

The final tab is the Design tab where you can apply to your Twitter page a template that includes a background image and a color scheme suited for it with one click. You can then customize the template to your own look with either a new background image (uploaded from your computer) by clicking on Change Background Image, or a new color scheme by clicking on Change Design Colors. The changes are not live online until you single-click the Save Changes button.

FIGURE 2.12

Custom backgrounds, provided they are kept to the basics, can give additional information about a user, but be wary about how they appear in a browser with sidebars (above) and without (below).

A Little Birdie Told Me...

Many Twitter users create custom backgrounds that tell visitors to Twitter a little more about themselves, what they do, and where they can be found online. Designing backgrounds like the one featured in Figure 12.12 is a clever way to give people additional information beyond the standard profile, but you should try to test the background in different screen resolutions and in browsers with sidebars collapsed and expanded. Otherwise you take a chance in having your additional information covered up by the Twitter interface.

Building the Network

When your profile is complete, it is now time to start building your network. With help from Twitter, though, you can start right away, as shown earlier in this chapter. You can also go to the top of your Twitter page and click on Find People, which gives you four options:

- **Find on Twitter**—This search option lets you look for people already on Twitter by username or their first and last name.

- **Find on Other Networks**—This option searches other networks such as Gmail and AOL for friends who have accounts registered with Twitter. After you log in, you can then follow them on Twitter.

- **Invite by Email**—Whether it is on a popular service like Yahoo, Gmail, or AOL, or on a private server, you can email anyone in your address book and invite them onto Twitter.

- **Suggested Users**—Look familiar? This is the offered option at the beginning of your registration, now offering a bit more as you have a complete profile. Twitter takes a look at the details of your bio, finds active Twitter accounts, and then makes suggestions. With each one you check, Twitter lets you know whom you are following when you click on the Follow button.

FIGURE 2.13

Now that you have Twitter the way you want it, it's time to build that network, and Twitter's Find People option is there to help.

This option is usually a popular one because Twitter features a variety of account all showing active use. It should not take long for people to find you. Within the first 24 hours of setting up the TweetMorris account, I picked up three followers. It's that easy to get your network underway!

A Little Birdie Told Me...

Mr. Tweet (http://mrtweet.net) calls itself "Your personal networking service" and also aids you in finding people on Twitter that it considers would be good match-ups for you. To sign up with Mr. Tweet, you simply follow @mrtweet on Twitter and then the service will contact you via DMs with suggestions on who you should follow. Services like Mr. Tweet are popping up everywhere and some will be discussed in Chapter 5, "Terrific Twitter Tools."

Along with what Twitter offers, you might decide to venture out into the Twitterverse, just to see who is out there. Much like Capt. Jonathan Archer of the (original) *Enterprise*, you are boldly going into the open spaces to make First Contact.

Don't be nervous. This is the easy bit.

Following Someone at Random on Twitter

1. If you are new to Twitter, click on the Everyone option on the right side. This shows you the public timeline of everyone on Twitter.

2. Scroll along the first page. If you find a tweet that strikes your interest, click on the username. Twitter immediately sends you to that user's home page.

3. Look over that first page of tweets. If this Twitter sounds like someone you want to connect with, go to step 4. Otherwise, click on the Home link at the top of the page and repeat steps 1 and 2.

4. Under the user's avatar is a button that says Follow. Click on it.

Congratulations! You just made your first random connection on Twitter. This is social networking at its easiest and at its finest. This is, however, following someone at random. What if you get a business card with a username on it? How do you find this person on Twitter?

Following Someone You Know on Twitter

1. With the person's username on hand, log into Twitter.

2. In the URL field of your browser, edit the address from http://twitter.com/home to http://twitter.com/username. (Examples: http://twitter.com/ITStudios, http://twitter.com/TeeMonster)

3. After the user's Twitter page loads, single-click the Follow button under the user's avatar.

Now comes the ominous emails you receive at random points throughout the day: *Someone is following you on Twitter.* That does sound a bit stalker-ish, sure, but that is what happens when someone clicks that Follow button on your Twitter home page. So you receive email notification that you are being followed by another Twitter user. What do you do now?

Following Someone That's Following You on Twitter

1. In your email notification, you see under Check out User Name's Profile Here: a URL for that user's Twitter home page. Single-click the URL in the email or copy the URL.

2. Your browser should launch automatically if the URL is active in your email, or launch your browser of choice and paste the URL you copy from the email into the URL field. You will find yourself at that user's Twitter home page.

3. Review that Twitter's opening page. If you think this is a follower you want in your network, click on the Follow button under the user's avatar.

From here, it is up to you. You start tweeting. You start communicating. You let your network know what you are doing in Twitter. That's all there is to it. From here, all you need to do is maintain your network, keep an eye on the activity, and participate in the chat or simply post your current status wherever you are, keeping those in your network informed.

So, come on in. The chat is always on, and you might learn something new before the day is done.

3

Talking on Twitter

You have the profile all filled out, and you have managed to sum up everything about yourself into a tidy little package for Twitter's benefit. You have also done some cyberscaping on your home page, and you have a sharp and snazzy little home page. The avatar is definitely your style, so you are ready to let the Twitterverse know that you are here and ready to communicate.

But what about that whole 140-characters-or-less limitation? That's kind of a drag not being able to really let it go on your first tweet, right? There is a science to putting a tweet together, a frame of mind where you have to try to boil down what you want to say and what you need to say, but do so with an economy of words. Characters and spaces, even. With Twitter keeping track of how many characters remain on call and how many must go when typing too much, you have to think differently about your method of communication when tweeting.

This chapter is less about embracing your inner-Social Media geek and more about embracing your inner editor.

Writing a "Tweet"

All communication on Twitter begins with the statement you type into the message field, or what Twitter refers to as a *tweet*. At this point I see people outside of the Twitterverse furrow or roll their eyes at how their message is reduced to a cutesy term. *"You tweet?"* they ask, usually followed by the slow shake of the head.

Yes, it's a tweet. You're using Twitter. Lighten up and let's communicate.

How hard is it to tweet? It might surprise you because you cannot necessarily speak your mind completely undeterred. You work within the parameters of 140 characters. When you include the spaces, that tends to be limiting in what you can say.

Editing Your Tweet

Let's take a look at something that could be a tweet, but we need to edit it down to the bare essentials without having it sound like a telegram from the days of the Wild West.

So let's say your first tweet is

> I'm awake this morning and waiting for the coffee to brew. I've got a big day ahead of me with lots and lots of items on the To Do list. Yes, it looks a little overwhelming, but I'm feeling confident and ready to rock!

This is a 218-character tweet. Although you do have services and applications that allow you a "cheat" and create tweets longer than 140-characters, Twitter in its current default setting simply cuts off the message after 137 characters with the last three characters being an ellipsis.

The main points of this tweet are

- You're awake.
- The coffee is brewing.
- Your To Do list is very full for the day.
- You're feeling overwhelmed by it all.
- You're confidence level is high and you are feeling mighty!

You want to say all this, but Twitter—while Twitter's web's interface allows you to type your message—won't let you send all that in a single tweet. (Some applications like Twitterific will not allow you to type past character 140.) You could space this single thought across multiple tweets, but some of your followers might miss part of the "complete" tweet and will be perplexed by what you mean.

So let's see if we can rethink this tweet:

> I'm waiting for the coffee to brew. Got a day ahead of me with lots of "To Do" items. Looks a little overwhelming but I'm feeling confident!

This tweet has been pruned down to *exactly* 140-characters after making logical edits:

- You're tweeting, so no need to let us all know you're awake.
- "Lots and lots…" can easily be trimmed down to "lots…" and the intent is still clear.
- If you're feeling confident, you can also safely assume you're ready to rock. Keep one sentiment. Cut the other.
- While you have eliminated some of the smaller subjects like "It's" the tweet still sounds as if you are having a conversation with someone. It's not choppy or disjointed.

To some Twitters this is a "perfectly sculpted" tweet, but I like to have wiggle room. I prefer to come in under character, so I'm not watching the counter on many applications and on Twitter running down like a bomb's LED clock. Let's take one more pass at this tweet and see if we can edit it even more.

> Awake. Coffee is brewing. Got a big day ahead with lots of "To Do" items. A little overwhelming, but I'm ready to rock! RAR!

This version of the tweet gets in the "I'm awake…" announcement, condenses "I'm waiting for the coffee to brew." to "Coffee is brewing.", rearranged and edited the "To Do" list section, and then—after condensing the final statement of being "ready to rock" I added in a "RAR!" for emphasis. All this, and I still have room for more.

That, to me, is a *perfect* tweet.

Posting Your Tweet

Now that you have the perfect tweet, what do you do with it? Well, you go on and you tweet it. For this next exercise, I'm going to give you something to tweet, and part of this is going to be a fun experiment in social networking as I will see—provided you play along—exactly how far-reaching this book becomes.

1. Go to http://twitter.com/home on your Internet browser. If you are logged in and you told Twitter to remember you, you should still be logged in. (If not, go ahead and log back into Twitter.)

2. In the field under What Are You Doing? enter in the following:

   This is my first tweet. Thanks for the help on this, Tee Morris and Que Publishing. #allatwitter

This tweet is 96-characters long so you should have plenty of space if you want to add in anything else like this page number, your current location, or even a quick "Hi, Mom!" Make sure that "#allatwitter" appears at the end of your tweet as pictured in Figure 3.1.

A Little Birdie Told Me...

Ending our tweet with #allatwitter has now made this "Social Media experi-ment" easier to track. Whenever you start or finish a tweet with a pound sign and a keyword, you create a *hashtag*, an informal tracking system for trends on Twitter that day, and for special events that are covered on Twitter. We go more into hashtags in Chapter 6, "Tracking Twitter."

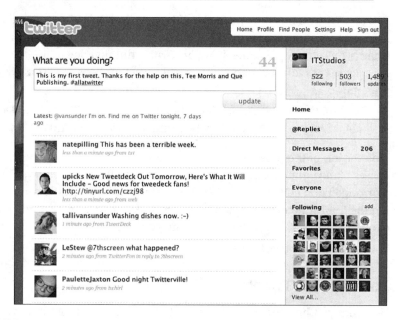

FIGURE 3.1

When you have your tweet composed, you are one click away from communicating with your community.

3. Single-click on the Update button. Your screen automatically refreshes and your message appears at the top of your visible time-line.

Your message is now out in the Twitterverse for those in your network and (depending on the security you have in place) the Public Timeline to see.

Type. Proof. Post. That's all there is to it!

Now that you are effectively tweeting, our next step is to see the response (if any) to your first tweet. In Chapter 4, we discuss how to retrieve tweets using third-party applications such as Twhirl and TweetDeck, but let's keep it simple and stick with our Twitter web page.

Following Followers

If you are curious to see a reaction to your tweet from the people you already know and network with, take a look at your Twitter home page immediately after logging in or click on the Home button. There is a good possibility you are already viewing Twitter in a mode where you can see only the tweets of your Followers. In the default setting for your Twitter home page, you receive the tweets of anyone you are following.

A Little Birdie Told Me...

This Following Followers mode shouldn't be confused with the Following section of your Twitter page. Twitter gives you and those visiting your home page the chance to look through the followers of your network. When you click Add, you are routed to the Find People option. "View All" begins with the most recent person you followed and works its way back to your first connection.

Reviewing your Followers tweets tends to feel slightly voyeuristic, but this is how social networking operates: You build a network and as if you are at a giant never-ending mixer, you enjoy the conversation. If something strikes your fancy, you chime in with a tweet. To keep up with your network, refresh your page at designated times. You might pick up on individual subject threads and contribute your opinion with a quick reply. Your updates remain at the top of the page until you refresh your page. Your updates, instead of remaining at the top of the Timeline, will then be interspersed across other tweets from your network, as seen in Figure 3.2.

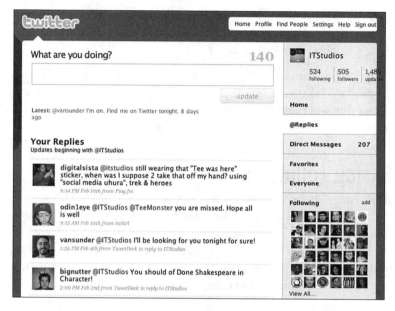

FIGURE 3.2

Viewing Twitter in the Your Replies mode filters out all other tweets in your network, displaying only those tweets directly replying to you.

Following @Mentions

Another option is to click on the Mentions (known by the older crowd in Twitter as "@Replies") option, the button at the right of your Twitter home page labeled at the "@" symbol and your username. While keeping tabs on those following you might feel voyeuristic, this viewing mode might make you feel slightly narcissistic. After all, when you review Twitter using @Mentions, it really is "all about you." This Twitter option displays only those tweets that are specifically addressing you. Most of the time, these tweets will be from people following you. Mentions can also come from people who have just started following you but are not following yet. There are also third-party applications that allow people to reply to you, and neither one of you are following each other. (This means they might not appear in your Twitter home page until one of you is following the other.) The @Mentions option is a great way to keep track of who is trying to get your attention, but the trade-off is you are now oblivious to other trends happening within your network, focused only on who is specifically addressing you. This might become necessary, though, if you are developing or have developed a large network. Focusing on mentions to you is a good way to filter out unwanted noise from the signal. (We talk more about Twitter's Signal-to-Noise Ratio in Chapter 9, "The Trouble with Twitter.")

What both Following Followers and Following @Mentions share in common is both encourage interaction. Whether it is someone in your network tweeting on a topic that strikes a passion, or if another Twitter's reply to you warrants another reply, you are not obligated to but *highly encouraged* to participate.

Let's get to know our network and how to talk to one another.

Replying to a Tweet

After you post your tweet, someone could ask you in a tweet, "Who is Tee Morris and what does he have to do with Twitter?" but the tweet will appear in your timeline like this:

> TeeMonster @ITStudios Who is Tee Morris, and what does he have to do with Twitter?

This is a reply or an @Mention in Twitter. An @Mention begins with (depending on the interface you use) a user's avatar, the username, your username preceded by an "@" symbol, and finally the tweet. By adding in the @ symbol and username, the reply is "flagged" by Twitter as an active account and is then recognized by the Twitter home page (and other third-party applications) as a reply to you.

1. Whether you are in the @Mentions mode or your Timeline window, find the tweet you want to reply to. Either type into the tweet field @username or hover your mouse over the tweet and single-click on the arrow visible on the right side of the shaded tweet.

2. In the open tweet field, enter in a reply by clicking on the arrow as seen in Figure 3.3. For the question from TeeMonster, the reply would look like this:

    > @TeeMonster Tee Morris is the writer of All a Twitter, available from Que Publishing. It's a great resource! #allatwitter

Fail Whale Says....

When coming up with a username for your Twitter account, it is a good idea to think compact and easy to type. Replies tend to be shorter for those with longer usernames (defined here as anything over 10 characters) as the 140-character limitation does include the username.

FIGURE 3.3

When you hover a cursor over a tweet, the tweet is shaded and offers you the option to either Favorite it (the star icon) or reply to it (the arrow). Single-clicking on the arrow adds in the @Mention command automatically into your tweet field.

3. Single-click on the Update button. Your screen automatically refreshes and the reply appears at the top of your visible timeline.

@Mentions provide you a quick connection to those following you, and you can give an @Mention to anyone on Twitter, even to people outside your network. Their response, if they are not following you back, may or may not appear; but you can still reach out. The effort is all part of social networking.

Something else to notice about the reply is that the reply was to @TeeMonster and not @teemonster. Although some third-party applications do not discriminate, others including Twitter.com do. If you want to assure the Twitter you are replying to does receive the reply, double-check your spelling of the username. The @Mention mode, in some clients, is case sensitive.

A Little Birdie Told Me...

In your home page's interface, you can click on the arrow icon to reply to someone. If you want to reply to more than one person with a single tweet, you simply give a space from the first @username and type in the second @username. You can reply to as many people as you like. Just remember to spell their usernames properly.

There is another form of replying called the Re-Tweet. This is more difficult to do from your Twitter.com home page but how a re-tweet works is you copy another Twitter's tweet or reply, paste it into your own tweet field, and then precede the tweet with either **RE-TWEET:** or **RT:** to let people know you are passing the tweet *along* your network. If the re-tweet allows room for it, you can add in your own comments in parentheses. A re-tweet would look something like this:

> RT: **@YourUsername** @TeeMonster Tee Morris wrote All a Twitter, from Que Publishing. It's a great resource! (I like it too!) #allatwitter

Although there is no one-click button or keyboard shortcut in your Twitter home page, you can find Re-Tweet functions built into third-party applications. Re-tweets are terrific methods in spreading a message, a link, or just something really cool throughout the Twitter network.

Replying to a Direct Message

As we work within the website, you might miss receiving a *Direct Message* or a *DM* as it is referred to in the Twitterverse. When you receive @Mentions, you can catch them either in the main Timeline, your network's Timeline, or in your @Mentions Timeline. Direct Messages are different. DMs are seen by you and only you (unless someone is looking over your shoulder, of course), are found not in your network's Timeline or @Mentions.

1. On your Twitter home page, single-click on the Direct Messages option. This takes you to your account's Direct Messages page. The tweets here are not posted on Public Timelines.

2. When you want to reply to a Direct Message, you can hover your cursor over it. Similar to making @Mentions, the Direct Message is shaded and offers two icons: an envelope (DM Reply) and a trash can (Delete DM). Single-click the Envelope icon, and you see in the Send drop-down menu that user's name.

A Little Birdie Told Me...

Unlike @Mentions that can be made to anyone in the Twitter network, Direct Message replies can be sent only to people who are following you.

3. In the message field, type in your Twitter response. Unlike @Mentions, the username you are replying to does not use up any characters in your 140-character setup.

FIGURE 3.4

Hovering your cursor over a tweet offers you two options: Reply to a Direct Message and Delete a Direct Message. To reply to a DM, single-click the Envelope icon, type your message, and then click the Send button.

4. Single-click on the Send button. You will be rerouted to previous DMs you have sent with a confirmation that your message has been sent.

Although this is a private means of communication on Twitter, keep in mind that there will be a delay between DMs and no notification on your home page that you have received a DM. You can keep your replies private; but if you need to have an important conversation with someone on Twitter, it would be a better idea to move the talk to Skype or some other chat application.

A Little Birdie Told Me...

Unlike @Mentions, you can reply to *only* one person with a Direct Message.

The web page you are rerouted to is an archive of your previous DMs. Scroll to the bottom of the messages, and single-click the More button to step back to the previous 20 DMs you sent. You can return to previously received DMs by clicking on the Inbox tab at the top of your DMs. And like the ones you have sent, you can also step back to earlier DMs received here.

Twitter also does this for the tweets you send on the Public Timeline, and your history of tweets are accessible in only a few clicks.

Your Twitter Archives

When you click on your avatar, Twitter takes you to your home page as others see it. This first page of tweets are your Archives, all your tweets dating back to the first one. Depending on how long you have been on Twitter and how frequent you tweet, your Archives can be a few pages or in the case of my TeeMonster account, several *hundred* pages. (My oldest archived tweet at the time of my writing this goes to late October, 2008. Such is the cost of being a Twitter "Power User" like me.)

Your Twitter Archives go back only so far. If you are a frequent Twitter or have been on Twitter for a long time, there is a good chance your Archives reach back to a point. If you hit the end of your Archives and delete the oldest one, you will not retrieve any dating before the last tweet of the final page.

You can manage your Archives by either making older tweets Favorites (which we talk about in a moment) or deleting older tweets. To delete an older tweet (the reason behind the deletion is your own), you simply hover your cursor over a tweet. Much like in making a reply, the tweet you hover over will become shaded, and offer you the earlier-mentioned options of Making a Favorite (the star) or Delete (the trash can). Single-click on the trash can to delete the unwanted tweet. You get a warning that you cannot undo a tweet delete. When you hit okay, the tweet disappears.

A robust collection of Archives does not impede your Twitter account's performance, but if you try to find a reference to something you said, weeding through dozens (okay, in my case, hundreds) of tweets might not be the most economic or fun thing to do. Depending on how often you tweet, you can manage your tweets to the essentials if you ever need that quick reference.

Your Favorites

Another option for having quick references on hand, even for yourself, is to make a tweet into a Favorite, a tweet that you consider a "Best Of" and you decide to bookmark in your Archives. One of my recent favorites came from actor Brent Spiner who tweeted on January 26 at 11:13 p.m.: "I believe all tweets are created equally."

This was a particular favorite for me as I replied at 11:21 p.m.: "RE: Tweets created equal. OH FOR GOD'S SAKE, JOHN, SIT DOWN!!!"

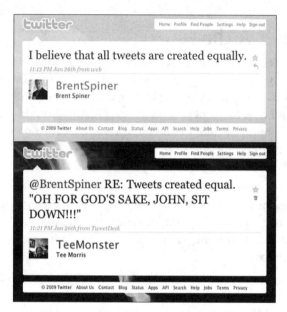

FIGURE 3.5

An exchange of tweets between actor Brent Spiner and Tee Morris, found in the Favorites of TeeMonster.

Many people know Brent Spiner as Commander Data from *Star Trek: The Next Generation*; but I am also a fan of his stage work, in particular when he played John Adams in a revival of *1776*. (No, he didn't @Reply me. Oh well, another time….) This quick exchange seen in Figure 3.5 made me smile, so I immediately went to Twitter and single-clicked on the star next to both tweets.

The star, once clicked, saves these tweets in your Favorites Bin. Although the Favorites feature of Twitter tends to be overlooked, this option can tell others a lot about you. Your Favorites, provided you are not protecting your updates, say a lot about what strikes your fancy. These tweets serve as an online scrapbook of favorite moments on a particular day. For those who are protecting their updates, the Favorites serve as a nice orientation to the person you have approved for your network.

So when you get into a groove with your network, consider your Favorites as a nice way to archive the quick wit and fun banter of the moment.

Now that you have taken some time to get to know your Twitter home page, we need to work outside the box. More to the point, we need to work outside of this home page. Sure, we're offered a lot of options, and Twitter is making it easy to figure things out. However, the real power in Twitter resides in the third-party applications I have eluded to throughout these first three chapters. It's time to take a closer look at what is out there, what options (and obstacles) they offer for Twitter, and how they can help you make the most out of your time in the Twitterverse.

4

Working Beyond the Website

So far you have taken an in-depth look at how Twitter.com works. You know how to set up an account, how to post a tweet, and how to interact with your network. You tap into your network and enjoy the banter, occasional links, and introductions to other Twitters from backgrounds and social circles other than your own. Now it's time to make your Twitter more efficient by working independently of its website.

According to *TweetStats* (found at http://tweetstats.com and covered in more detail in Chapter 6) well over half of Twitter's membership use Twitter.com as their primary application. This is surprising, if not a touch perplexing, as the first thing recommended to me by members of my community was to install a third-party application. Why? Perhaps the biggest hindrance of Twitter.com is in retrieving tweets. Something comes across your desk, you take some time out to watch *Burn Notice*, and then, on refreshing your Twitter window, you find you have missed a *lot*. As you attempt to catch up, you wonder if there is an easier way to get new tweets from the network.

Twitter's developers considered this, and released into the wilds of the Internet some of Twitter's protocols, inviting other programmers to create their own *Application Programming Interfaces (APIs)* particular to the demands of Twitter. The end results were innovative third-party applications that brought Twitter to a higher level of performance.

There are many third-party applications available for Twitter, and I could easily write a new book about all these applications and what they do. (Que, you have my phone number...and my Twitter account as a matter of fact!) Because I have only one chapter, I'm going to hit some of my favorite Twitter clients (another name for third-party applications for Twitter), showcasing their strengths, flaws, and why you should invest the time into working with them.

Twitterific

This was my first Twitter client, which has continued to improve in its performance from update to update. I recommend it for use on both desktops and iPhones for anyone beginning with Twitter.

Twitterific (Free download, with an optional USD$14.95 registration for an "advertisement-free." version, available at http://iconfactory.com/software/twitterrific/), created by The Iconfactory, is a quick to install and easy-to-run Mac-based client that brings the content of your Twitter account to you. Within minutes you can set up your Twitterific to be running in the corner of your desktop—your network's tweets, replies, and direct messages all coming to you without having to press Command-R on your keyboard once.

Installation and Setup of Twitterific

Much like Twitter, installation and setup of Twitterific is simple and easy. The Iconfactory recommends, though, you log out of Twitter first. Following installation and login through Twitterific, you can then log back into your Twitter home page if you want to change any of your profile settings, Swap out your avatar, or build on your network.

1. Download a copy of Twitterific from The Iconfactory.

2. Click-and-drag the Twitterific folder into your Applications folder, and then launch Twitterific by double-clicking on it.

3. After Twitterific launches, you are asked for an Account and Password. Type in the necessary username and password, and then single-click on the Login button.

4. Your tweets are then gathered from your network, organized as "most recent" at the top to "oldest" at the bottom. You can scroll along your Timeline using Twitterific's scrollbar located on the right side of the window.

FIGURE 4.1

Twitterific from Iconfactory brings tweets directly to your desktop and offers you the ability to reply or DM directly from its own interface.

5. At the bottom of the interface is a blank field asking What Are You Doing? Single-click inside this field to type in a tweet, @Reply, or DM. As you type, a character countdown window appears to the right of the field, keeping you updated on how many characters remain in your tweet.

6. To send your tweet, simply press the Return or Enter key on your keyboard.

7. To the left of where you compose your tweet, you have three icons: a house, wrench, and two arrows making a circle. Single-click on the wrench to access the preferences of your Twitterific.

A Little Birdie Told Me...

Take a closer look at your Twitterific GUI (Graphic User Interface) and focus on the bottom left corner. The Home button (the house icon) takes you to your home page on Twitter. The Configure button (the wrench icon) helps you customize and set up preferences for Twitterific, and the Refresh button (the curved arrows icon) manually refreshes Twitterific for you.

8. Under the Tweets window, you can set up Twitterific to
   - Download tweets *from the people you follow*
   - Download tweets *from the public timeline* (Everyone on Twitter)
   - @Replies
   - Direct Messages
   - *Automatically refresh* Twitterific at various time intervals
   - *Show notification* that new tweets have arrived
   - *Hide Twitterific* after new tweets arrive
   - Play a notification sound (And because it is Twitterific, it is a bird call.)

   Set up Twitterific to your desired specifications and then move on to the Window tab.

9. In the Window tab, you decide how Twitterific displays your tweets and itself amid other open applications and windows. You can also set up a hotkey (your own custom keyboard shortcut) to bring Twitterific to the front of your monitor or send it back. Set up Window to your specifications, and then proceed to the System tab.

10. Under System, you can set up Twitterific to automated functions and behaviors on your computer, such as auto-login and status updates in various Voiceover Internet Protocol (VoIP) applications. Set up Twitterific to your preferred settings and then click OK.

A Little Birdie Told Me...

The initial download of Twitterific is a free application. It works fine without paying the $14.95 registration, but with every refresh of tweets, a paid sponsor appears in the window. If you want your Twitter feed to be ad free (at least, from The Iconfactory), you can pay for the registration code that blocks the advertising. In the About tab, located in the Configuration window, you can go straight to The Iconfactory to pay the registration fee. You can then return to Twitterific, click on Configure Twitterific, and then click on the Register tab to enter in the registration code provided by The Iconfactory.

Twitterific is now up and running; and instead of constantly refreshing or constantly reminding yourself to refresh your Twitter window, Twitterific does this for you, keeping you in the know of what is happening in your corner of the Twitterverse.

What I Like About Twitterific

- **Replies and DMs are color-coded**—This might seem like a tiny detail; but when you build up a network and you have many tweets come in, this is a helpful detail. Replies (shaded in brown) and DMs (shaded in blue) pop out and are hard to miss.

- **Extensive shortcut commands**—The keyboard shortcuts are extensive and can help you do a lot of easy-and-quick things on Twitter instead of trying to retype names for replies and DMs, knowing where and how to click to get to users' home pages, and the like. The shortcuts can found at http://iconfactory.com/software/twitterrific/ at the bottom of the page.

- **Ability to reply to multiple people in one tweet**—With Twitterific, you simply click on a tweet from that user, press Command-2, go to another user's tweet, press Command-2, and repeat this until you have everyone in your tweet you want included in the reply. Their usernames appear in the tweet field in Twitterific's interface.

- **Easy installation**—Download, copy into your Applications, launch, login. That's really about it. How much easier do you want it?

- **Ease of use**—The basics of Twitterific are easy to figure out.

What I Don't Like About Twitterific

- **Unexpected Rate Limit Errors**—If you are a frequent Twitter, Twitterific might not be a great application because it tends to suddenly throw up a *yellow*-shaded tweet, telling you that you have exceeded your *rate limit* (number of requests) for tweets. Twitterific can sometimes run for weeks without this happening, and then other days it creeps up and gets "stuck" in this error. Even on the days when I am not frequently tweeting, it still gives me this error.

- **Interface lacks icon shortcuts**—The earlier mentioned keyboard shortcuts are extensive and can help you do a lot of easy-and-quick things on Twitter, but there is little you can do conveniently if you don't know where they are on the website or if you don't have them memorized. So unless you can easily get back to iconfactory.com, you are more-or-less stuck with what you can recall or access in Twitterific's interface.

- **Interface lacks a built-in Retweet feature**—It's difficult enough trying to copy and paste a tweet from the web page into your feed, but on Twitterific it can be even more difficult. Whereas other applications like Twhirl and TweetDeck do offer Retweet functions, Twitterific does not.

- **Available for the Mac only**—Don't get me wrong: I love my Mac and I'm a faithful Mac user. I think Twitterific is a cool application, and I think it's a shame it's not available for the Windows crowd. Yes, there are other apps out there for Windows users, too, but Twitterific is cool and should be available for the big three: Mac, PC, Linux. Not this time.

For my first year on Twitter, I used Twitterific with Twitter and found it to be the only way to tweet. Everything for my basic Twitter needs was now integrated into my desktop into a simple, slick little application. I didn't think it could get any better than this, and I grew comfortable (if not slightly addicted) to working in Twitterific.

The problem is that Twitterific is available for the Mac crowd; and while in my perfect world, there would be a Mac running smoothly in every home, I know that there are just as many passionate Windows users out there who would love to get into the joy and rapture of a Twitter client for the desktop.

Perhaps one of the best things concerning Twitter allowing developers a look under the hood was the opportunities it offered to create a terrific application that would not only run on a Mac but also on a Windows machine, and offer an option for the Linux users. We have covered one of the long-time veterans of the Twitterverse, but now we look to a new player in town. This is an application that means business, just from the sound of its name!

DestroyTwitter

DestroyTwitter (http:/destroytoday.com/projects/destroytwitter) launched on January 1, 2009, and started the year with an aggressive bang. Developed by Jonnie Hallman, he came up with the name from his own mantra of "destroying today." In his own words, he explains, "To destroy today is to make the most of the day—destruction as a form of creation. This is my carpe diem."

If Jonnie does believe in creating chaos, his creation is one of the fastest-growing, attention-demanding, and all-out-impressive desktop clients for Twitter.

FIGURE 4.2

Launched on New Year's Day, 2009, DestroyTwitter set out to change the way people were tweeting on Mac, Windows, and Linux.

There are many, many options available in DestroyTwitter, and when you think you have learned everything there it to know about this sleek application, the creative mind behind DestroyToday.com has simply begun pulling you down into the maelstrom of its creative madness.

Installation and Setup of DestroyTwitter

Although Twitterific offers the quick-and-easy setup, DestroyTwitter has an extra step involved before installation and setup. You need to have Adobe AIR installed on your computer. Without Adobe AIR, DestroyTwitter can't run. Fortunately, Adobe AIR is free to download at http://get.adobe.com/air.

A Little Birdie Told Me...

Adobe AIR, in a nutshell, takes online content and delivers it to your desktop in real-time fashion. In other words, it brings the Internet to you without you needing to use a browser. The development behind Adobe AIR builds off the same languages as found in successful web applications, so AIR is a new idea based on tried-and-true concepts. AIR works with current developer resources to create custom-built applications that run on popular operating systems.

What you need to know about this download is that it is free, safe, and has the support of Adobe behind it.

Although downloading "one more add-on" to make DestroyTwitter run properly can put people on edge, the power and the potential of this new player of Twitter desktop clients is immediately evident within your first few tweets.

1. Download a copy of Adobe AIR from Adobe Systems. You can follow the link provided above.

2. Install Adobe AIR on your computer. When installation is verified, return to DestroyTwitter's home page and download the latest version.

3. Install DestroyTwitter and follow the login procedures for your account. You do not have to be logged out of Twitter to log on with DestroyTwitter.

4. When you initially log in, you are greeted by a single column of tweets from your network, several tabs across the top and bottom of its user interface (UI). With DestroyTwitter up and running, let's configure it.

5. At the bottom-left portion of the UI is a tab labeled Preferences. Single-click this to access your Preferences. Here, you can

    • **Setup API usage**—Users can select varying times and requests to Twitter.com for tweets, @Replies, Searches, and DMs with a click-and-drag over highlighted bars.

- **Application**—These preferences control how DestroyTwitter launches and appears when running.

- **Workspace**—You can decide what options you want active or inactive for your workspace. *Activate Wider Workspace now.*

- **Themes**—You can download user-created themes from DestroyTwitter's home site that easily plug into your client. Simply click on the theme of your choice to activate it.

- **Rules**—Similar to filters in other applications, you can apply to your network viewing privileges or restrictions for specific users.

- **Canvas**—By default, DestroyTwitter fills a canvas with 20 tweets per column. Here, you can increase that number.

- **Tweet/Message**—In this set of options, you decide how your tweets appear, how they are time-stamped, and even designate a larger or smaller font size for your messages.

- **Notifications**—These preferences enable or disable various notification methods.

- **Debug**—If DestroyTwitter acts "odd," you can begin troubleshooting the problem through the options offered here.

- **Account**—Want to make a quick change to your Twitter Profile? You can do it from your DestroyTwitter Preferences.

After you set up your Preferences, simply single-click on the Home tag in the upper-right corner of the UI to have the main interface slide back into view, this time in the Wider Workspace mode displaying three columns:

- **Home**—This is your network's timeline. Those you follow on Twitter all appear here.

- **Replies**—Anyone in your network or outside of it replying to one of your tweets appears here.

A Little Birdie Told Me...

In some instances you might notice a pair of arrows (>>) appearing to the right of a Replies' timestamp. Single-click it and a smaller window slides up from where the Compose Tweet User Interface (UI) would appear. This is a Dialogue feature that enables you to view a *thread* (topic) covering a series of tweets related to that specific reply.

- **Messages**—These are DMs sent to you. Only you can see these postings.

6. As you roll over your tweets, you notice they are highlighted and options appear in the lower-right corner of your tweets. You can

- Save (Favorite)
- Reply
- Retweet
- Delete (Messages only)

FIGURE 4.3

DestoryTwitter's Preferences show not only the inner-workings of DestroyTwitter, but also offers options for editing your profile and reveals details on any user recently accessed from your Twitter stream.

7. Single-clicking a user's avatar or name slides your tweets away, revealing the Preferences options, as seen in Figure 4.3. To the right side of the UI under User are user details along with networking options. Single-click Home to return to your tweets.

8. To send a tweet, single-click on the Reply option on any of your tweets, or single-click the speech bubble in the lower-right corner of your UI. A tweet interface slides up from the lower-left corner of the UI. Single-click inside this field to type in a tweet, @Reply, or DM. As in Twitterific, a character countdown window appears at the upper-right of the field, keeping you updated on how many characters

remain in your tweet. If you exceed your limit, the tweet box high-lights with a red border, displaying how many characters you are over.

9. Other options you have in the Tweet window include

    •   **Enter and Shorten URL**—Type in or paste a URL in this field and then single-click Shorten to trim your URLs into smaller shortcuts, preserving valuable characters.

    •   **TwitPic**—You can choose a photo from your computer, upload it to TwitPic, and include a link to the photograph inside your tweet.

A Little Birdie Told Me...

In the latest version of DestroyTwitter, you can now click-and-drag photos into tweets. Find the photo you want to include, click–and–drag it into the interface, and automatically the Tweet UI slides up. You can then drag the photo into the tweet field, and DestroyTwitter (with the help of TwitPic) takes care of the rest.

By the way, these URL Shorteners and TwitPic are all part of the Twitter experience, and you can find out more about them in the next chapter.

    •   **Tweetshrink**—This feature quickly scans your tweet and con-denses it where it can. For example, characters becomes char, You becomes U, to/two/too becomes 2, and so on. It might not get you under the character limit, but it can give you a head start.

    Click Submit or hit Return/Enter on your keyboard to send your tweet.

10. Click Search in the upper-right corner of the UI to activate a special Search feature that allows to search through Twitter (both in your network and the Public Timeline for any topics of conversation peo-ple might be tweeting about). Also featured in this window are your Saved (Favorites) tweets and Groups which highlights specific people from your followers whenever they tweet. To return to the main UI, click on the Home tab, and your network's public tweets slide back into place.

As you see with DestroyTwitter, there is a simplicity to the interface but an elegance in getting around the application. DestroyTwitter offers you a lit-tle more in the way of options than Twitterific.

What I Like About DestroyTwitter

- **Availability for Mac, Windows, and Linux**—That is a fantastic trait, and I applaud DestroyToday for making this application so accessible.

- **Profile control**—I find it a nice touch that you can make edits to your profile in DestroyTwitter. Sometimes, it can be tougher to dig into your Twitter home page and edit using Twitter's interface than by simply clicking on the Account tab in the UI. It's not a perfect feature because you cannot change the profile picture (yet), but it is a nice feature to have.

- **Elegant interface**—Compared to the other desktop clients out there, DestroyTwitter makes the Twitter experience almost ballet-like with the way options slide in and out. Sure, you can disable this interface animation, but why would you? I smile and think about movies like *Clue* and *Murder by Death* where walls and paintings are sliding back to reveal secret passageways. DestroyTwitter turns Twitter into a delightful whodunit-mystery in the style of Agatha Christie. You want to know what this feature does? You will have to *"put ze candle BACK!"* as Mel Brooks would say.

What I Don't Like About DestroyTwitter

- **Tweetshrink**—Sum ppl may like usin this 2 mak tweets tiny & EZ 2 get in a lot, but I think this is NoyeN.

  I hate it with a passion when people tweet like this. Tweet intelligently, please. So, yes, Tweetshrink is not a feature I embrace.

- **Monitor space needed for Wider Workspace option**—DestroyTwitter does not need the amount of space I allocate for it (I have the Wider Workspace option active, which gives me the three columns of Home, Replies, and Messages); but if I work with this feature deactivated, I have only one column visible with only the desktop notifications to alert me of Replies and DMs. DestroyTwitter is at its optimum best in the wider workspace but that means taking up a good amount of desktop space.

- **Motion sickness with Single Column view.** As I love the sliding panels feature (and yes, I know it can be deactivated) of DestroyTwitter, it is a bit like watching *Cloverfield* (only with fewer monsters) when you move from option to option of the client. I got a touch dizzy now and then. Another reason I'm not a fan of the Single Column view.

- **Performance of DestroyTwitter is inconsistent**—With all the various clients I have test driven both before and during writing this book, I hate to say this, but DestroyTwitter has been the least stable. Maybe if I disabled my adored sliding doors option, emptied the cache more often, and didn't work in the Wider Workspace option, it wouldn't be as much of an issue; but sometimes the application crashes unexpectedly (and each time for a different reason), or the UI just locks up. I can access the Tweet interface but cannot leave the Preferences or Search option. And when you access a user, a different user's details are accessed. When the application is rock solid, it runs like a champ, but out of the other clients I have implemented and worked, this one tends to be the quirkiest.

Perhaps the bad seems to outweigh the good here, but after I got into a frame of mind to work with DestroyTwitter, I find it a really nice client. There is a good application in DestroyTwitter, I believe, and with all the different applications I have tested and implemented, I think this will only get better with time. At the printing of this book, it has only just turned six months old and it is already learning lessons as the "Groups" feature is definitely an inspiration from another popular client, TweetDeck (reviewed later in this chapter). There is still plenty of time for DestroyTwitter to build its reputation, and currently the people who use it do love it.

I like DestroyTwitter. I like it a lot. Do I love it? Well, there is another client that holds a special place for me on my desktop; and I figured that out when I broke away from DestroyTwitter to fire it up and grab a few screen captures from it. There's just something about this next application I genuinely adore.

When I first started with Twitterific, I felt like all my Twitter needs were taken care of. My home page was a base of operations where I could follow new users, change my profile, or fine-tune my first impression there. Twitterific allowed me to stay in touch with my network by retrieving my tweets for me. At that time, I believed with these resources that the Twitter experience could not get any better.

Then I got turned on to *Twhirl*.

Twhirl

At the beginning of 2008, Twhirl (http://www.twhirl.org) introduced itself to the Twitterverse and exploded in its popularity in April of that same year. Twhirl offered many of the cool capabilities that came in Twitterific but also went beyond as DestroyTwitter does by design.

FIGURE 4.4

Twhirl established itself as a presence in 2008 and quickly became one of the most popular Twitter clients in use.

Twhirl offers a great deal more in its interface and an expanded integration with other online services such as TwitPic, FriendFeed, Ping.fm and Seesmic. With its intuitive approach to Twitter, it's no wonder this application has become a must-have of the Twitterverse.

Installation and Setup of Twhirl

Similar to DestroyTwitter, Twhirl needs to have Adobe AIR installed on your computer. Fortunately, a direct link to Adobe AIR is provided at Twhirl's website.

1. Download a copy of Adobe AIR from Adobe Systems. You can follow the link from the Twhirl home page to the download location on Adobe's website.

2. Install Adobe AIR on to your computer. After installation is verified, return to Twhirl's home page and download the latest version.

3. Install Twhirl and follow the login procedures for your account. You do not have to be logged out of Twitter to log on with Twhirl.

4. When you initially log in, there is a lot of activity. Tabs pop up, chimes might go off, and your screen fills with tweets. All this is perfectly normal. Now that Twhirl has your attention, you can configure it.

5. At the bottom of the interface, much like in Twitterific, is a blank field. This is your tweet field in Twhirl. (If your tweet field is not visible, click on the speech bubble icon located on the bottom-left corner, to the left of the Home button.) Single-click inside this field to type in a tweet. As you type, a character countdown window keeps you updated on how many characters remain in your tweet.

6. To send your tweet, simply press the Return or Enter key on your keyboard, or single-click the Send Update icon (the single checkmark located underneath the character countdown) in Twhirl.

Fail Whale Says...

If you go over 140-characters, the tweet field is shaded in red, and the counter goes into a negative number countdown, telling you how many characters you have exceeded in your tweet. If you press Enter, Return, or the Send Update icon, the tweet sends, but does not truncate, stopping at the 140-character point. The tweet doesn't appear complete either on Twhirl or your Twitter archives.

7. At the top-right corner of Twhirl, you see a wrench icon. Single-click on the wrench to access the Configuration pane.

8. Under the General window, you can set up Twhirl to

    - Open this account when Twhirl launches

    - Keep Twhirl visible (forefront window) at all times

    - Hide Twhirl when minimized

    - Spell-check tweets (a blessing for Twitters like me!)

    - Access Twitter profiles either in Twhirl or on their user home page

    - Format retweets in a specific fashion

    - Use Twhirl and Twitter to update your status in other social networks

    Set up Twhirl to your desired specifications and then move on to the Visual tab.

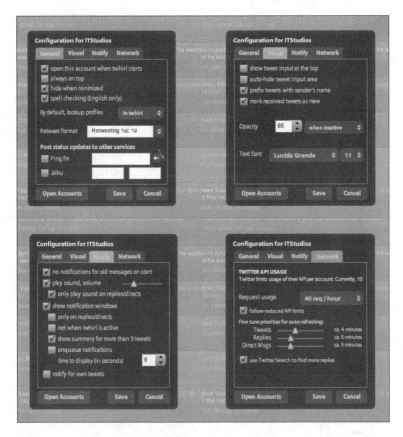

FIGURE 4.5

By single-clicking on the wrench, you can configure Twhirl to run the way that best suits you and your work environment. The various options for Twhirl are spread out across four tabs: General, Visual, Notify, and Network.

9. The Visual tab is where you set up specifications for your tweets and some of the Twitter interface by

   - Placing the tweet field (or tweet input as Twhirl calls it) at the top of Twhirl, or leaving it at the bottom
   - Offering to auto-hide tweet field
   - Identifying tweets with avatar and username, or avatar only
   - Marking tweets as "new" with a small star in the top-right corner of the tweet
   - Adjusting the transparency of Twitter when inactive (and active)
   - Choosing your display font

   Set up Visual to your specifications, and then proceed to the Notify tab.

10. Notify is (apart from one of my favorite features of Twhirl) where you control Twhirl's attention-getter methods. When new tweets arrive or if anyone replies to you, either open to the network or privately you can have Twhirl

    - Notify or not notify you of previous messages accumulated on launching Twhirl
    - Set a volume level for its notification chime and whether you want it for all new tweets or only ones directed to you
    - Display smaller pop-up windows (under particular circumstances such as Twhirl's activity, @Replies and DMs, and such) of incoming tweets
    - Notify you on your own tweets

    Set up Notify to your specifications, and then go to the Network tab.

11. The final tab is the Network tab, and here is where you can set up technical preferences of Twhirl. Depending on how often you tweet, you can have Twhirl make more or less requests from Twitter per hour. You can also increase the delay between auto-refreshing. Although that does allow for fewer requests per hour, it means more tweets to review depending on the size of your network. Set your preferences here accordingly.

12. Single-click the Save button to apply your configuration settings.

This is the most setup you have done (so far) for any of the applications you have worked with, and at first glance this might seem more involved than you anticipated for anything involved with Twitter. Twhirl is worth the eye for detail as you see in my breakdown of why Twhirl remains one of my top choices for Twitter.

What I Like About Twhirl

- **Notification pop-ups**—In noise-sensitive environments, this feature is simply fantastic. Whether you are interested in everything in your network or only in the @Replies and DMs, it is subtle and unobtrusive how you can have a single or group of windows fly up into the lower corner of your desktop. It is also a highly effective means of multitasking with Twitter.

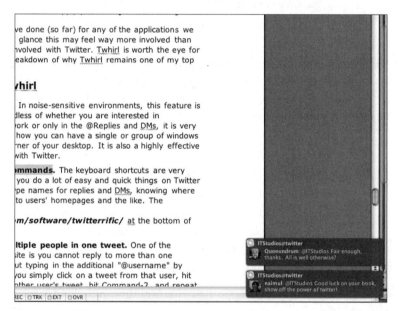

FIGURE 4.6

Twhirl can be set up to send you @Replies and DMs as tiny pop-ups on your desktop, seen here alerting me while I'm in Microsoft Word.

- **API Usage meter**—In the bottom right corner is a tiny icon that looks like two computers networked together. Hover your cursor over it to see a quick overview of your API requests and (more important) its health. If you're at 100 percent, you have a good, strong rate exchange between Twhirl and Twitter. If your health starts to slip, it might be time to return to the Network tab in Configuration and change your settings. This feature helps avoid the unexpected rate usage errors that occasionally crop up in Twitterific.

- **Twhirl is available for Windows**—Something that both sides of Mac-Windows users can agree on: This is a fantastic Twitter client. I'm glad to see something so awesome offered to both Mac and Windows users—brings both sides closer together in a We-Are-the-World kind of vibe.

  Maybe? Possibly? Well, I'm an optimist....

- **Spell-check for tweets built into Twhirl**—From the bottom of my heart: thank you.

- **Slick and intuitive interface**—Twhirl's strongest feature is how easy it is to do any action within Twitter. Simply roll over the avatar of a user and you see four clickable options: Send reply, Send DM, Favorite, or Retweet. Single-click on any of these options, and that action is carried out. If you click on the camera icon, you can instantly load an image directly to TwitPic and post. Single-clicking the chain link offers you a window for a full URL to be shortened. You can even follow new followers without ever leaving Twhirl.

FIGURE 4.7

Hovering your mouse over a user's avatar offers four options: Send Reply, Send DM, Favorite, or Retweet.

- **Ability to run more than one account**—Something I cover in Chapter 11, "Taking Care of Business," is the importance of maintaining two accounts. However with many of the applications and Twiiter itself, you can be logged on to only one account at a time. Twhirl, however, allows you to set up multiple accounts and run each account in separate windows. If you decide, then, to have a professional account for Social Media suggestions, software and hardware reviews, and upcoming podcast episodes, and run a second account for *Battlestar Galactica* episode discussions, the best place in DC for tapas, or personal rants on headlines in the news, Twhirl makes maintaining both accounts easy and effortless.

- **Twitter Search and TweetScan built-in**—With all the preceding features, Twhirl goes one step further incorporating Twitter Search and TweetScan, two services I go into more detail about in Chapter 6, "Tracking Twitter." Clicking on the magnifying glass underneath Twhirl's tweet field allows you to access these powerful search engines for Twitter, allowing you to scan previous tweets for terms that match your interests or pertain to you specifically.

- **Automatic updates and Twhirl alerts**—Twhirl.org, on releasing an update, notifies you both when you launch Twhirl and in your interface that a new version is online and ready to install. Upgrades take only a few seconds, and then you are brought back into the conversation. Twhirl also makes available in your window announcements of scheduled outages at Twitter, possible Twhirl glitches, and other possible service disruptions. Along with these alerts, links are provided offering additional information.

What I Don't Like About Twhirl

- **Replies and DMs do not pop out from the rest of tweets.** If you blink, you might easily miss @Replies and DMs in Twhirl. They tend to be shaded in gray, the *same* shade of gray; and they lack that eye-catching trait that works extremely well in Twitterific.

- **Too compact for Larger Networks.** Twhirl is a great client for anyone new to Twitter or has a network of less than 1000 followers. Once you clear that milestone, it tends to get more difficult to keep up with your network. I still use Twhirl for my professional account (@ITStudios) but I know that when I break into a larger network, I may outgrow this favorite client of mine.

Yeah, that's it—8 to 2. What can I say? Twhirl is one impressive client and extremely powerful in what it does and how it does it. I recommend it over Twitterific and a solid alternative to DestroyTwitter.

The next application, though, in the summer of 2008, set out to do things completely different on Twitter; radically changing people's approach to online networking, and in less than a year's time, it quickly gained popularity with power users and perhaps an infamous identity within certain circles. Some swear by it while other loathe its "intent," but whatever side of the fence you are on, you cannot deny the rocket-like ascent of TweetDeck among the Twitter community.

TweetDeck

It has been called the "best approach" to Twitter as well as Twitter's "cheat" but TweetDeck (http://tweetdeck.com) has earned itself a dedicated fanbase. For my own part it is not uncommon to see the familiar tweet "Giving TweetDeck a try...." What I find most telling about the new users of TweetDeck are the comparisons people make to it and Twhirl.

Both applications have a great deal in common, and for some users it is a flip of the coin between which client to use. The real question of whether you would use TweetDeck depends on what kind of Twitter user you are and what is the size of your network.

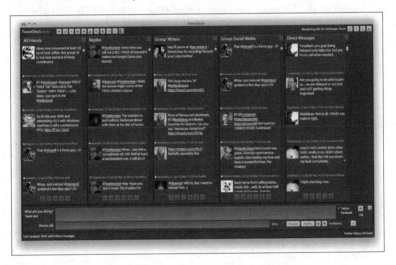

FIGURE 4.8

For Twitter's power users, TweetDeck gives you the ability to organize your Followers in categories, with other options built-into the application.

TweetDeck is a powerhouse, but to really tap into what TweetDeck can do for you, the initial setup takes some time, so make sure you allocate some time for this when you first install it on your desktop.

And something else you might want to consider: an additional monitor. Seriously.

Installation and Initial Setup of TweetDeck

Similar to Twhirl and DestroyTwitter, TweetDeck needs Adobe AIR installed before it can get to work. Without Adobe AIR, TweetDeck can't run. Follow http://get.adobe.com/air to Adobe AIR's download page on Adobe.com.

1. If you haven't already, download a copy of Adobe AIR from Adobe Systems and install it on your computer. When verified, return to TweetDeck's home page and download the latest version.

2. Install TweetDeck and follow the login procedures for your account. You do not have to be logged out of Twitter to log on with TweetDeck.

3. When you initially log in, TweetDeck's tweet field and main interface are located at the top of the screen. If you want your tweet field located at the bottom of the screen, click on *(Wait for it!)* the wrench icon to access your Settings. Under the General tab, you can

   • Set your tweet window at the bottom of TweetDeck.

   • Have a Notification Window appear at the top of your (primary) monitor to let you know of new tweets.

   • Play your computer's alert sound on receiving new tweets.

   • Narrow columns in TweetDeck. (You'll find out why in a moment.)

   • Hide previously loaded tweets and direct messages from past sessions on restarting TweetDeck.

   • Open user profiles in external browsers as opposed to using TweetDeck.

   • Use an "autocomplete" functions for when typing out usernames.

   • Auto include hashtags when replying to tweets.

   • Show preview information for short URLs.

   • Set maximum number of tweets to appear in one column.

   Try out a few of TweetDeck's specifications, and when you're happy with the look of TweetDeck, click on the Colors/Font tab.

4. Under Colors/Font, you can tweak and adjust the colors of your TweetDeck from its current steel-gray theme to your own custom look. Try out a few color schemes, and when you're happy with your own look for TweetDeck, click on the Twitter API tab.

A Little Birdie Told Me...

Single-clicking the TWEET COLORS button turns your custom color scheme into a tweet you can share with your network. The RESET COLORS reset your theme back to TweetDeck's default colors.

5. The Twitter API tab is like Twhirl's Network tab where your requests to Twitter per hour (your Twitter API limits) are set. You can increase or decrease the delay between auto-refreshing or turn off Twitter updates all together by single-clicking the Turn Off Twitter Updates button. The Total percentage number you see is how "close" you are cutting it with your current settings to your API limits. After you set your limits to settings that work best for you, click on the Services tab.

Fail Whale Says...

By default, you API Limits are set to 75 percent. Although that is fine for the average user, for power users who have thousands (or tens of thousands) in their network, it is easy to exceed the default setting and slam the brakes on your tweeting habits. I recommend resetting your API limits (based on the combination of delays that work best for you) to fall between 50 percent to 60 percent to decrease the amount of your requests to Twitter, thereby staying well within your set limits.

6. The Services tab offers quick links to TweetDeck Support and Twitter Counter, and an option to select your primary language to take advantage of the Google-powered translator built into TweetDeck. When this final pane is set, single-click the Save button to return to TweetDeck.

Although you probably found the setup with Twhirl intensive, you are about to get deep into TweetDeck's features. It feels as if you do less tweeting with TweetDeck and more of making TweetDeck behave the way you want it to. As I mentioned at the beginning of this section, TweetDeck needs some "undivided attention time" before you see exactly what makes it such a major player in the Twitterverse.

Setting Up Groups in TweetDeck

The biggest appeal of TweetDeck is how you can take all your followers and set them up in Groups. When you establish groups, TweetDeck creates for a new column. This way, you can set up your TweetDeck to not only follow your network but also follow specific groups of people within your network.

1. In the top-left corner of your TweetDeck window, you have a toolbar of features. From left to right, these tools are

    *   Access Tweet Field (speech bubble)
    *   View All Friends (globe)
    *   View @Replies (curved arrow)
    *   View Direct Messages (envelope)
    *   View Favorites (heart)
    *   Create Groups (User-User)
    *   Twitter Search (magnifying glass)
    *   View TwitScoop (mini TwitScoop icon)
    *   View 12Seconds updates (12)
    *   View StockTwits ($)
    *   View Facebook Updates in separate column (the Facebook icon)

    Out of all these many tools, single-click on the Create Group icon. Your tweet field collapses, and a window appears to the right side showing all active members of your Twitter network.

2. In the Add New Group window, give your group a name.

3. Scroll up and down your network and check those Followers that best fit within this grouping. After you check and double-check this group, single click on the Save Group button.

4. TweetDeck creates a new column featuring your group. Double-clicking on the group name accesses the group, and you can add to the group and change the group's name if you like. You can also arrange your columns by going to the toolbar at the bottom of your group's column and single-clicking the Move Column Left button (the left arrow icon) or the Move Column Right button (the right arrow icon).

Fail Whale Says...

TweetDeck, even as you create a new group, still receives tweets. If a tweet comes across your TweetDeck that you'd like to reply to or retweet, *don't*. If you do, TweetDeck closes the Save Group window and returns you to the tweet interface. Your new group, even if you have names selected, will not be saved until you click the Save Group button.

FIGURE 4.9

When creating a group, you must identify them by a name (that is, Family, Coworkers, Gaming Club, and so on) and then go through your Followers and check their names to include them into the group you are creating.

5. If you receive a tweet from someone that should be in your group, clicking on their username in one of their tweets pulls up a Profile window giving you full statistics of that user from the time he registered on Twitter to how many he is following and how many followers he has. At the bottom of the Profile window are two options: Unfollow and Add a Group (User-User icon). Click on Add a Group and a new window appears. Select the group or groups you want this user associated with and then close the window. That user is now part of your groups.

FIGURE 4.10

You can use TweetDeck to view details of user profiles, follow people, and assign them to your various groups.

Now you see why the earlier-mentioned option of Narrow Columns in TweetDeck's General Preferences was a good choice to make. TweetDeck has other amazing features that take Twitter to a higher level of performance (such as Facebook integration, URL shorteners, hashtag integration, etc.), and the learning curve between other clients and TweetDeck is nonexistent. Within minutes of setting up columns and groups, you can begin tweeting with this powerful desktop application.

What I Like About TweetDeck

- **Best Interface of any Twitter application**—Rolling over a user's avatar brings up four options: Reply, Direct Message, Retweet, and Other Actions. Under Other Actions, you have a wide array of options. In your tweet window, you have the ability to shorten a URL, access TwitPic, condense a tweet that is more than 140-characters, use Twitter to update your Facebook status, and view recent hashtags used in your session. And don't forget the earlier-cited tool-bar that offers you even more interactivity with other Twitter services. For a program that is still in beta, TweetDeck is Twhirl after a few months of intense workouts at the gym.

- **User management**—If your Twitter network starts to really take off, it might be hard to keep track of tweets from friends and family while others joining your network are colleagues and associates from professional circles. If you are involved with media (television, film, literature, theatre, and such), you might want to have a separate column set up specifically for Fans, and TweetDecks makes this kind of organization easy and effortless.

- **Availability for Mac, Windows, and Linux**—TweetDeck is a power-house of an application, and it is nice to find it a triple-threat.

- **Spell-check for tweets built into TweetDeck**—As if it couldn't get any better!

- **Hashtag support**—Hashtags have been cited before in this book and will be again in Chapter 6 where we delve deeper into what they are and how they work, but TweetDeck has incorporated some intuitive options for them. With the previously mentioned Recent Hashtags options located on the bottom-right side of the tweet field, TweetDeck automatically adds into a reply a hashtag if the original tweet is already tagged, thereby continuing the trend. This is forward-thinking on the part of TweetDeck developers and a nice option.

- **Information and options given on viewing user profiles**—I like knowing details about those I connect with or are about to connect with. As @Replies can come into your feed from people who are not following you, TweetDeck's User Profile window is a nice feature to access because it gives you a full report of who that user is, how long (and how frequently) someone has been tweeting, and what their recent tweets are. You can also follow (or not follow) someone here, and (as mentioned previously) add that user to a group.

- **Automatic updates and alerts**—Similar to Twhirl and DestroyTwitter, TweetDeck notifies you when a new version is online and ready for installation. Upgrading take only a few seconds and remains an option until you okay the upgrade.

And now we come to the downside of TweetDeck. It is hard to believe that there are any downsides to the most popular Twitter client, but there are. I have only three hang-ups with TweetDeck…

…but they are *whoppers*.

What I Don't Like About TweetDeck

- **TweetDeck takes up an entire monitor**—It could be debated on this
  point, but to take advantage of the Groups you create and the multiple columns its GUI offers, you should have TweetDeck running on a
  separate monitor. That way, you can set up columns for your network, your groups, replies, and DMs. Otherwise, you are limited to
  the Single Column option TweetDeck offers if you want or need to
  multitask between windows. To see other columns in this mode, you
  need to scroll horizontally.

FIGURE 4.11

*After researching TweetDeck (and a sale at Micro Center) Tee's desk is now rivaling the bridge of
Serenity with the left monitor running Twhirl and Firefox, the center monitor showing his work,
and the right monitor running TweetDeck.*

 Fail Whale Says...

TweetDeck has a great memory, so when a crash happens it still remembers
your Groups. However, if you close a group, you are warned by TweetDeck that
when a Group is closed (the only exceptions being All Friends, Replies, and
DMs), the Group is closed. So if you want to view TweetDeck in single column
view and start closing Groups to conserve space, you might be doing more
harm than good.

- **TweetDeck is "cheating" on Twitter**—Again, the whole point of
  Twitter is *social networking*. You connect with new people, some old
  friends from college and others complete strangers who are interested
  in something to say. In theory, you network with those you follow.
  However, when your Followers are numbering into the tens of
  thousands, how do you effectively communicate with all these
  individuals?

For some users, the solution is TweetDeck. Set up Groups and filter out from the noise (those not quite on your priority list of people to pay attention to) the signal (the people that you hang on their every character when they tweet). The All Friends column becomes the main feed for everyone, so technically you can say you "follow everyone in your network" while you build up the numbers.

Is this really social networking or has Twitter (via TweetDeck) become a game of numbers and popularity?

Perhaps that last item is debatable and should be saved for a later conversation (or a later chapter such as Chapter 12, "Anti-Social Media"), but TweetDeck in a short amount of time has become a powerful tool of Twitter. If you have a monitor to spare, I recommend taking advantage of this amazing application.

I know there are many, many others, and if I had the time and the room in this book I would go into some of these other favorites, such as Friendbar, FriendFeed, and Tweetie; but with these, you can explore on your own the different means available out there for bringing Twitter off the home page and automatically onto your desktop.

We are not done, though, with working beyond Twitter.com. Because of its popularity boom, developers have been creating a wide variety of services for the Twitter community, offering everything from music exchange to photo swapping to tweeting-on-the-go. These are the tools built to make Twitter even more interactive and, in some cases, portable.

5

Terrific Twitter Tools

You are now up and running with Twitter; if you work your account from clients like TweetDeck or Twhirl, you develop and stay in touch with your network 140 characters at a time. After a free exchange of tweets, you might discover what the appeal of this service is. Part blog, part chat application, part resource exchange—Twitter and its third-party clients change online communication with each tweet.

But who says Twitter has to stop with just clever tweets, cool avatars, and fascinating followers?

Along with the clients mentioned in Chapter 4, "Working Beyond the Website," online services crop up everywhere, catering to the Twitter crowd with a variety of online tools to go above and beyond what the desktop clients offer. Some of them are essential for management of your Twitter accounts. Others are just plain fun. In this chapter, we are taking our Twitter one step forward by looking at ways of improving our network, exchanging bloated URLs more efficiently, and incorporating Twitter directly into a popular blog interface. This is a look at my personal favorites from a wide array of websites offering innovative and diverse options for Twitter.

Mr. Tweet

Designed for Twitters who want to build their network fast and efficiently, or maybe for new users who are in search of people sharing opinions and outlooks similar to their own, *Mr. Tweet* (pictured in Figure 5.1 and found at http://mrtweet.net) bills itself as your online Personal Networking Assistant. Based on what you tweet and who is already in your network, Mr. Tweet heads out into the Twitterverse and finds other Twitters that share opinions, likes, and interests. It's your on-call specialist dedicated to making your Twitter better, stronger, faster.

Mr. Tweet helps you easily build meaningful relationships by looking through your network and tweets. He will regularly:

1. Suggest good people and followers **you are missing out on**

2. Recommend you to enthusiastic users **relevant to you**

3. Regularly update useful stats of your **Twitter** usage

Follow Mr. Tweet

That is all you need to do. After you follow him, he will send you a DM with what he finds for you!

FIGURE 5.1

Mr. Tweet takes the fear out of networking by looking online for Twitters like you.

Starting with Mr. Tweet

Mr. Tweet sets itself apart from other similar services in that the site does not ask for any passwords or usernames. Instead Mr. Tweet asks you to follow him, and based on your archived tweets, your online activity, and the people you follow, the service notifies you either with a Direct Message (DM) or an email update. The networking from there is all up to you.

1. Go to http://mrtweet.net and click on the Follow Mr. Tweet logo.

    Also featured on this page are endorsements, a quick breakdown of what Mr. Tweet can do, and FAQs. If you still have a few questions behind the why's and how's of Mr. Tweet, take a look here.

2. Watch your DMs. You will be notified (maybe in the same day, per-haps in a few days) when Mr. Tweet has something for you to review. Click on the link provided in the DM, and your browser opens a page, similar to the one seen in Figure 5.2, at mrtweet.net.

Mr. Tweet : your personal networking assistant :

New: Increase your reputation by getting **credible** recommendations from good people

Hi! If you think I add value to your network, do drop me a recommendation at http://mrtweet.net/ITStudios?gr Much appreciated!   Get Recommended

If you know someone great, be sure to recommend them too!

Hi Imagine That!,

Here's what I found for you. What would you like to do today? (By the way, I update these every 2 weeks.)

1) See good people beyond my network (200)

2) Review followers I am not following (33)

3) My own profile and usage stats (0 recommendations)

FIGURE 5.2

After looking though your Archives and monitoring your public tweets, Mr. Tweet creates a page of relevant Twitters matching up within your profile.

3. The first link you are provided in your report from Mr. Tweet is Influencers in Your Network, Twitters that Mr. Tweet thinks are relevant to you based on the content you tweet.

4. In Figure 5.3, Mr. Tweet recommends Twitter for you to follow. You also can review on the left side a series of statistics for that user that summarize the following:

- **Reciprocity**—Habits this Twitter practices such as frequent follow backs, replies to those not within his or her network, and so on

- **Updates**—A daily average of frequency in updating

- **Links**—How often this Twitter posts URLs

- **Conversations**—How often this Twitter gets into conversations with his network

From these stats, you can deduce if you would like to invite this user into your network.

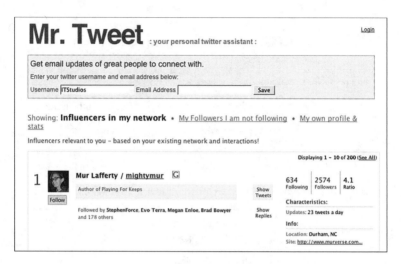

FIGURE 5.3

Mr. Tweet's results include a breakdown of average replies, link exchanges, and updates for the Twitter users recommended to you.

5. Click on the username (usually underlined and in purple) to visit his Twitter home page. From there, you can decide if you want to follow that user or not.

 Fail Whale Says...

Just underneath the user's avatar, you see a Follow button. While the steps I give you might seem more than just simply clicking on the "Follow" shortcut, there is a reason behind it. After clicking the Follow button on Mr. Tweet, you are asked for your Twitter password. When any online third-party service asks for a password, security becomes a concern. Although I have not heard any complaints about Mr. Tweet (and its creators even address this matter at http://blog.mrtweet.net/addressing-privacy-concerns), I prefer to remain cautious. Hence, the extra steps depicted here.

6. The second set of results Mr. Tweet provides is a friendly reminder of people who are following you, but you are not following back. With the same extended statistics as seen in the first set of results, you can reconsider following them or get a reminder as to why you are not following them.

7. The last set of results is your *Twitteristics*, pictured in Figure 5.4. These are your own statistics alongside your profile in Mr. Tweet. Not only are you given a set of statistics, Mr. Tweet also gives you an assessment of how you use Twitter from a user standpoint, how engaging

you are, and how hard you work to connect others with outside resources. These statistics can be sent across your network in a tweet by clicking on the Share This! button.

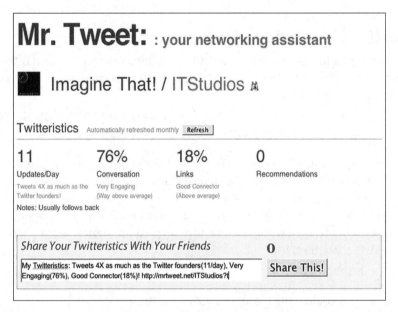

Mr. Tweet: : your networking assistant

Imagine That! / ITStudios 🦾

Twitteristics Automatically refreshed monthly **Refresh**

11	76%	18%	0
Updates/Day	Conversation	Links	Recommendations
Tweets 4X as much as the Twitter founders!	Very Engaging (Way above average)	Good Connector (Above average)	

Notes: Usually follows back

Share Your Twitteristics With Your Friends 0

My Twitteristics: Tweets 4X as much as the Twitter founders(11/day), Very Engaging(76%), Good Connector(18%)! http://mrtweet.net/ITStudios?| **Share This!**

FIGURE 5.4

How do you hold up in your Twitterisitics? Mr. Tweet tells you straight up how you measure in your interaction with the Twitterverse.

8. Scrolling down this page, you can also review *Recommendations* or make recommendations yourself. These are 140-character versions of the endorsements you would find on LinkedIn (http://www. linkedin.com) where you give a quick nod to a colleague or someone you admire on Twitter. Your recommendation is then sent out to your network, and Mr. Tweet notifies you.

Mr. Tweet can work with you to help build and even thoroughly screen potential members of your network. While you wait for your account's latest update, you can always pick up the latest Twitter news and tweeting tips at http://blog.mrtweet.net, Mr. Tweet's official blog.

Mr. Tweet is simply the first in what will be some of the add-ons you will want to take advantage of online. These tools are here to help you not only improve your network but also help you in making the most of your

140 characters. This next tray of our Twitter toolbox is dedicated to helping you swap the coolest of online resources with your network without costing you too heavily in valuable, available characters.

Shorten URL Services

When you first start Twitter, the 140-character limitation seems a little hard to get used to; but after a few baby steps, it's a cake walk, until you get to a link like this one:

> http://www.amazon.com/Case-Pitchers-Pendant-Billibub-Baddings/dp/1896944779?ie=UTF8&s=books&qid=1213066870&sr=1-1

This leaves you with only 27 characters left to type. If you want to do a book review or something like that, it would have to be really short like *"Great read. Go buy now,"* which isn't much of a review (a great endorsement, don't get me wrong!) because it doesn't even give a title or an author name to it. Wouldn't it be nice if we could shorten that massive URL to something like:

> http://is.gd/kuDQ

Then you could write a proper TwitReview around it like:

> The Case of the Pitcher's Pendant is Tee Morris' latest Fantasy-Mystery novel. http://is.gd/kuDQ Just as good as the series' first book.

That's right. Both http://www.amazon.com/Case-Pitchers-Pendant-Billibub-Baddings/dp/1896944779?ie=UTF8&s=books&qid=1213066870&sr=1-1 and http://is.gd/kuDQ are the same link, but the latter is a shortened version of the original.

Is.gd

Is.gd (found at http://is.gd/ and yes, that's it. Even their home URL is shortened…) is one of many services that shortens URLs for Twitter clients, blogs, and other online services that allow for embedding URLs.

1. Find a URL (blogpost, webpage, and such) that is particularly long. Single-click in the URL Address field of your browser and then press either Command-A (Mac) or Control+A (PC) on your keyboard. Then press Command-C (Mac) or Control+C (PC) to copy the URL.

2. Go to http://is.gd in your browser and paste (Command-V [Mac] or Control+V [PC]) into the empty data field the URL in its full, unaltered form.

3. Single-click on the Compress That Address! button.

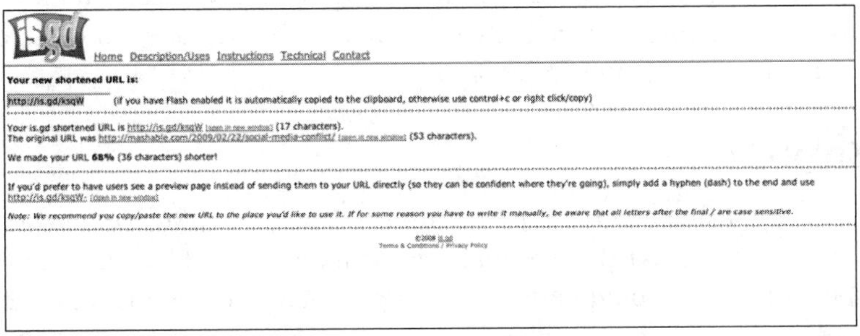

FIGURE 5.5

Is.gd takes incredibly long URLs and condenses them to compact, character-conserving addresses.

4. Your browser is redirected to a Results page. In the top-left part of the page, you see a new, shortened URL under the Your New Shortened URL Is header. Copy this URL and then use it in your tweet.

The way is.gd works is it keeps a record of the unabridged URL you submit and then assigns an original alphanumeric alias to it. When another Twitter clicks on to the is.gd-created URL, the alias accesses the unabridged URL in is.gd's records, sending the curious Twitter to where you originally want it to go.

Many of the Twitter clients online have is.gd built directly into their interface. For example, to use is.gd on a client like TweetDeck

1. Find a URL (blogpost, webpage, and so on) that is particularly long. Single-click in the URL Address field of your browser and then press either Command-A (Mac) or Control+A (PC) on your keyboard. Then press Command-C (Mac) or Control+C (PC) to copy the URL.

2. Under the tweet field, you will see the Shorten URL field. On the right side of the Shorten URL field is a triangle pointing down. Single-click that triangle to reveal a menu of various URL-shortening services. From the options offered, select is.gd. Paste the URL in its full, unaltered form into the empty field (Command-V [Mac] or Control+V [PC]).

3. Single-click on the Shorten button.

4. The is.gd-shortened URL appears in your tweet field wherever your cursor happens to be in that tweet composition.

Is.gd is just one of many URL-shortening services you can find online. The others go by various names but accomplish the same results: a manageable URL for your 140-characters limit. The other services, however, offer something beyond the basics of is.gd.

SnipURL

If you are like me or other friends and colleagues of mine who love sharing the same resources over and over again, it would be great to have a spot online that could maintain a running record of your favorite haunts and have them ready and waiting for you. This is what sets SnipURL (http://snipurl.com) apart from is.gd. Although is.gd maintains its database sight unseen, SnipURL allows for you to set up an account, manage your own SnipURLs, and even browse the *snips* of other users.

1. Go to http://snipurl.com and in the upper-right portion of the webpage, single-click Register to set up your account. After a username and password is set up, you can then set up your account to parameters that best fit your usage. After making changes, click on Save Changes at the bottom of the page and then single-click on the Create Snips tab at the top of the page.

2. Find a URL (blogpost, webpage, iTunes Store address, and so on) that is particularly long. Single-click in the URL Address field of your browser and then press either Command+A (Mac) or Control+A (PC) on your keyboard. Then press Command+C (Mac) or Control+C (PC) to copy the URL.

3. On the SnipURL home page, you see the Long URL field. Paste (Command-V [Mac] or Control+V [PC]) the URL in its full, unaltered form into the empty field.

4. Single-click on the Snip It! button.

5. Repeat steps 2–3 a few more times, but this time enter in a quick keyword related for your link in the Nickname field. In the Title field, type in what the link pertains to. When using the optional fields, make sure to click the Snip It! button.

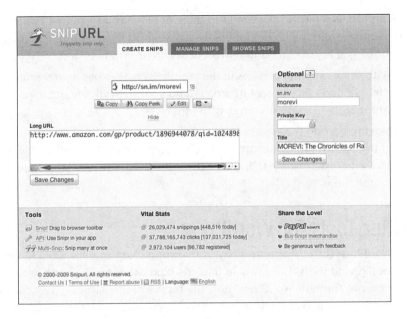

FIGURE 5.6

SnipURL gives you the ability to customize the condensed URLs with nicknames and labels, making them easier to share with others.

6. Underneath the newly created snipped URL, you can either

   - **Copy**—Copy the URL on to your clipboard.
   - **Copy Peek**—Copy the URL on to your clipboard with visual notification of what you copy and where it goes to.
   - **Edit**—Edit the nickname, title, or original URL before snipping.
   - **Paste Options**—Various locations where you want this snipped URL pasted.

7. Click on the Manage Snips tab, and on the right side of the interface you see See Snips From options. Click on Today to see the snipped URLs you created.

   You can click on the Edit button here and set nicknames and titles here.

8. If you do not see the recent snipped URLs that you assigned nicknames to, click on the Sort menu either on the last snipped URL or at the top-right section of the page and select either Nickname or Title to see all the snipped URLs created.

SnipURL is a terrific place to keep track of all your past shared Twitter resources, and the ability to make each SnipURL your own makes it easier for people to circulate and retweet across their own networks.

With these essential services under your belt, Twitter becomes a more effective and efficient tool in broadening your network and increasing your ability to share resources with others.

Moving beyond the website does not necessarily stop here. As I mentioned at the opening in this chapter, there are hundreds of tools all developed for Twitter users, some to increase their efficiency whereas others are just for the fun of it.

Twitter Tools for WordPress

WordPress (http://wordpress.org) is the world's largest self-hosted blogging tool, giving users the ability to host the blog either on their own web server or through WordPress' host site (http:wordpress.com). They can do this for free as WordPress is part of the Open Source movement, making the service completely community-driven. It is this community that continues to develop tools (also known as Plug-ins) that take WordPress beyond its default settings, and what allows developer Alex King (http://alexking.org) to offer Twitter Tools (http://alexking.org/blog/2009/02/18/twitter-tools-16), a handy, versatile, and powerful plug-in for bloggers and podcasters in the Twitterverse.

Installing Twitter Tools

First, we need to install Twitter Tools into our WordPress blog. If you have ever worked with plug-ins before on WordPress, you know this is as simple as drag-and-drop and then log into WordPress. If you are new to running a WordPress blog, this might make you a touch nervous. No need to worry. The process is swift, simple, and painless.

Fail Whale says...

If you blog with WordPress using WordPress.com, you are not going to like what you read next. Twitter Tools (and plug-ins for WordPress on a whole) is not available for blogs running through the dot-com location. You need to have WordPress installed either with the download received from WordPress.org or with a one-click install offered by some hosting companies like Dreamhost or WebHostingBuzz. So if you are hosting your blog through WordPress.com or some other blogging service such as Blogger or LiveJournal, you cannot install or use Twitter Tools.

1. Go to http://alexking.org/projects/wordpress and scroll down to where you see Twitter Tools header. Click on Download to download Twitter Tools onto your default location for downloads on your computer. If needed, open the ZIP file to expand the Twitter Tools folder.

2. Open your FTP program and access your site hosting the WordPress blog. Go to wp-content > plugins and upload the Twitter-Tools folder.

3. After the Twitter-Tools uploads, go to your browser and log into your WordPress blog. When your Dashboard loads, look on the right side of your screen for the Plugins tab. Single-click the tab.

4. When your Plugins page loads, scroll down until you see Twitter Tools. In the farthest-right column, single-click on the word Activate to turn Twitter Tools on.

If that was your first plugin installation, congratulations! It's just that easy to extend the capabilities of your WordPress blog. (So go shopping now. When you get a chance, check out some of the other really cool add-ons that are out there!) With Twitter Tools running, we need to set it up to the Twitter account this blog will be affiliated with.

Configuring Twitter Tools

On activating Twitter Tools in the Plugins, a link is provided for you to access Twitter Tools Options. These options can also be reached by going to either:

*   Settings > Twitter Tools
*   Write > Tweet > Twitter Tools Options

You'll see a long list of options and even a route back to the developer's website. All these options allow you to get Twitter Tools to work in parameters best-suited for your blogging and tweeting needs.

1. The first two fields are for your username and password so enter in the account you want Twitter Tools to work with. Single-click Test Login Info to verify that your username and password are verified, as seen in Figure 5.7.

2. On a blog post being published, select the Enable Option to Create a Tweet When You Post in Your Blog? to compose a tweet that says

    New Blog Post: (Title of the Entry) (Condensed URL)

    Select Yes from its menu and also for Set This on by Default? option.

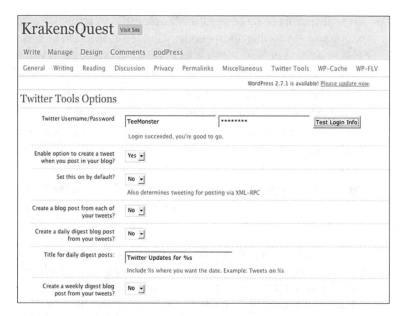

FIGURE 5.7

After entering in your username and password, test your login to make sure everything is verified and ready to go for Twitter Tools.

3. The following options are variations on the theme of turning your tweets into blog posts.

- **Create a Blog Post from Each of Your Tweets?**—If you use Twitter as a microblog or post on occasion, this takes your daily or on-the-blue-moon post and turns it into its own post.

- **Create a Daily Digest Blog Post from Your Tweets?**—For the more frequent Twitters, this option collects your tweets at the end of the day and puts them all together into one blog post.

- **Create a Weekly Digest Blog Post from Your Tweets?**—This is the final option for turning your tweets into a blog post. Twitter Tools takes all your tweets from the week and turns them into one blog post.

- **Title for daily digest posts** and **Title for weekly blog posts**— These options offer you the option to customize the title for the daily or These options offer weekly blog posts based on your tweets.

Make sure before customizing the title that you do not delete the %s because that is code that automatically enters in the daily or weekly date of the tweets.

Fail Whale Says...

Before thinking how terrific it would be to take advantage of these options, consider how often you tweet. For a short period, I was running with daily digests on Imagine That! (http://imaginethatstudios.com), thinking that the activity on the blog was going to be a good thing. This was before I got an email from Evo Terra (@evo_terra) of Social Media Triage (http:// socialmediatriage.com). He simply asked me *"Have you ever looked at your digest? What does it add to the content and aim of your blog?"*

This is why he is my friend.

Much like tweets that do little to contribute to the community you are cultivating, blogs can also be more noise than signal. Before you turn any of these digest features on, consider how you use Twitter and how often you tweet. If you are a frequent Twitter and are engaging more than simply posting updates and references, maybe these digests and these microblog posts are only cluttering the aim and intent of your blog. You want to be certain when using Twitter with other Social Media initiatives that they are complementing and not hindering one another.

4. The following options are organizational attributes for your tweet-composed blog posts:

    *   **Order of Tweets in Digest?**—You can either set your tweets to appear from oldest to most recent, or most recent to oldest.

    *   **Category for Tweet Posts**—If you have a number of categories for your blog, you can either file them into one uniform category or go into WordPress and create a category specifically for your Twitter stream.

    *   **Tag(s) for Your Tweet Posts**—Just as with full blog posts, you can tag your Twitter-composed posts or digests with specific keywords.

    *   **Author for Tweet Posts**—This is a feature best used when your blog has multiple authors, or this option simply defaults to admin if you are its sole author. When the blog post is created, the option selected here is listed as the post's author.

5. The final options here are tiny details that can make digests shorter, assist widgets, and even send a little love Alex's way:

    *   **Exclude @Reply Tweets in Your Sidebar, Digests, and Created Blog Posts?**—Any exchanges you have with other Twitters are excluded and only the tweets directed to the open network are compiled for the daily post, daily digest, or weekly recap.

- **Tweets to Show in Sidebar**—When the Twitter widget is activated in your template (found under Design > Widgets), you can decide how many tweets are visible.

- **Create Tweets from Your Sidebar?**—If you really want to tweet from your blog, this option offers you the interface to make a tweet happen.

- **JS Library to Use?**—This is a javascript library that Twitter Tools needs to access to run. Leave this setting on its default.

- **Give Twitter Tools Credit?**—This is where you can give developer Alex King credit for all this awesomeness. There should be only one setting for this option: Yes.

6. After you set up Twitter Tools to your specific needs and wants, single-click the Update Twitter Tools Options button to accept the settings.

With these options set, you can now tweet from your blog by either creating a post (and automatically notifying your network with an automated tweet), or you can go to Write > Tweet in your WordPress Dashboard and compose a tweet in the field provided.

The various tools we covered here have been geared for productivity on Twitter, on increasing your network and broadening your resources; however, you might also find many, many more tools available online at blogs such as Helmiasyraf.com (http://sn.im/twittertools01), Woork (http://sn.im/twittertools02), and smartech (http://sn.im/twittertools03). Some of these tools are variations of Mr. Tweet, is.gd, and Twitter Tools. Some of these tools focus on increasing your number of followers. Some help you avoid spammers and other "black-listed" accounts. Search in the blogosphere, and you are sure to find a tool seemingly custom-designed for your own social networking needs.

 ### A Little Birdie Told Me...

As I type this, a tweet just came across my TweetDeck referencing *Smashing Magazine*'s "50 Twitter Tools and Tutorials" at http://sn.im/twittertools04 geared specifically for web developers. Not only can you find new tools appearing for extending Twitter's capabilities, but you can now truly make Twitter your own from the ground up in its implementation and integration into you blog or website.

And then there are those tools in Twitter that are out there that are just for plain fun.

TwitPic

In all the various Twitter clients covered in this book, you may see the icon of a camera or a button (or link) labeled TwitPic. This is your client's fast and furious photographer's connection to the free website, TwitPic http://twitpic.com.

TwitPic is exactly what you think it is: it's Flickr (http://flickr.com) for Twitter. Perhaps it does not have the same capabilities of Flickr or other online photo albums, but TwitPic does allow you to easily share photos with others, either through the website, your desktop Twitter client, or your mobile phone.

The good news about TwitPic is that the setup is...well, already done. Simply go to http://twitpic.com and login with your Twitter username and password. You can then click on the Home link at the top of the page to reroute yourself out of the home page (a variation of the Public Timeline) to be directed to your TwitPic home page.

Unlike the TwitPic home page you see in Figure 5.8 (http://twitpic.com/photos/TeeMonster), you probably do not have any pictures uploaded. So, provided you have a portable drive or a folder on your computer with a few pictures suitable for sharing with friends, let's get some pictures into your TwitPic account.

FIGURE 5.8

A home page on TwitPic is not a far cry from a Twitter home page because it is pulling from the Twitter account you used to log into TwitPic.

Uploading Pictures on TwitPic

1. Go to http://twitpic.com and log in with your Twitter account settings. After you log in, single-click on the Upload Photo link at the top of the page to go to the Upload and Post a Photo interface.

2. Click on the Browse button to browse your computer for a photograph. When you find a photo you want to share on your Twitter network, click OK to return to TwitPic.

3. In the next field, enter in any information (funny caption, location, or information) for the photo. Then click the Upload button.

The photo is uploaded onto your TwitPic (and in its original size, TwitPic resizes it for preview purposes in the same way Flickr does), and then a tweet featuring a TwitPic URL and your caption appears in your Public Timeline. If the picture is a vertical shot and uploads horizontally, viewers can rotate it to an upright position. After uploading if you decide that you would rather not have the photo displayed, simply click on your Twitter Username in the upper-right portion of the browser window, and that will take you to your collection of photos. When there, single-click the Delete (trash can) icon grouped with the photo you want to delete.

Fail Whale says...

Although you can send images via TwitPic with your DMs, only the DMs accompanying them are kept private. The image itself is made public, so if you are thinking of saucy (or downright naughty) pictures attached to DMs, keep in mind that the photo will be present in a *public* TwitPic stream. The Privacy settings in TwitPic are not discriminating enough to omit pictures accompanying DMs.

This is the process for uploading photos directly with TwitPic.com, but how about uploading pictures to TwitPic from other Twitter clients? Although the icons or buttons might differ in appearance, they essentially follow the same process to help you add images to your Twitter feed.

Using DestroyTwitter as a benchmark, let's throw a picture into our feed!

Using TwitPic with Twitter Clients

1. In the lower-right corner of DestroyTwitter is a speech bubble. Single-click that to access the tweet interface. In the interface's lower-left corner is an option for TwitPic. Single-click it.

2. Through your computer's operating system, find a picture you want to share with your Twitter network and single-click the Select button.

A progress bar appears that gives you the progress of the photo's upload.

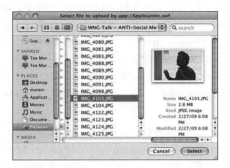

Twitter clients such as Twhirl, TweetDeck, and DestroyTwitter (pictured here) allow you to upload and tweet a photo from your computer, all directly through the client's interface.

3. When the TwitPic URL appears, you can then compose your tweet around the URL. When you finish, send your tweet.

With many mobile phones, TwitPic integration is built into the client's GUI, usually appearing as a Camera icon. Follow these same steps and you can TwitPic while on the go.

For more on taking your Twitter on the road, look at Chapter 6, "Tracking Twitter."

A Little Birdie Told Me...

TwitPic can appear to be a fun add-on to your Twitter habits, but it can also serve as a powerful tool for photojournalists and news media professionals; and in some cases, Twitter and TwitPic can turn you into an ace reporter the likes of Clark Kent and Jimmy Olsen had never seen.

On January 15, 2009, Twitter Janis Krums (@jkrums) was on a ferry crossing the Hudson (probably tweeting the commute away as those who tweet on-the-go tend to do) when he noticed US Airways Flight 1549 coming in for a landing. In the Hudson. After the plane came to a halt in the water, Janis' ferry changed course to pick up survivors. As they pulled up alongside the ferry, Janis took what would be the first photo published of The Miracle Landing (http://twitpic.com/135xa), appearing first on TwitPic.

TwitPic is more than just a place for people to share their spur-of-the-moment photography-by-phone, but a visual link for Twitter on what is happening in the world. Anywhere. Any time.

Twitters everywhere now have ways and means to bring their followers into the action, adding a visual aspect to their tweets. Tweets can now "speak 1,000 words" with the integration of TwitPic, and you also have a new tool to build your network with. Other Twitters visiting your TwitPic home page can leave comments on the featured photograph, automatically generating a tweet featuring the photo's TwitPic URL. Now, your photo is shared with networks other than yours, and Twitters who are not following you have a way to get to know you a little better and follow you in turn.

It tends to surprise people exactly how much there is to Twitter and in exploring the variety of services online that extend the capabilities of the home page where the average user doesn't get beyond.

The downside to all these wonderful tools and extensions, though, is your time investment in Twitter. Although I tend to be called a bit of a Twitaholic (and I mean, come on, is 30,000+ updates really the sign that there's a problem?), I admit that users can easily lose themselves, their attention, and their productivity to the various tangents, conversations, and comments made in the Public Timeline.

And that's in your own network, not in the Public Timeline's option of following everyone.

So how effectively and efficiently are you using Twitter? Can you improve your tweeting habits, or is it time for an intervention? Mr. Tweet, cited earlier, does offer an assessment of your Twitter habits, but there are different services online dedicated to evaluating your behaviors and trends in the Twitterverse, hopefully offering you options, critiques, and strategies to improve your network.

6

Tracking Twitter

Regardless of whether you are the Twitter user that is doing this for fun or for the promise of profit, users everywhere like to have an idea of how they measure up. This is nothing new, really, as many of us grew up with Billboard charts and Neilsen ratings tracking what we were listening to on the radio and what we were watching on the television. At the movies, careers are made with the box office receipts. Authors strive to break into *The New York Times* Bestseller Lists. It's all about numbers, ratings, and the interested parties keeping tabs on you.

Social Media, in the same vein, also has its ways and means of keeping score, beyond that simple set of counters on your home page. Tools are accessible that keep score on when you or your username is dropped in a conversation, and other tracking tools keep tabs on you so that you can have an idea of how you are using Twitter. This all might seem kind of Big Brother in its description, but these websites are more than just about the ratings, the buzz, and the attention you might (or might not) be getting.

These tools are designed to make you a better and more efficient Twitter, and these tools can help you in making your network a stronger one. Here, we learn how to track trends and topics with a variety of search techniques. We use a URL shortener to track the number of hits our link is receiving. Then, we have a safe and effective evaluation of our own habits on Twitter. This is the reason we track Twitter: to grow and increase our (positive) impact on the community.

Twitter Search

There is a lot happening on Twitter. Especially if you are now running TweetDeck, Twhirl, or some other client, you know that people are tweeting up a storm in the Twitterverse. It could be easy to blink and miss something important to you, or perhaps someone replies to you and you miss it for some reason (because, you know, there is a world happening off and away from your computer). And if you have worked hard to build up a network, it might be even harder to filter out the noise from the signal.

FIGURE 6.1

Twitter Search is the Google of Twitter, giving you the ability to search terms, usernames, and people mentioned in feeds across the network.

With Google-esque efficiency, Twitter Search (http://search.twitter.com) can search throughout all Public Timeline tweets the keywords, names, and places you enter into the Twitter Search field.

1. Go to http://search/twitter.com and type into the empty data field a term you want to search in the Public Timeline. Single-click on the Search button.

   This might seem like all there is to Twitter Search, but I have one more trick to show you....

2. In the top-right corner of the search results, you see an RSS logo followed by a Feed for This Query link. Single-clicking that automatically takes you to your default RSS reader, allowing you to subscribe to this query as a feed. When new instances of this search appear in the main Twitter feed, you receive notice in your RSS reader.

A Little Birdie Told Me...

In case you were wondering how suddenly, you are hit with a tweet from a complete stranger concerning a tweet you had made only moments ago, now you know. By subscribing to a Twitter Search, you can receive via RSS the Twitter-version of a Google Alert and find out who is tweeting what about you or topics of interest to you. Twitter Search is another way you can grow your network: searching on terms of like interest, subscribing to them with an RSS reader, and then reviewing users who tweet about them.

Twitter Search is a service that has quickly become a cornerstone of how to keep an eye and ear on buzz words and hot topics in the main feed. It is so essential to making Twitter work that many Twitter clients have actually built it directly into their interfaces.

For example, if you were to launch Twhirl right now...

1. In the Twhirl interface, you see a row of various icons. The farthest right icon along the bottom of the interface is a magnifying glass, tagged Search when you roll your cursor over it. Single-click on Search to access Twitter Search.

A Little Birdie Told Me...

Along with Twitter Search is a similar tool called TweetScan (http://tweetscan.com). Resembling the same setup as Twitter Search, only with a Search Cloud greeting you at the home page displaying the most recent and popular search terms, you can follow the same steps for TweetScan as you do for Twitter Search. When your query hits appear, you can also subscribe to the search results via RSS by clicking on the RSS link in the upper-right corner of the search results. TweetScan is another offering, and whichever service you use comes down to personal choice. If you prefer TweetScan over Twitter Search, Twhirl gives you that option. When you click on the Search tool, you see to the left of the data entry field a menu with Twitter Search as the default option. Single-click the menu, and you will be offered the option to switch to TweetScan if you so want.

2. Type your search term into the data field and press Return or Enter on your keyboard. Your results appear in your Twhirl window.

3. In the top-right corner of the Twhirl window, you see an Activate button. Single-clicking this button stores this search term and searches it when accessed, similar to subscribing to a query via your RSS reader. When new instances of this search occur, you can access them in Twhirl's Search window as seen in Figure 6.2.

FIGURE 6.2

Twitter Search in Twhirl allows you to not only access the power of Twitter Search remotely from your desktop, but also allows you to store previous searches for later access.

Twitter Search can keep you in the know of what people are talking about in your circles of interest; and with some Twitter clients, its capabilities are now available on your desktop. Go exploring with Twitter Search and discover how it can influence not only your network, but also your overall habits on Twitter.

Bit.ly

In Chapter 5, "Terrific Twitter Tools," I covered URL-shortening services, but the URL-condensing website Bit.ly (found at http://bit.ly/) is covered in "Tracking Twitter" as it is a little different and more involved than the other URL-shortening services. Bit.ly is like Is.gd as it shortens websites, and it is like SnipURL as it maintains a database for you. Bit.ly, however, offers one more option not found in either of the previous URL shorteners: You can now track traffic visiting that website once the link is live.

First, you have to set up an account for yourself. That might seem a little unsettling for some users (especially for the ones wearing the tin-foil hats), but it's a free account and allows you to access some of the more dynamic features of Bit.ly, such as URL Tracking.

1. Find a URL (blogpost, webpage, and such) that is particularly long. Single-click in the URL Address field of your browser and then press either Command-A (Mac) or Control+A (PC) on your keyboard. Then press Command-C (Mac) or Control+C (PC) to copy the URL.

2. Go to http://bit.ly in your browser and paste the URL (Command-V [Mac] or Control+V [PC]) into the empty data field in its full, unaltered form. You are also offered an option to create your own customized URL.

3. Single-click on the Shorten button.

4. Your URL is then shortened in both its own window and in a field offering you to tweet directly from your Bit.ly account. If you have not set up your Bit.ly account for Twitter, you can do so right now by single-clicking on Sign Up, located in the upper-right corner.

   Regardless if you tweet from here, click the Copy link to get the link on your clipboard.

5. Go to your browser and paste into the URL field your Bit.ly URL, adding at the end of it a plus sign. (For example, you copied http://bit.ly/TeeOnFB but in your browser you entered http://bit.ly/TeeOnFB+.)

6. Press Return or Enter on your keyboard to view statistics on traffic you're generating.

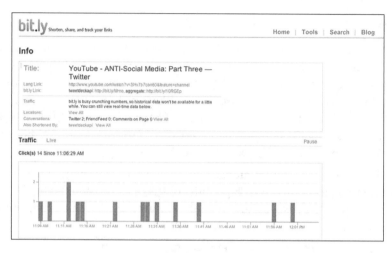

FIGURE 6.3

Bit.ly tracks statistics of the traffic you are generating through the links you tweet, including origins of the traffic, retweets of the links, and any additional Metadata associated with the original link.

In real time, Bit.ly reports statistics based around the link you have shortened and tweeted. You are given, as seen in Figure 6.3, a bar graph that progresses across your screen with increased traffic. You also get a breakdown of where your hits are coming from in the world. As a marketing and business tool, this gives you a terrific assessment of the online activity your Twitter presence is generating.

Bit.ly also gives you a running tally of recent shortened URLs you have created. Instead of rendering a new one or searching past previous tweets, you can simply click on the Home link to see previous links of yours. This is a handy feature, but Bit.ly is not unique in offering this to its registered users.

TweetStats

Perhaps one of the earliest of the Twitter evaluators out there, TweetStats (http://tweetstats.com) takes a look at your account and breaks down your usage into a variety of categories that tell you who you're talking to, when you're online, what your peak hours are, and also what you're talking about. It's a quick glance of what kind of Twitter you are. The developers keep the interface simple and (most important) safe and secure, making it a popular self-evaluation tool for many Twitters.

1. Go to http://tweetstats.com and enter your Twitter username in the text field provided.

2. Single-click the Graph My Tweets! button. You will then be told to wait a few minutes as TweetStats looks at your overall history and gives you a breakdown of your Twitter habits. The results appear something similar to Figure 6.4.

Fail Whale Says...

If your updates are protected, TweetStats cannot look at your usage and give you an evaluation. This is the trade-off in not asking for passwords. If you want to be assessed, your timeline must be public, not protected.

3. After reviewing your data, single-click on the Tweet Cloud tab at the top of the results to view a tag cloud of your most commonly tweeted terms.

4. If you want to send these results as a tweet, single-click on the Tweet This link at the top of each result page. You are then rerouted to your Twitter home page with a tweet all set and ready to send.

TweetStats has the capability to go back to the beginning of a Twitter account *(Wow, have I really been on Twitter for two years!?)* and give you a breakdown of that user's basics. This is hardly private information that anyone can access, mind you, and considering the less-than-sensitive information being shared here, no password is required. All you need to do is punch in a username and review the results.

The various graphs you find at TweetStats cover

- **Tweet Timeline**—This is a monthly bar graph that shows the progression of your tweeting habits, from your humble beginning to whatever level your tweeting reaches. TweetStats also gives you your average tweets per day based on these statistics.

- **Tweet Density**—This is a useful statistic for people who try to contact you using Twitter. Tweet Density is a breakdown of when you are on Twitter, on a daily and weekly basis. The darker, thicker portions of the graph are the times your tweets are most frequent.

- **Daily and Hourly Tweets**—From the time you first logged onto Twitter to the point where you asked TweetStats to look at your account or the account of the username you entered, TweetStats looks at the timestamps of your stream and reports the days and hours where you are tweeting the most and the least.

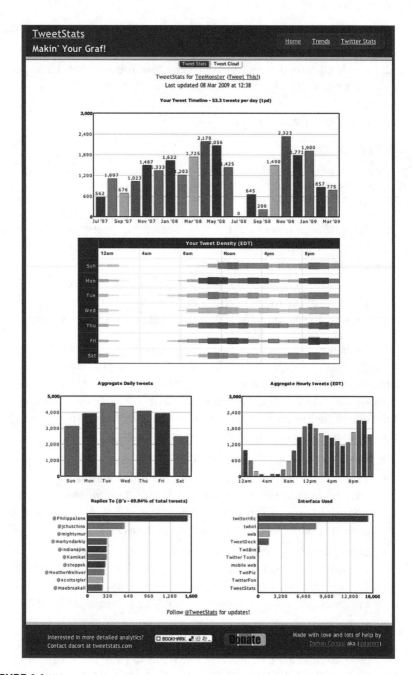

FIGURE 6.4

TweetStats is a quick and simple graphic representation of when you tweet, what you're using to tweet with, and even what your popular tweet topics are.

- **Replies To**—On this graph, you see your Top Ten list (sans David Letterman and The CBS Late Night Orchestra) of people you're replying to. For people wanting to broaden their network, this is a handy tool to review potential additions to their network. For the user, this graph also features a percentage of tweets that are @Replies.

- **Interface Used**—I find this one endlessly fascinating as I see at a glance which Twitter client I am using the most. For new users, this can provide a nice breakdown of various tools available for Twitter, especially if (like me) the Twitter user in question likes to test spin other applications.

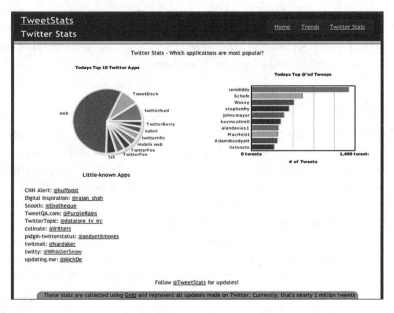

FIGURE 6.5

Twitter Stats provides you a graphical representation of popular Twitter applications and users receiving the most @Replies.

TweetStats, along with assessing individual statistics, offers Trends and Twitter Stats (pictured in Figure 6.5) in the upper-right corner of its website. These links cover the entire Twitter network. Under Trends, TweetStats gives you the top ten daily and current topics (keywords and/or hashtags) discussed across Twitter's Public Timeline. Underneath the graphs are tag clouds of popular terms from the day and of all time (alright, at least the most popular trends dating as far back as Twitter allows TweetStats to go).

Maybe there isn't a lot of "useful" information here, but there is lot of cool trivia. This is a neat way of staying in the loop on what are the hot topics of the network.

The Twitter Stats page, on the other hand, is a terrific resource for people who are searching for a different Twitter client. Clicking this link gives you on the left side a pie chart of the most popular Twitter clients currently in use. On the right, you have the top users being @Mentioned, giving Twitters an idea of who is currently enjoying traffic on the network.

TweetStats has been around for some time and continues to still be a rock-steady and reliable resource for you (and others) to get a good cross section of what is happening on Twitter and how you are tweeting within all that. However, as it is with technology and with the Internet, new services are constantly appearing, and what is terrific about the Twitter network is how its members will keep you in the know.

Twitalyzer

While working on this chapter, Susan Kuhn Frost (@SweetSue) pointed me in the direction of a new Twitter assessment service that dedicates itself to not only give you an honest look at how you're tweeting but also goes into how you can improve on your Twitter habits. Twitalyzer (found online at http://www.twitalyzer.com/ and pictured in Figure 6.6) breaks your tweeting down into five categories:

- **Influence**—Arguably, Twitters who are using Twitter as a networking and promotional tool are striving for this. People like Gennefer Snofield, Robert Scoble, Jeff Pulver, and Deborah Cole Micek can simply tweet, and people take notice. Although others might call this "popularity," Twitalyzer refers to this impact on Twitter as "influence" or an average assessment of your number of followers, the number of times you are retweeted, the number of times you retweet others, how often your username is referenced by others, and finally your number of weekly updates.

- **Signal-to-Noise Ratio**—This, for me, is the most important aspect of Twitter you should develop and nurture. Up to this point, I've talked about Signal-to-Noise-Ratio, and now I (and Twitalyzer) am going into exactly what that means. Signal-to-Noise (or SNR) goes into the quality of your tweets. There are Twitters who swap online resources and advice, reply to those who query them, and share stories of past and present. There are also Twitters who make comments about the sandwich they are making, where they are driving to, and what they are watching on television. Then there are accounts that do nothing but promote their websites, their products, or their services. The quality of what you are tweeting goes into the SNR ratio. The higher the quality of tweets, the stronger your signal is. If people are tuning you out, your tweets are regarded as noise. Twitalyzer defines a signal as how much you connect with other Twitters, how URLs and referenced and used in tweets, whether you incorporate *hashtags* (explained later in this chapter), and how often you retweet others.

- **Generosity**—Twitalyzer defines Generosity as how much you are sharing (or retweeting) others, passing along in your network their links, opinions, and advice and creating within *your* network awareness of *their* work.

 Fail Whale Says...

While Twitalyzer states in its definition of Generosity that *"Incidentally, if you retweet more frequently, you'll also increase your signal-to-noise ratio as well...,"* I argue that simply retweeting others incessantly increases only the noise in your Twitter SNR. There comes a point where retweeting others becomes regurgitation. Show that you have your own resources, your own thoughts, and share them on Twitter. You can find out more about Signal-to-Noise Ratio in Chapter 9, "The Trouble with Twitter."

- **Velocity**—As you might guess, this is your frequency of tweets. Twitalyzer works your number of tweets against a theoretical maximum of Twitter's API limits. Depending on the frequency of your tweeting, you might find your velocity incredibly high or low, but simply tweeting to get the number of updates up does little for your SNR. The influential Twitters out there (some mentioned in this book) do update their Twitter and use the tools here to stay in the loop of discussion and keep their network in the know. Velocity works both ways: You can only increase awareness of yourself or your business through continued tweeting, but you should consider the quality of your tweets.

- **Clout**—This is the one that makes me smile a bit as this is Twitalyzer's measure of Tweet Cred (what tech bloggers call your street credibility on Twitter) as determined by traffic outside your account. The more people who reference you by account name (@TeeMonster, @ITStudios, and so on), the higher your clout.

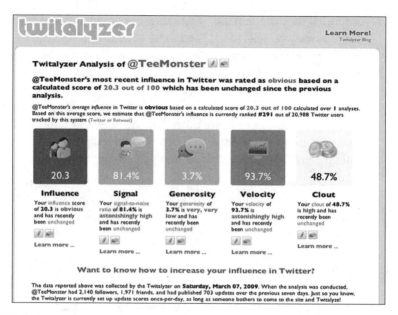

FIGURE 6.6

After entering a username into Twitalyzer, your account is assessed on several characteristics that affect your presence in the Twitter community.

The developers keep the interface simple and (most importantly) safe and secure.

1. Go to http://twitalyzer.com and enter your Twitter username in the text field provided.

Fail Whale Says...

The problem you have with TweetStats and protected updates also applies with Twitalyzer. Twitalyzer does not work with protected updates.

2. Single-click the Twitalyze button. Your account will be assessed, and then your results appear on your browser.

3. Click on any of the pencil icons associated with a category to send your results across your network as a tweet.

4. Over time, you can return to Twitalyzer, repeat steps 1–2, and then scroll down for progress analysis and compare-and-contrast with other Twitters using Google Motion Charts.

Twitalyzer is a terrific place to get a breakdown of your Twitter account, but its real power comes out after you make return visits to assess the growth of your account over time. The comparison tools, not only against yourself over time but also with other Twitters, can give you various goals and benchmarks on what to gauge your own growth and development on Twitter.

Fail Whale Says...

There are many, many online Twitter assessments out there. One reason Mr. Tweet, TweetStats, and Twitalyzer are highlighted here is they are services that are 100% safe. In other words, they do *not* ask you for a password. This is something you should be wary of when visiting any online service, particularly if they are offering to assess your Twitter trends for free. If a password is required for this service, it is best to avoid such online courtesy. For more on the darker side of Twitter, see Chapter 12, "ANTI-Social Media."

Both TweetStats and Twitalyzer focus on tracking and assessing your effectiveness on using Twitter. Now, to wrap up this chapter on terrific Twitter tools, we combine the assessment of TweetStats and Twitalyzer with the search engine effectiveness of Twitter Search and TweetScan. This is a tool that has been mentioned in passing in this and previous chapters and is one of the essentials in tracking awareness, themes, and trends on Twitter. I refer to *hashtags*.

Hashtags

To really understand what hashtags are, you have to step back in time to the early days of Twitter. In the first year, "tweet themes" (sometimes referred to as *memes*) were shared throughout the network, both my own and in the public streams. Usually, memes were labeled with similar introductions like "On Our Feet" or "Solidarity" accompanied with a relevant tweet. The only problem was, though, that doing a search on "Solidarity" or "On Our Feet" would get other tweets unrelated to the meme in question.

October 23, 2007, though, changed the way we track topics on Twitter when Nate Ritter (@nateritter) posted updates concerning the San Diego fires. His tweets concerning the wildfires sweeping through Southern California started or ended with #sandiegofire (which he used as—at that time—sandiegofire was the third hot tag listed on Flickr), which gave all of his tweets an easily searched, easily distributed common term. His intent was to use this form of grouping (as blogger and tech legend Stowe Boyd would call it) as a mechanism to bringing people together.

Thus, hashtags (the home site featured in Figure 6.7 and found online at http://hashtags.org) were born.

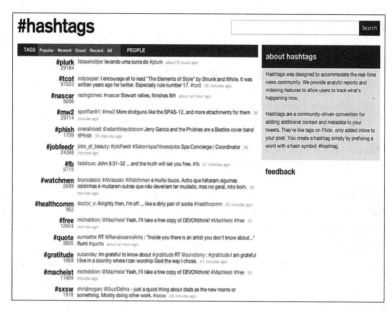

FIGURE 6.7

Track trends that you start or raise awareness of a cause with hashtags.

Hashtags, some complain, use up valuable characters from your 140-character limit. Others get aggravated over the fact they are easily forgotten when you are composing a tweet. Like any new practice, you simply have to get into the habit of working around them; and when you want to raise awareness or visibility on Twitter, you really should use hashtags.

Hashtags are free. There is no real setup involved. They are easy to incorporate and even easier to use.

1. In Twitter or on your preferred Twitter client, compose the following tweet:

   "Right now, I am learning how to use hashtags. Thank you, Tee Morris for teaching this."

   Do not send this tweet just yet.

2. At the end of this tweet, add #allatwitter and then send your tweet.

3. To track who else is using the hashtag you have just incorporated, go to http://hashtags.org and perform a search in the Search field, located in the upper-right section of the website.

A Little Birdie Told Me...

When performing searches on hashtag.org, the # and case sensitivity is not mandatory. If you use the right hashtag, the search results are the same.

That's all there is to it to incorporate hashtags. The only hard part with hashtags is remembering to add in the hashtag at the end of your tweet. Although it doesn't matter if you use upper- and lowercase letters for your hashtag, what is important is that you use the same hashtag and it is simple and easy to remember. So while the following hashtags are considered the same

- #allatwitter
- #AllATwitter
- #ALLATWITTER

These hashtags will not offer the same search results

- #All A Twitter
- #All_A_Twitter
- #All-A-Twitter

The rules of thumb to follow when it comes to hashtags are simple:

- Use a simple, quick, easy-to-recall, and (if possible) small keyword for your hashtag.
- Remember to be consistent with it, and make sure others are consistent with it.
- Remember to add it to the end of your tweets.

A Little Birdie Told Me...

The latest version of TweetDeck (v0.25b) will, when you reply to a tweet that has a hashtag in it, automatically add in the hashtag at the end of your reply. (Nice touch, guys! I love that!)

Hashtags, along with the other tools mentioned here, are all powerful additions to your Twitter account. You now have ways and means of increasing your community, improving your networking skills, and raising awareness for your causes and movements. This is all part of the potential found in social networking. And even beyond these tools, there are many, many others available, both geared for the lighter side of Twitter and for the professional approach to networking. The ones featured here are terrific springboards and the essentials you should have when working with Twitter on whatever level you are at. Whether you are a beginner or a seasoned veteran of social networking, the websites here are your portals to other tools, some variations on themes we've covered here. Consider the sites covered here as stepping forward with Twitter, to unlock the potential and make it a powerful tool that can make amazing connections happen.

7

Twitter to Go

To those of us really into Twitter, this is a bizarre addiction. There is something about connecting with friends and colleagues, and about being in the know and kept in the loop, that is quite appealing. It is something we develop and nurture a need for, and we don't even realize this addiction is happening until we step away from our computers. That's when the fingers tap nervously on our knees and the wrist twists again and again to reveal the watch. Are we home yet? Can't traffic move any faster? What's the holdup with the commuter train? *Doesn't anyone understand I need to get online so I can check Twitter?!!*

Yes, there are those who understand. This is why we have Twitter for mobile phones.

Fail Whale Says...

Before getting all into tweeting from your favorite mobile device, whatever make and model it is, take a look at your surroundings and ask yourself, "Is this okay?" If you are waiting for the local metro rail or enjoying a cup of coffee in a café, then sure, tweet away. In a *social* situation, whether it is family gatherings or a night out with friends or a date (yes, it's been known to happen), whipping out the Twitter and snickering at whatever joke flashed into your stream might be a faux pas of epic proportion. Just remember that *Twittiquite* is key.

Now, if it's a particularly *bad* date, all bets are off. Tweet for help.

We have many versions of mobile phones on the market, and there are still new and innovative makes and models emerging as I work on *All a Twitter*. In this chapter, I focus on two contenders in the wireless communications arena: the BlackBerry and the Android

G1. These trademarks of modern data transfer face off in the Twitterdome like proud, armor-clad warriors. Standing aloft, these titans of tomorrow's technology today are showered with praise from the tweet-hungry masses while they survey one another, taking stock of their value and potential in what they bring to Twitters around the world....

(Okay, this is the last time I write while *NFL Films* plays in the background.)

Twitter for the BlackBerry

On December 18, 2008, Research in Motion reported its subscribers to this—the first mobile phone to be considered a *smartphone*—reached the 21 million mark. It was a sticking point with our 44th president, Barack Obama, and the Secret Service. It was first introduced in 1999 and revolutionized in 2002 the way we handle wireless data transfer and communication, and even offers its own server to allow for integration into a company's network. I am talking, of course, about the *BlackBerry* (http://na.blackberry.com/eng/).

FIGURE 7.1

The BlackBerry (their latest model, Storm, pictured here) first introduced to the market a mobile phone that went far beyond what phones of the day could do.

What sets the BlackBerry (and other smartphones like it) apart from the SMS option for Twitter is that now, instead of using SMS (text only) for tweeting, you can now use the data network (3G, for example) to send messages back and forth. In other words, you are not in an Internet-like setting but truly *on* the Internet. Now tweeting from your phone, depending on the client, behaves as if you never left your desktop computer.

A Little Birdie Told Me...

Installation for a BlackBerry application is the same for all these Twitter clients. You can either download the application on your computer and install it with a manual sync, or you can perform a wireless download and installation. From there, the basics of logging in and tweeting do vary.

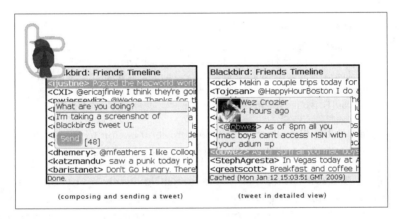

(composing and sending a tweet)   (tweet in detailed view)

FIGURE 7.2

Blackbird is a no frills, easy-to-use client for the Blackberry, presenting Twitter in a streamlined text-only format.

Blackbird

Some prefer the Joe Friday approach to Twitter: *"Just the facts, ma'am."* This is what Blackbird (http://dossy.org/twitter/blackbird) offers for BlackBerry users more into the simplicity and less on the avatars and aesthetics of Twitter. Blackbird sends and delivers tweets in a lean, text-only interface.

Getting Started with Blackbird

1. Download from http://dossy.org/twitter/blackbird your copy of Blackbird and install. Upon launching Blackbird, you will be asked to log into Twitter. Do so.

2. Click on the BlackBerry's trackball or Menu button to access Blackbird's main menu. Click on the Friends Timeline option to access tweets from your network.

3. Using the trackball, scroll down and find a tweet in your timeline and press the Enter/Return key to access this tweet. Details of the tweet, including the user's avatar, become visible.

4. To post a tweet, click the BlackBerry's trackball or Menu button to access Blackbird's main menu. Click on the Send Update option to access your Compose Tweet window in Blackbird.

5. Compose your tweet and then press the trackball again to access the Send option in the Compose Tweet window.

A Little Birdie Told Me...

If you want to see this particular exercise in action, you need to look no further than http://peek.snipurl.com/bbirdaat. BlackBerry and Twitter user @all-macallmike features this application in his video tutorial on how it works. (You might need to pause and replay parts of the clip a few times. His Finger Keyboard Fu is quite strong.)

6. Click the BlackBerry's trackball or Menu button to access Blackbird's main menu. Click on the Refresh option to refresh your tweets.

This is Blackbird in a nutshell. No razzle. No dazzle. Your tweets, delivered fast and simple. By delivering avatars only when a tweet's details are accessed, the application runs on the barest of resources. You can access websites and user profiles provided in tweets via the BlackBerry browser, but beyond that Twitter is operating on bare bones. If all you want are the basics from Twitter, Blackbird is your best option.

Although there are a variety of different options from client to client, the basics of accessing menus and options in these clients remain the same. By clicking on the BlackBerry's trackball, you access and scroll through the various features, select what you like to do, and then press the Return/Enter key to perform the action. Accepting that, let's take a look at some of the other clients available for the BlackBerry that inch closer to the Twitter experience of a desktop application.

Twibble

Blackbird is a terrific client if you are not one for the eye candy associated with Twitter, but what if you wouldn't mind something visually sweet to

savor? Don't worry. Some Twitter addicts across the pond in Germany created such a Twitter application that runs with the efficiency of Blackbird
but with just a hint more panache and flair. This is *Twibble*
(http://www.twibble.de/twibble-mobile/), a mobile Twitter client that offers
more than just text and the occasional avatar.

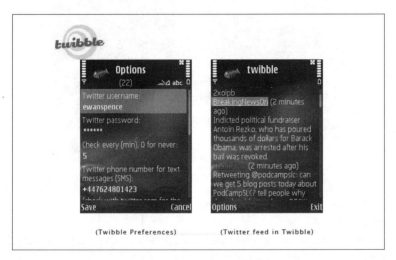

(Twibble Preferences)   (Twitter feed in Twibble)

FIGURE 7.3

*Twibble is a mobile client for the BlackBerry (and other Java-enabled smartphones) that simu-
lates the Twitter experience from your desktop.*

Twibble offers to its BlackBerry users many different options for mobile
tweeting:

- **Interface options**—Quick shortcuts provided for @replies, follow
  requests, mark as Favorites, retweets, and so on.
- **Auto Refresh**— Receive tweets automatically after preset time lapse.
- **Notification**—Configure twibble to vibrate when new tweets arrive.
- **TwitPic Integration**—With a few taps, photos can be uploaded into
  TwitPic and offered in your feed.
- **Keyboard shortcuts**—Popular options accessed via keyboard short-
  cuts, similar to a desktop computer.
- **Themes**—Twibble offers different interface themes.
- **Integrated timeline**—Followers' tweets, @replies, and direct mes-
  sages display in a single list, organized from most recent (top) to old-
  est (bottom).
- **Web access**—URLs contained in tweet are live and accessed via
  BlackBerry's default browser.

(Twibble Mobile)   (Twibble Desktop)

FIGURE 7.4

Twibble Mobile (left) sports a more simplified GUI for the BlackBerry compared to Twibble Desktop (right) that is built for your computer's operating system.

Keep in mind, this is Twibble Mobile, not Twibble Desktop. The desktop version of Twibble features options not available for the mobile version, including visual extras such as user avatars. Before installation, make sure you are downloading the right version of the software needed for your BlackBerry.

Tiny Twitter

Tiny Twitter (http://www.tinytwitter.com) may strike you, at first, as something akin to Blackbird in its extremely minimalist website. There's not much to it, but this is the nature of Tiny Twitter. Much like the home page for Twitter.com, Tiny Twitter keeps things simple but manages to give you everything you need to start.

FIGURE 7.5

Tiny Twitter offers a cross between the Twitter interface found in desktop clients and using SMS to retrieve and send tweets on your network.

Tiny Twitter, with a single-click of the trackball, gives you the following options:

- Update your feed.
- Compose and send a tweet.
- Access URLs featured in tweets.
- View @Replies and your Inbox (that is, DMs).
- Delete a selected tweet or all visible tweets.
- View a specific user's timeline.
- Edit Tiny Twitter Preferences (profile, font, auto-refresh, and such).

Unlike Blackbird and Twibble, little is available online about Tiny Twitter. I wanted to offer more on Tiny Twitter, and this is when I turned to my Twitter community and asked, *"Anyone out there using TinyTwitter?"* You could call this a "Hail Mary" on Twitter.

And just as a promising wide receiver of the Fighting Irish, someone responded.

Ben Wassink (@bwassink) is a designer for print and web and is on his way to become something of a Mac snob. He is also someone in my Twitter network who comments, shares links, and replies to others in his own network. In other words, he participates.

As I did with my own comments about desktop clients for Twitter, I have broken Ben's perspective on TinyTwitter into a similar breakdown. So let's get a user's experience in tweeting from his BlackBerry, his direct quotes appearing in italics.

What Ben Likes About Tiny Twitter

- **Auto-refresh**—This is a feature you would think is readily available for many of the mobile clients, but not so. Ben likes that Tiny Twitter takes care of the tweet retrieval. *"You can set your sync settings options being never, 4 minutes, 15 minutes, 30 minutes, every hour."*

- **Emulates desktop interface**—Tiny Twitter offers the option for you to view your Twitter stream as you would on a desktop client. *"Tiny Twitter displays both users' avatars and full tweets. You can also @reply and DM users through a convenient interface menu. You can also select an individual user and view their timeline."*

- **Efficient startup process**—One of the problems with many Twitter clients, both desktop and mobile versions, is they clear all previous tweets on shutting down. Tiny Twitter, however, works a little differently. *"When you quit Tiny Twitter, the application saves your feed, speeding up its launch on the next start up."*

- **Convenient Inbox for Direct Messages**—*"There is an 'inbox' for all of your Direct Messages, so you don't have to search for them."* Instead of having DMs distributed throughout your Twitter stream, Tiny Twitter ensures your privacy with this feature.

What Ben Doesn't Like About Tiny Twitter

- **Unostentatious interface**—*"This could be a plus or a minus but the interface is very 'plain'."* Although you do have the option of viewing avatars and full tweets, the interface—from a visual perspective—is a bit barren.

- **Accessing URLs is cumbersome**—Tiny Twitter does offer you live links featured in tweets, but getting to the website can be a bit clumsy. *"...to get to featured URLs, you open the Tiny Twitter menu, select 'access links,' then find the tweet with the URL, and* then *select the link."*

- **Auto-refresh should be user specified**—Although Tiny Twitter does offer an auto-refresh function, its settings—depending on your sleep preferences for the BlackBerry and your use of Twitter—might go untried. *"I think the sync settings could be more loose or perhaps even user-specified. I'm not sure that they actually update unless you're on the application all the time."*

FIGURE 7.6

Ben Wassink (@bwassink) takes his Twitter to go with Tiny Twitter, an application available for the BlackBerry.

Ben remains a Tiny Twitter user and is quite happy with the application when he's on the go. (To satisfy curiosity, he is a TweetDeck user when parked at his desktop.) Tiny Twitter might not be the same as actually working in Twitter on your desktop, but it still offers the interactivity and community Twitter nurtures, making it a good recommendation in bringing Twitter to your BlackBerry.

However, if you want the most popular Twitter client for the BlackBerry....

TwitterBerry

In the same vein of my "Hail Mary" of *"Anyone out there using TinyTwitter?"* I also asked, *"Is anyone tweeting on a BlackBerry? If so, what do you use?"* In the next hour I got hit hard with replies; and compared to Ben's one answer for Tiny Twitter, I received ten for this BlackBerry-friendly client.

TwitterBerry (http://orangatame.com/products/twitterberry/) is easily (in my Twitter networks) the most popular client for the BlackBerry. Provided you run BlackBerry OS 4.1.0+ (or OS 4.2+ for TwitPic support) and connect to the Internet via BlackBerry Internet Browsing Service, a BlackBerry Enterprise Server, or a direct data connection, this free client offers full integration with Twitter, including integration with TwitPic.

A single-click of the trackball brings up the main menu in TwitterBerry, offering you these options:

- Update your feed
- View Friends Timeline
- View @Replies
- View DMs
- Review Friends List
- Show Full Menu

The Full Menu option also allows access to

- Public Timeline (that is, everyone)
- Your Account's Timeline
- Sent DMs
- TwitterBerry Preferences
- TwitterBerry Information (version, developers, and such)

Getting Started with TwitterBerry

1. On your BlackBerry, launch your browser and visit http://orangatame.com/ota/twitterberry/ to download and install your copy of TwitterBerry. Upon launching TwitterBerry, you are asked to log into Twitter. Do so.

2. You are automatically sent to the default Twitter welcome screen, asking, *"What are you doing?"* You can compose your tweet here.

FIGURE 7.7

TwitterBerry, the most popular of Twitter clients for the smartphone, provides users with both Twitter and TwitPic integration.

3. Click on the BlackBerry's trackball or Menu button to access TwitterBerry's main menu. Click on **Update** option to send your tweet.

4. Click the BlackBerry's trackball or Menu button to access the main menu again. Click on the Full Menu option to explore the other features of TwitterBerry.

A Little Birdie Told Me...

You might notice on the more feature-rich, graphic intensive clients such as TwitterBerry that it might slow down in performance when compared to desktop clients or the actual website. Keep in mind that the performance of your mobile client, whatever platform you're on, will be based on the speed of your smartphone's data network.

Much like with Tiny Twitter, I wanted to cover more than just the features I got from its website. So I called on my dear friend, Heather Welliver (@HeatherWelliver), a singer, voice actress, and cohost of the Grailwolf's Geek Life (http://grailwolf.com) podcast. She is cited earlier in *All a Twitter* as an SMS Twitter that has made the jump from a standard mobile phone to a BlackBerry. She is also an active voice in the Twitter community and offers her own viewpoint on what does and doesn't work for her in TwitterBerry, and a side-by-side comparison between using SMS and using TwitterBerry for Twitter.

FIGURE 7.8

By clicking on the Full Menu option, TwitterBerry gives you more options to choose from for your tweeting tendencies.

What Heather Likes About TwitterBerry

- **Closer to the true online experience**—Although TwitterBerry is hardly TweetDeck or Twhirl, it is one step closer to emulating Twitter versus tracking community members using SMS. *"I was using SMS, so all I had to go on was pure text. Seeing avatars and timestamps are a wonderful change. TwitterBerry also keeps track of how many characters you have remaining, similar to my Twitter home page."*

- **Auto-refresh**—Much like Tiny Twitter, TwitterBerry takes care of collecting tweets from your feed. *"I have TwitterBerry refreshing every ten minutes, so I can control the flow of content coming in. This makes it easier for me to track with conversations."*

- **Ability to track entire network**—With SMS, users assigned specific people in their network to come into your phone via text. For wireless customers on limited text messaging plans, this could get expensive. Now, with TwitterBerry, the entire network is visible. *"This is really nice as you can see the beginning of a thread or topic versus with SMS where you pick up only part of conversation. So tweets that were once filtered out are now available to me."*

- **Active URLs**—With any links (TwitPic, news articles, and so on) arriving with tweets, TwitterBerry makes them active and easily interconnected with both TwitterBerry and the BlackBerry browser. *"The URLs open in my BlackBerry browser and I can easily switch between TwitterBerry and the browser, so I never lose my place in the conversation."*

- **Convenient Interface for @Replies and DMs**—*"If I see someone's tweet in my stream, I can single-click it using the trackball, and I automatically get two options: Reply or Direct Message. I love that."* So now, with TwitterBerry, you can easily reply to a tweet the best way warranted.

FIGURE 7.9

Podcaster and vocalist Heather Welliver (@HeatherWelliver) made the jump from using SMS to track Twitter to using TwitterBerry, and still she finds cons within the pros. (Photo courtesy of @Choochus and @VividMuse)

What Heather Doesn't Like About TwitterBerry

- **Features promised that do not work**—*"TwitterBerry has some extra features like Remove People from My Network, Make Favorites, and Follow,* *for example, that give me error messages every time."* TwitterBerry does offer a Support Forum if you run into problems. You can also track the various changes and improvements to each version. Still, promised features denied can be frustrating.

- **Filtering unavailable**—One of Heather's favorite things about TwitterBerry is also something that makes her Twitter experience on the BlackBerry a bit of a challenge. *"Everyone in my network is now delivered, whereas with SMS messages I could easily filter out certain 'Tweet-Happy' followers. While you can filter using desktop apps, you can't do that with TwitterBerry."*

- **Visual limitations**—Not all BlackBerry models have the portrait-to-landscape capabilities as the Storm, so visuals are lacking. *"With my BlackBerry Pearl, there are a lot of visual limitations both in the interface and in the browser. The avatars are unable to be viewed in detail and graphic-heavy websites like Bitstrips, AppleGeeks, and other web comics are not worth accessing."*

Heather's experience with Twitter, particularly with TwitterBerry's ease-of-use and emulations of both Twitter's home page and various third-party desktop clients, is no longer limited to being at her computer. Twitter for Heather, Ben, and many other users now happen anywhere and everywhere, or at least everywhere BlackBerry data exchanges can occur. Considering the addictive nature of BlackBerry (as is made evident by the nickname CrackBerry its community dubbed the device), it stands to reason that there would be such Twitter clients available.

The BlackBerry truly can be called the first of the smartphones, and like gunslingers of the Old West, there will always be the young upstarts who want to prove their salt by besting the legends of the quick draw. The newcomer to the world of smartphones is such an upstart, capturing the attention of such people as award-winning author Neil Gaiman (@neilhimself) and basketball legend (and also, affirmed tech geek) Shaquille O'Neil (@the_real_shaq). Already the newcomer has been met with equal praise and criticism, but it is also building a following that cannot (nor should not) be ignored.

And yes, the following have made their way onto Twitter.

Twitter for the G1

In October 2008, three heavy hitters would rise to the challenge of creating the next big thing in smartphones. With HTC designing the hardware,

Google creating the operating system, and T-Mobile as its carrier, the *Android G1* (or HTC Dream for some overseas clientele, and found online at http://www.androidg1.org) emerged as the new contender in the smartphone arena, offering some of the cool features of the iPhone with the keyboard of a BlackBerry, all in a compact design.

FIGURE 7.10

T-Mobile's G1, the first phone to be powered by the open source Android operating system, is the newest competitor in the smartphone market.

The *T-Mobile G1* and its Android operating system Market promises the best of both worlds (iPhone and BlackBerry) but with its own unique approach to wireless data exchange. With the open source nature behind Android, developers are encouraged to create applications that will truly make G1s an integral part of users' lifestyle.

This lifestyle integration, thankfully, includes Twitter.

Twidroid

Twidroid (http://twidroid.com), developed by Ralph Zimmermann and Thomas Marban, brings to the G1 a full Twitter experience though its easy-to-use interface and wide array of options.

A single-click of the menu button or the menu button on its touch-sensitive screen accesses Twidroid's main menu, offering to its users these options:

- Create new tweets, @Replies, and DMs from a single-line tweet field at the top of its interface.
- Receive tweets from your Followers, @Replies only, or DMs.
- Access detailed user profiles.
- Easily follow (or drop) a user to your network.
- Auto-completion of usernames you are sending tweets to.
- Integration with Android's gallery for sharing, and for uploading and tweeting via TwitPic and Phodroid.
- Options for interfacing with other Twitter-compatible APIs.

Other features of Twidroid include

- Interface compensation when working in both landscape and portrait mode
- Background notifications (similar to Twhirl) for replies and direct messages
- Integrated Search, Nearby, and GPS location options
- Native URL-shortening
- Custom notification sounds
- *Buzz* feature that allows you to view today's most talked about stories on twitter directly in the app. (courtesy of twittersphere.com)

FIGURE 7.11

Twidroid (its initial setup and launch screens featured here) takes G1 users into the Twitterverse with many terrific features and options.

Getting Started with Twidroid

1. On your G1, launch the Android Market and search for Twidroid to download and install your copy

2. When the Twidroid appears, launch it and touch the Setup button to launch.

3. Enter your username in the **Twitter ID** field and your **password** in the next open field. Then select how often you want Twidroid to retrieve new tweets for you from the drop-down menu of options.

4. A download window appears giving you a progress bar of tweets downloading from Twitter to your G1. When you have your previous tweets loaded, you can then tap into the blank field on the top of your interface and (with that slick G1 keypad) type in your tweet.

5. To reply to someone in your network, simply tap on that person's tweet and then select either the @Reply or DM option.

With the G1 being so new, it was difficult for me to find users in my immediate circles that were avid Twitters, but in the Twitterverse I called on Annette Holland (@daNanner), a project coordinator based out of California and a proud G1 user who loves to tweet. When she is behind her desktop, she floats between the workhorses TweetDeck and DestroyTwitter. When searching for something to take Twitter on the road with her, Twidroid was her first choice.

What Annette Likes About Twidroid

- **Easy Navigation**—*"It's very easy to perform basic functions from here. With one click, I find all the options accessible in a desktop client."* Twidroid is able to go above and beyond other mobile applications on account of the hardware. With the basics (composing of tweets, replies, DMs, preferences) kept to the touch-screen interface, higher functions can be assessed through the keyboard as well as the application's GUI.

- **Auto-refresh**—Unlike applications that download-for-pay, the free Twidroid collects tweets from your feed immediately from Setup. *"You can determine the settings, and its nice that Twidroid warns you that more frequent updates will use up the battery faster."*

- **Tracking options**—Keeping a sharp eye on the details and what Twitters want in their own mobile tweeting experiences, Twidroid developers considered what to offer its users in the way of options to reply. *"I like that I have options to follow my own network, follow replies, or simple review Direct Messages. Twidroid also keeps me up-to-speed on how many new tweets I have waiting for me."*

- **Notification options**—Twidroid notifies users by either vibrating the phone, sounding a chime, or using a visual cue courtesy of Android's built-in LED. *"Instead of the standard colors for battery life, the Android LED will flash blue when I receive tweets. A nice little detail."*

- **Twidroid's cache can be designated by user**—*"This is really nice for people with a lot of followers as cache can fill up pretty quickly. Also, by making it the SD card, Twidroid loads and runs faster."* Offering this preference to users, cache memory for messages, avatars, and other details needed to render tweets can be stored elsewhere than internal G1 memory space. Users can redirect Twidroid to store cache on an SD card up to 16GB in size. (Woah!)

- **Twidroid's developers are always listening**—*"I don't have a lot of issues with Twidroid as the developers address them all with every upgrade."* Between the forums and the ability to reach out and feedback to the developers on Twitter (@twidroid), the creative minds behind Twidroid are striving to make the application better.

FIGURE 7.12
Power Twitter Annette Holland (@daNanner), took her tweets on the road with her shiny new G1 via Twidroid and TwitterRide.

A Little Birdie Told Me...

There might be those rare occasions when you want more than just the 140-character reply from the developers or the grumblings of a user on an application's user forum. The good news is a quick search online (hey, why not—on your Google-powered G1) can offer review blogs and Android discussions that might give you resources to consult and opinions to ponder. So don't think you are working on your own with the G1. There are many helpful users out there to call upon.

What Annette Doesn't Like About Twidroid

- **No distinction between tweets**—*"There is no way to distinguish between new tweets and old ones."* When new tweets arrive there is no distinction between the tweets that were on screen previously and the ones newly arrived. (An example of a timestamp on new versus old tweets can be seen in Figure 7.5 of Tiny Twitter.)

- **Problem retrieving replies following Twitter upgrade**—With the change at Twitter changing @Replies to @Mentions, some clients were "confused" by the change, leading to missing replies. *"Since that update, Twidroid does not include all my replies since the update to Twitter API on March 30th, 2009."*

- **Battery life**—So what is the cost of the auto-refresh and receiving your tweets often? *"I like to refresh often, and that sucked my battery dry. Quickly."*

As Annette is a project manager and specializes in solving problems for people, she does not limit her Twitter habits to just one G1 application. Annette and I had a talk about another mobile client she uses. The host website for this application might keep things strictly to the facts and very little else, but don't let that fool you. This mobile Twitter client can take you for one sweet ride.

TwitterRide

The website where *TwitterRide* is found at (http://twitterride.net) describes the application as a simple and fast Twitter client for your Android G1, but I would argue that TwitterRide is selling itself short. (Well, it's not selling itself at all. It is also a free application.) Engineering mind and client creator Satoshi Tanimoto does keep the interface simple and the performance fast, but this is not SMS, Blackbird, or a bare-bones approach to Twitter.

FIGURE 7.13

Although TwitterRide describes itself as "simple and fast" its features and performance rivals Twidroid.

The basics of Twitter are all there:

- Create new tweets, @Replies, and DMs in a tweet field at the top of its interface.
- Receive tweets, @Replies, and Direct Messages from Followers.
- Access User Profiles.
- Integration with Android's gallery for sharing, and for uploading and tweeting via TwitPic.
- Quick access to Trends and Search Twitter.

These are the features you come to expect from Twitter clients, whether they are desktop or mobile devices like the G1. TwitterRide, however, doesn't mind adding a few extra perks to its interface:

- Built-in version checker to alert users of upgrades (which can be deactivated in Preferences).

- Auto-refresh runs when you post a new tweet.
- "Nearby" feature offered in GUI.
- Options available for Favorites management.
- Background notifications (similar to Twhirl) for replies and direct messages that also work as a shortcut to TwitterRide.
- Advanced features offered when showing User Profiles including a Follow/Unfollow button.

Getting Started with TwitterRide

1. On your G1, launch the Android Market and search for Twitterride to download and install your copy.
2. Launch TwitterRide, and when prompted enter your Username and your Password in the provided fields. Tap Verify Credentials to check your username and password.
3. You can then select the Use a Notification Icon as a Quick Launcher option if you want the background notification to do so. After you are set, tap Save to continue to the TwitterRide GUI.
4. When your previous tweets have loaded, click the Menu button on your G1 to access the main menu for TwitterRide. Select the Post option to compose a tweet in the interface.
5. When the tweet is ready, tap the Send option.
6. To reply to someone in your network, simply tap on that person's tweet and then select either the @Reply or DM option in the Post interface. You can also make this an open tweet by deselecting any of these two options.

What Annette Likes About TwitterRide

- **Fast load time**—*"It's much faster than Twidroid, even with the amount of Followers I have in my network."* As Twidroid seems to lag slightly on larger numbers, TwitterRide doesn't blink at the larger numbers of some Twitter networks.
- **Intuitive interface**—TwitterRide not only auto-refreshes tweets but also does so after you compose your tweets. There is also color-coding for new tweets and @Replies, and different options are available in a tabbed interface. *"I love the fact that you can auto-refresh when you post. And I still find the color-coding of new tweets one of its best features."*

- **Complete user's details and follow options offered** —With an avatar and both User Name and Real Name, TwitterRide gives accessed usernames their bios and a variety of other details, including the option to reply to their tweets or follow them in return. *"It's nice to have the ability to follow, unfollow, or block from my phone."*

What Annette Doesn't Like About TwitterRide

- **Integration of photos and TwitterRide sluggish**—*"Photos uploaded to TwitPic take over a minute to upload and tweet. From the G1 interface it is still faster to snap a photo and then share it via email to TwitPic."* Whenever incorporating media other than text into a tweet, that can cause a slowdown in performance, but because other clients can manage TwitPic integration, the sudden drop in TwitterRide's performance is noticeable.

- **Battery Life**—Much like Twidroid, TwitterRide does take a heavy toll on the G1's battery. *"With this latest update (1.2.0), I can't tweet for hours on one battery charge like I could before."*

- **Response to touch-screen inconsistent**—The G1, much like the iPhone, offers its users a slick touch-sensitive screen. This doesn't mean that the interface always works. *"Sometimes, I have to tap a feature or option several times before it finally engages."*

So this is how we take our Twitter even farther away from the keyboard and take the act featuring 140-characters on the road. When it comes to working on the go, however, you might wonder exactly where the third contender for the title of "Champion of the Twitterdome" is. Yes, we have explored the options for the BlackBerry and even gave the G1 newcomer a bit of time and attention. But where is the other?

Actually, it is plugged into my MacPro, resting up from today's tweeting and gearing up for another day out in the world. It's now time to look at how we tweet on the iPhone.

8

iPhone, Therefore iTweet

It was named *Time*'s Best Invention of 2007 and ranked highest by JD Power and Associates for Business Wireless Smartphone Satisfaction in 2008. Although the Blackberry might have revolutionized the mobile phone in what it could do, the iPhone changed everything in the way mobile phones were designed and interfaced with their users, interacting with their lives. I still couldn't buy into the iPhone when it came on the scene in 2007; but when I became an owner of one in 2008, I understood, and now I can't go anywhere without it.

FIGURE 8.1

The 800-pound gorilla of smartphones from Apple and AT&T, the iPhone.

iPhone users are as passionate about their phones as Mac users are passionate about their computers (present company included!), and tens of thousands of applications are available on the iTunes Application Store. Games. Extensions for other iPhone applications. Books (including one of my fiction titles!) and other pleasant diversions.

Applications are also available for the iPhone focusing on social networking, and some are made for bringing Twitter to you iPhone-style. So this chapter is for the iPhone users. Not only is Twitter made ready and available on our iPhones, but clients exist—both for free and for a small fee— that rival the power and capabilities of popular desktop clients. We focus on the set-up and the interfaces that seamlessly bring Twitter on the road with the iPhone.

A Little Birdie Told Me...

Similar to the Blackberry, installation for an iPhone application is the same across the board. You can either download the application on your computer and install it with a manual sync, or you can perform a wireless download and installation. From there, the basics of logging in and tweeting vary.

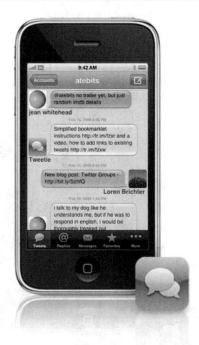

FIGURE 8.2

Tweetie, developed by atebits, takes advantage of the graphics and pizazz of the iPhone and replicates all the fun of a Twitter desktop client.

Tweetie

Tweetie (download for USD$2.99, available at the iTunes Application store with additional information found at http://www.atebits.com/software/tweetie/) brings to the iPhone a compact and innovative interface that outshines my first iPhone Twitter client, *Twitterific*. (Go with what you know! But if you don't know Twitterific, hop back to Chapter 4 and read up on Twitterific.) Tweetie brings all the capabilities offered to you by a client like Destroy Twitter or TweetDeck (which, like Twitterific, you can find out more about in Chapter 4), and even a few capabilities that would be welcome to a desktop client.

Setup of Tweetie

When you first launch Tweetie, you will be walked through the login procedure commonly found in setups for many Twitter clients, but in this exercise we take advantage of a feature not found in all Twitter clients.

1. After purchase, download, and installation, launch Tweetie and enter in your Username and Password. Type in the necessary username and password, and then touch the Done button in the lower-right corner.

2. Your tweets are then gathered from your network, organized as "most recent" at the top to "oldest" at the bottom. You can scroll along your Timeline by dragging your finger along the height of your screen.

FIGURE 8.3
Tweetie offers you different ways of viewing your tweets, either in a traditional Twitter layout or something closer to iChat.

3. Before tweeting, return to your iPhone's home page for a moment and touch Settings to get to your Phone and Application Settings. Scroll down to the bottom of the screen for the preferences on Tweetie.

4. Set up Tweetie here with

   • **Themes** you want to use for Twitter interface

   • **Font Sizes** best for your comfort level of reading

   • **Display Name or Screen Name** so that you can identify those easily on Twitter

   • **Integration** with other Twitter services like TwitPic or Mobypicture

   • **Advanced Features** such as Multiple Accounts, Sound Effects, Landscape Keyboard, and how many tweets initially load

   While you set up Tweetie to appear the way you want, make sure to activate the Advanced > Multiple Accounts feature.

5. Launch Tweetie again. Before tweeting *(Wait for it!),* touch the Accounts arrow in the upper-left corner. This takes you to your Twitter Accounts page.

6. Touch the + button in the upper-right corner to add in details of a second Twitter account. This procedure automatically logs you into the new account. To return to the original account, simply click on the Accounts arrow and touch the account you want to track with.

A Little Birdie Told Me...

Why have more than one Twitter account? If you decide to run a second Twitter account for your business, or are recruited to head up a Social Media initiative at your day job, you might want to consider the advantages of a second account. For one thing, the "professional" account might be a better place to talk shop whereas the "personal" account can be where you tweet how a recent episode of *EUReKA* has made that series your favorite television show. Find out more about the reason behind multiple accounts in Chapter 11, "Taking Care of Business."

7. *Now, let's tweet!* Touch the Compose button in the top-right corner of the interface. Go on and type up your tweet and touch the blue Send button in the top-right corner.

FIGURE 8.4

The Compose button found in many of Tweetie's screens (this one is the More option on your menu bar) accesses the interface for typing up tweets.

8. Scroll to the top of your list of tweets and touch the Refresh icon (a circular arrow) at the top of your tweets. This retrieves new tweets for you.

From here, the best way to get to know Tweetie is to play. Whether it is on a commuter train or during a lunch break, tune out the outside world and start playing with it. The trick of Tweetie's interface (as covered in the following section) is exploring the various features and the features nested within features. I am not exaggerating when I say this tiny $3 application does a *lot*, including a few things that many desktop clients do not do. So go exploring and see what tools and toys work for you!

What I Like About Tweetie

- **Viral tweeting**—Touching the icon in the lower-left corner of an expanded tweet (a tweet that has been tapped open) allows you to repost (retweet) a tweet, post a direct URL to the tweet in your feed, or email the tweet to people not on Twitter or to yourself for later reference.

- **Ability to switch from account to account**—For many desktop and mobile Twitter clients, to log into a different user account requires you to log out and then log in under different credentials. For Tweetie, you enter in the account information once and then in two taps of the screen you are in the new account. Quick, simple, and oh so efficient.

- **Visually stunning and highly interactive interface**—In this application, windows slide back to reveal details of users, tapping avatars fade up from black profile pictures in full resolution. Touching and dragging a single tweet aside reveals options for replying, user profile, or creating favorites. Part of the fun in this application is simply seeing what does and doesn't slide away, and what surprises are awaiting you behind every window.

- **Options, options, options**—Where do I begin on this one? Did you know that when you double-tap on an @Mention (referred to as an @Reply in Version 1.3.1, featured here), you can review the conversation tweet-by-tweet by clicking the In Reply to (username) button? Did you also know you can click on the More option at the bottom of the screen and access a tool called Nearby that looks for active Twitters in your area? Did you also know under the same option you can look up what Trends (hashtags, common keywords, and such) are happening across the Twitter network? All this (and *still* more) is happening in Tweetie.

What I Don't Like About Tweetie

- **Options, options, options...where are they again?**—You might notice that one of Tweetie's biggest perks is also one of its greatest shortcomings. Many of the cool features offered by Tweetie are hidden, mentioned only in passing on the website but with no explanation as to how they work or where they are. This turns the application into something like a treasure hunt where you do something by accident, find something new or unlock a new feature, and then you spend a good portion of the day trying to figure out how you did whatever it is you did to get that cool feature. This kind of hunt-and-tap-or-swipe might have been a lot of fun when playing *Myst* but I really don't want to search for my features.

- **Updates are out of sequence**—In its features, Tweetie promises to Remember Scroll Position on Launch and Reload but for me (and I was in version 1.3), I found myself scrolling back to the last tweet I recognized before my own appeared. Twitterific for both desktop and mobile kept track of where I was better than this. Additionally, Tweetie would either post replies out-of-sequence or lose tweets altogether. This meant missed @Replies and unanswered DMs.

- **No alert sound or notification for new tweets**—On every refresh I had to keep an eye on my Twitter stream because I was given no audio or even visual indication that new tweets had arrived. Perhaps it does sound a bit of a nit-pick but considering other clients do this, I would assume that Tweetie would follow suit. I was wrong.

- **No Auto or Global Refresh**—For everything Tweetie has to offer, the fact it does not offer an auto-refresh for retrieving tweets is shocking. What makes this last point a real deal breaker for me, though, is the lack of global refreshing when you do retrieve new tweets. When you refresh your Twitter stream, you might notice when you visit @Replies that there are no new tweets there, even though you saw one or two replies arrive in your Friends stream. This is because when you refresh your Friends Tweet stream, that is the only Twitter feed you update. @Replies and DMs are separate feeds; at least this is how Tweetie regards them.

Tweetie leaves me torn a bit because I see its potential as a mobile client, and wow, does it offer the features. I particularly find myself drawn to the visuals that remain untouchable by other clients. The lack of an auto-refresh feature, though, is tough for me to let slide; but this does not mean that Twitters are sharing my mindset. The application tops the iTunes Application Store charts for paid downloads, and iPhone users remain supportive of it as a way of taking Twitter with them.

The good news is that you have choices and although iPhone users sang the praises of Tweetie in my network, another client was brought to the forefront. I have also been playing around with this client as well, and see why this is the *other* paid download that users rave about.

Twittelator

From Stone Design (http://www.stone.com) comes the other heavy hitter, *Twittelator* (available as a free download or in a Pro version for USD$4.99 from the iTunes Application store with additional information found at http://www.stone.com/Twittelator/). Developer Andrew Stone offers two versions, a Lite version and Pro version.

FIGURE 8.5

Offered as both a paid and free download, Twittelator (Pro version's interface on left, Free on the right) brings to your iPhone a fully loaded Twitter experience.

As seen in Figure 8.5, there is a slight difference between the Free version and the Pro. At first, I started using the Free version; but on paying a visit to Twittelator's homesite, I found at http://www.stone.com/Twittelator/Pro_versus_Lite_Features.html a full list of features that were exclusive to the Pro version. Here are just a few options that sold me right away:

Writing Tweets

- Landscape mode for easy typing.
- Toggle Private/Reply with tap of user's name in the tweet.
- Options to Retweet, Email tweet, and send link to Instapaper available.
- Option to access recently used hashtags now available.
- Option to access recent Friends and @Mention other friends in same tweet now available.
- Option to shorten URLs using bit.ly, piurl.com, href.in, is.gd, or .ws.

- Add a photo (including high resolution images) to your tweet via TwitPic, Pikchur.com, yFrog.com or moby.
- Option to turn tweet confirmation on or off.

Reading a Tweet

- Large readable font size.
- Thumbnail of featured photos (TwitPic, MobyPic, Yfrog, and Pikchur) appear with accompanying tweet.
- Tap bubble to review a conversation (from initial tweet to most recent reply).
- View your Twitter stream, and DMs you have sent.
- Turn on/off auto-refresh of new tweets.
- Option to refresh all view options on new tweet retrieval.

Based on these (and other really cool) features outlined at the earlier-referenced URL and because I manage more than one Twitter account, I went on and spent the $4.99 for Twittelator Pro. Since that investment, I have turned on at least five people in my TeeMonster network on the application and even convinced a few people to make the jump to the Pro version after writing a review for AppleiPhoneApps.com (http:// appleiphoneapps.com). For *All a Twitter*, the screen captures and features seen here will be coming from Twittelator Pro. If you are using the free version of Twittelator, some of these features may not be available.

Believe me when I tell you, Twittelator Pro will be smartest $5 you will spend at iTunes. Go on, jump in with both feet, purchase Pro, and read on! But if you are still not convinced, visit http://www.stone.com/ Twittelator/Pro_versus_Lite_Features.html for a full comparison of the Free download's capabilities versus the Pro upgrade.

Multiple Account Setup and Tweeting in Twittelator Pro

Much like in your initial launch of Tweetie, you will be prompted for login found in setups for Twitter clients on your first launch of Twittelator. Also like Tweetie, you can enter in multiple accounts. So if you run more than one account on Twitter, let's enter in a second here in Twittelator.

1. After purchase, download, and installation, launch Twittelator Pro and enter in your Screen Name and Password. Type in the necessary user name and password, and then touch the Next button in the lower-right corner.

2. Your tweets are then gathered from your network, organized as "most recent" at the top to "oldest" at the bottom. You can scroll along your Timeline by dragging your finger along the height of your screen, or you can tap the top toolbar to scroll up one page.

3. Before tweeting, go to the bottom of your Twittelator interface and touch More to go to the More Options page. Touch your current username (marked with a key icon) at the top of the list.

FIGURE 8.6

Twittelator Pro offers you the ability to float between different Twitter accounts, review Trends, perform a variety of Searches, and even set up Subgroups, all with the More option.

4. Touch the Add Account button in the lower-center portion of your interface to add in details of a second Twitter account. Touch Done to complete the login. You now have a new account added to Twittelator. Touch the account you want to monitor.

5. Click on the Friends icon to return to your Friends Timeline.

6. Touch the Compose button in the top-right corner of the interface. Type up your tweet and touch the blue Send button in the top-right corner.

A Little Birdie Told Me...

Before you really get into composing your tweet, turn your iPhone around to view the screen in Landscape mode. It doesn't matter which way your turn it, but go and see what happens.

Sure, I'll wait.

Pretty cool, huh? You can now compose tweets with a Landscape Oriented Keypad, making tweet composition that much easier. You also have available here all the terrific add-ons you can give a tweet such as TwitPic, Current Location, special characters (also known in typographical circles as Dingbats), and even a special Copy/Paste feature. Sadly, you cannot view your tweets in Landscape, but this is just another slick feature available (and oh so easy to love!) in Twittelator Pro.

7. When you see a reply to you or want to reply to someone, touch the Twitter's name once to access a variety of ways to reply:

    - *Reply* for the standard @Reply to a tweet.

    - *Private* to send a DM to this person.

    - *Re-Tweet (RT)* for retweeting this selected tweet across your network

    - *Email Tweet*, which launches your iPhone Mail program and composes an email featuring this tweet.

    - *Copy Tweet*, which copies this tweet and allows you to paste it in a tweet of your own, or edit accordingly to send out on your network (a variation of a Retweet).

    - *Favorite Tweet* for making a place for this tweet in your own personal Hall of Fame.

    - *Copy Link* for when a tweet features a URL. With this option, you can copy just the featured link of a tweet and use it in tweets of your own.

    Touch your desired option, and if you need to, compose your accompanying tweet and touch the blue Send button.

8. Touch the Settings icon (a gear icon) at the bottom of your screen to access the various preferences available for Twittelator. Between Image Options and Sub Groups is the Autorefresh Tweets option where you can activate or deactivate automatic retrieval of tweets.

Now comes the time for you to explore. Instead of tinkering with Tweetie on your commuter train or lunch break, you tinker with Twittelator. Similar to Tweetie's interface there are features nested within features; but in putting together this review and in spending some quality time with its latest version, I am concluding this was time (and money) well spent. Even Subway's $5-Foot-Long can't compare to the satisfaction I'm getting from Twittelator.

What I Like About Twittelator

- **Ingenious, intuitive interface**—Twittelator has all the visual and interactive perks of Tweetie, but unlike Tweetie the interface is easier to navigate and find what you want and what you need. For example, if you want to track with a conversation, you simply touch the speech bubble to the right of a tweet. Same with viewing TwitPic; you touch on the thumbnail of the featured image. Also, some things have become simplified. If you touch a tweets avatar once, you are asked if you want to view the details of that user (or other users featured in the tweet) . Whichever option you choose accesses that user's details. A single tap of the avatar brings up a more detailed version of the profile picture. A single tap of name puts you into reply mode. The paperclip (signifying an attached URL) opens included links. This is what a truly intuitive interface should be. Logical. Progressive. Elegant.

- **Auto-refresh**—Two words: thank you.

- **Landscape keyboard for composing tweets**—Four words: thank you very much.

FIGURE 8.7

One reason to consider Twittelator Pro is the Landscape Keyboard feature, making tweets even easier to type.

- **Notification of new tweets in the menu bar**—When you access your preferred view option (Friends, @Replied, DMs), the icon is given a tiny notification number (as seen in other iPhone apps) that tell you how many tweets have arrived and remain unread. Very handy, very efficient.

- **Ability to track conversations**—I first saw this on Tweetie and cannot rave enough about this feature, but Twittelator has perfected this in its latest version. To access this feature, you touch the time signature/speech bubble next to an @Reply. Your page switches to Conversation mode with all the tweets pertaining to the reply. What a fantastic feature!

- **Subgroups**—Twittelator took one of TweetDeck's most powerful attributes, the capability to create Groups within your Followers and adapted it for an iPhone application. With Subgroups (found in the More option of your menu), you can now organize your followers into various categories much like you do in TweetDeck. After you tap the Subgroups option, you either press the + icon to create a new group or tap on the Edit option (the blue-white icon) of a pre-existing group to add to it. Simply scroll through your network and add people into your subgroup. This is a terrific way of "increasing the signal strength" within Twitter's occasional noise.

What I Don't Like About Twittelator

- **Tweet notifications could use a tweak**—This might seem like a slight nit-pick on my part, but (again, like Tweetie) I am so impressed with the application on a whole that I'm surprised at the details overlooked. I love the fact that when I launch Twittelator, I'm notified of new tweets both with audio and alert icons, but after that I am notified only in my current view option, unless I turn on the Refresh refreshes Favs option. I was unaware of this until it was brought to my attention on the website.

  And the notification sound? If you offer me a choice in themes, I'd like a choice of audio, too. (The nostalgic aspect of me misses the Twitterific chirp.)

Apart from the one gripe, that is it. Twittelator has proven to be akin to the TweetDeck of mobile Twitter, and the more I play with it the more I love it. For the investment, you cannot beat it. This is money well spent on iTunes, and time well spent in getting to know this application.

But what if you really want to keep the five dollars spent on a Twitter client for a movie rental for the AppleTV or for four of your favorite songs? Well then, it's time to turn to the free downloads in iTunes' Application Store. Along with Twittelator Lite, there are free options such as Twinkle, the minimalistic Tweeter, and the old friend of the Twitterverse, Twitterific. Other free applications like Whrrl, WhosHere, and fring offer functionality with Twitter and other social networking services to keep your networks up to speed on where you are, what you're doing, and who you happen to be hanging out with. The great thing about these options is they are all free-of-charge, so giving them a spin comes down to you wanting to sit down to get to know what they do, how they do it, and how effective and efficient is the interface.

When I think of a free download that is all this and more, only one application comes to mind.

FIGURE 8.8

A favorite with the iPhone crowd is the feature-rich and cost-free download, TwitterFon.

TwitterFon

Developed by Kazuho Okui (http://naan.net) and available as a free download, TwitterFon (http://twitterfon.net) is one of the most intuitive and easy-to-use Twitter clients available anywhere, and one I would also rank as high as favorites like Twittelator Pro and Twhirl.

One of the main reasons TwitterFon impresses me so much is that it is the only free Twitter client I have used that offers in its Preferences an auto-refresh command. TwitterFon can retrieve tweets for me every 3, 5, or 10 minutes; or I can completely disable auto-refresh. That is a little touch all iPhone-Twitter clients should come with, in particular Twitterific because it is has perhaps one of the longest reputations of all Twitter clients in the community.

Setup and Tweeting in TwitterFon

1. After purchase, download, and installation, TwitterFon takes you to the Settings page where you enter in your Username and Password. You can access this page by returning to your iPhone's Home screen, tapping on Settings, and accessing the TwitterFon preferences there. After a username and password is accepted, you can now jump into Twitter via TwitterFon.

2. Along the bottom of your screen are the following options:
   - **Friends**—Your network of followers
   - **@Mentions**—any tweets that reference you
   - **Messages**—Direct Messages sent to you
   - **Favorites**—Your Hall of Fame of tweets you want to keep on record
   - **Search**—Twitter Search on TwitterFon

   If you have new tweets arrive, whether they are new tweets in your network, @Replies, or DMs, these icons are tagged with a tiny alert indicator telling you how many you have.

3. Your tweets are then gathered from your network, organized as "most recent" at the top to "oldest" at the bottom. You can scroll along your Timeline by dragging your finger along the height of your screen.

4. When you want to compose a tweet, touch the Compose Tweet icon in the upper-right corner of TwitterFon.

5. After you compose your tweet, tap the Send button in the top-right corner. You can close the window in the middle of composing the tweet by tapping the Close button in the upper-left corner. This will not delete the tweet but pause its composition.

6. To delete a tweet you're composing and start over, touch the Trash Can icon located to the lower-left corner of the Compose Tweet field. If you change your mind before typing again, you can touch the Undo button that appears to restore the deleted tweet.

7. In the lower-right corner of the Compose Tweet field you have

    - **Character Counter**—Starting at 140 and counting down.

    - **Current Location**—If Google Maps can find you by your iPhone, you can tweet your location.

    - **TwitPic**—Tap the camera icon to tweet a picture. Your TwitPic URL appears during the sending of the tweet, so keep the accompanying tweet with it short.

    Touch your desired option and if you need to, compose your accompanying tweet and touch the Send button.

FIGURE 8.9

With a single tap on a tweet, user details and various response options are available.

8. Touch a tweet you want to reply to and your screen slides away to show you a variety of options for this tweet including

- Make a Favorite
- In-reply-to: (which reveals the Conversation)
- Reply
- Send a DM
- Retweet

You can also access a user's details or timeline from here as well.

What I Like About TwitterFon

- **TwitterFon feels like a real desktop client, not an iPhone app—** Perhaps it does not offer all the various options of a client like TweetDeck or Twhirl; but in its compact design, TwitterFon preserves the looks and feel of a fully tricked-out Twitter desktop client. Avatars are present. Profiles are easily accessed with a single tap. (More on that later.) Various viewing options (Viewing @Replies, viewing DMs, Twitter Search) are all available in a toolbar underneath. When composing a tweet or an @Reply, TwitterFon offers GoogleMaps to give your current location and TwitPic to send photos from your phone to your network. You also have a People Finder so that you can sift through your network, and a Delete feature that even offers an Undo option. So far, it is as if you have never left your desktop Twitter client of choice.

- **Color-coded tweets—**This might seem, at first, to be a purely trivial perk, but it actually is a strong trait of TwitterFon. Considering how users scan tweets, TwitterFon took an extra step by color-coding everything new that is retrieved, in that Twitter-blue we all know so well. @Replies are shaded in a pastel green, making them pop out from the sea of cerulean blue. New DMs, although not present in your Friends Timeline, pop out even harder against previously viewed DMs because they are highlighted in a bronze color. You can remove the new tweet color by switching to a different option in the toolbar.

- **Alert notifications in toolbar—**When new tweets arrive, both at the launch and throughout your session, you are notified exactly how many new tweets are unread by a small red icon labeled with the number of updates.

- **Full tweet options with a single touch and easy-to-touch icons—** When that pastel green catches your eye or possibly a new tweet inspires in you a 140-character reply, TwitterFon, with a simple tap on the tweet in question, reveals the friendliest of user-friendly interfaces. Your Friends timeline slides aside to show an array of options, all easily accessed with large buttons. Directly to the left of the tweet is a star icon, allowing you to Favorite the tweet. Directly below the tweet's bubble are the options to reply, send a DM, or retweet.

- **Auto-Refresh—**As with Twittelator, Twitterific automatically retrieves your tweets. Considering Twitterific and Tweetie (download-for-pay applications) fail to do that, it is quite nice that there is a free application that does. And while you work on what kind of reply you want to make, TwitterFon is still collecting tweets so that you are not inundated with new content on returning to your Twitter stream.

- **Alphabetical Follower search list—**The People Search on Twhirl, for example, works in the order of whom you last followed or who followed you, the same way on Twitter.com. On TwitterFon, this list is alphabetical. Alphabetical. To quote the animated brewers of the Guiness commercials: *Brilliant!*

- **Stable performance with ingenious GUI—**Navigation in TwitterFon is intuitive, clever, and easy to figure out; its screen transitions back and forth are smooth and slick. Maybe I'm just one for the bells and whistles, but I do like the visual eye candy Okui has added. With all its eye-popping pizazz, TwitterFon remains a rock-solid application, having never crashed or locked up my iPhone at any given time.

What I Don't Like About TwitterFon

- **Options for DMs inconsistent with TwitterFon's overall performance** —DMs do not appear in your main timeline at all. You are notified of a DM in the toolbar, but I would prefer the DMs also appear in my Friends window as well. Another peeve in the DM department is when you reply to a DM, you suddenly switch into an iChat-style visual mode, similar to when you use SMS on an iPhone. I find this a little jarring, and in some situations I have forgotten I'm in Twitter, thinking I was using SMS. I would prefer to stay in the TwitterFon GUI, simply for sanity's sake.

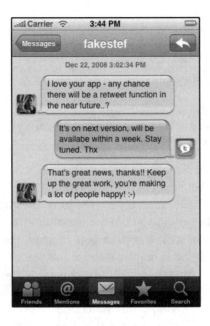

FIGURE 8.10

With all the things about TwitterFon that are Twitter-centric, the step back to the SMS/iChat-like display is a bit disorienting.

- **No audio alert** —There is one bell and whistle is missing from TwitterFon, and it is just that: *a bell* or *whistle*. Although Twitterific does have its signature chime and bird tweet alarm, and Twittelator gives the quick click that new tweets have arrived, TwitterFon offer no options for an alert sound anywhere. It's a small detail; but considering all the other details TwitterFon initiated, I'm surprised this one was overlooked.

With only those two tiny hang-ups, keep in mind that TwitterFon is free. The developer isn't even asking for a donation. (He should!) Additionally, TwitterFon's developer gives this free download plenty of attention, upgrading it often enough where I feel comfortable it is still up-to-speed-and-expectations, but I don't worry about its stability. TwitterFon is not just a good Twitter client for the iPhone, but it is a good Twitter client, *period*. It easily stands tweet-to-tweet with the Adobe AIR-powered power-houses of TweetDeck and Twhirl, and outperforms many of the pay-for-download Twitter applications. I recommend without hesitation or reservation this application to any iPhone user connected to Twitter.

Fail Whale Says...

Now with all these wonderful options for tweeting on the go, do not think for one second that tweeting while driving is a smart thing to do. It's not. In fact, tweeting while *walking* can have its own dangers. When you tweet on the go, whether you are on foot or behind the wheel, remain aware of your surroundings at all times. Mobile tweeting is better for commuter trains, public transportation, and locations not conducive for computers. Safety first, for yourself and for the real-world community.

If you are already suffering a Twitter addiction, I hate to be the enabler here, but this is not going to help you curtail, in any way, your fix for following your Followers. You need to rely on your own sound judgment and etiquette to make certain you are not tweeting within mixed company and appearing like some rude tech geek immersed in his or her iPhone or BlackBerry. And no, it is highly doubtful you will be let off with a warning from the police if you tell them "I wasn't texting, I was *tweeting!*" (It wouldn't surprise me if in the next six months someone will be the first fined for a DWT—Driving While Tweeting.) There is a great big world out there, and you want to make sure that even with the power of Twitter to go, you don't miss out on anything special or place yourself in danger on account of divided attentions.

Still, there is something very, very cool about being able through Twitter to take your network with you wherever you go. Sometimes, it's the TwitPic of a sunset or a random thought of appreciation that can go a long way with your community—and maybe even turn around someone's day.

9

The Trouble with Twitter

By now, you are up to speed on what Twitter is, how it works, and what you can do to build your community. This sounds like a well-spring of opportunity; but while it might promise happy places, unicorns, and gumdrop rain showers, Twitter is still a work-in-progress. This was an experiment in text messaging back in 2006 when Jack Dorsey developed for media search engine and directory Odeo, a method of sharing user statuses across its network. From this experiment came what Dorsey, Evan Williams, Biz Stone, and all of us call Twitter. Could Twitter's creators have foreseen the immense popularity of this service? Considering that Complete.com in February 2009, ranked Twitter as the third-largest social networking platform (just behind Facebook and MySpace, respectively), it's hard to say. Only Dorsey, Willams, and Stone really know for sure what they were thinking the moment they went live with Twitter. However, I would dare to venture to say they knew their undertaking wouldn't be easy. Especially when you consider that between February and March of 2009, *Social Times* (http://bit.ly/SocialTimes) reported that Twitter's membership grew 33 percent just within the United States. Mashable.com (http://bit.ly/AYxn) reported that 2008 Twitters experienced a 752 percent growth in unique visitors. With this kind of traffic, it's a bit naïve to think there won't be the occasional fender bender, beltway backup, or road construction slowing you down.

That's what this chapter is all about: growing pains and the best way to deal with them.

The Double-Edged Sword of Success

Although the outages appear to be under control and occur only at the odd moment here and there (and it is relative, but it usually happens to me when I'm *really* into a conversation with someone), this does not mean that Twitter is an error-free service by any stretch. This is all part of success, particularly if you underestimate its level. With the demand out on its server, Twitter finds communication between the left hand and the right hand difficult. This is when confusion and hilarity ensue; only the hilarity is absent.

These are some things that might happen without warning while you're tweeting. Keep an eye out for these odd moments in your day.

The Fail Whale

"Towards thee I roll, thou all-destroying but unconquering whale; to the last I grapple with thee; from hell's heart I stab at thee; for hate's sake I spit my last breath at thee."

Perhaps those of you who have, in fact, tackled this literary classic recognize this quote from Herman Melville's *Moby Dick*. For my fellow geeks, you're probably flashing back to Ricardo Montalban's dying words in *Star Trek II: The Wrath of Khan*. However, on Twitter, the Great White Whale is an icon we are all too familiar with.

Almost as iconic as Twitter's cerulean blue bird, the *Fail Whale* strikes terror and frustration into the hearts of Twitter users everywhere. The Fail Whale, seen in Figure 9.1, appears when Twitter traffic—unique visitors, timeline chatter, direct messages, and API requests from other clients—goes above and beyond their servers' capabilities.

This image of a whimsical whale carried aloft by birds has become synonymous with Twitter, even appearing outside the network on T-shirts, rock buttons, and animated in "The Twouble with Twitter" (http://bit.ly/TwoubleTwitter) from Current (http://current.com). Between 2007 and 2008, the Fail Whale seemed to pop up far too frequently to users' liking. Tech critics lambasted Twitter for poor service to users around the world relying on Twitter to deliver. Even today, tweets fly in protest whenever the Shamu of Social Media comes up for air....

My thoughts on the Fail Whale: This, too, shall pass.

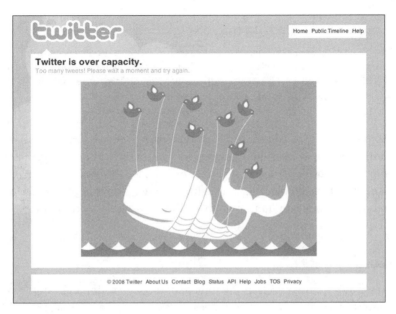

FIGURE 9.1

The Fail Whale usually makes an appearance, much to the grumblings of Twitter users, when the servers exceed their capacity.

I remember in January 2008, Twitter went offline and stayed offline for hours. Skype was also running on my desktop, and my friends there were in a right panic. Twitter was down! We're cut off! No transmissions were coming in from Colony LV-426! Quick, send in the Colonial Marines!! The next day, Twitter was back online. Balance was restored, and yet the criticism flew on the shoddy performance of Twitter, particularly during high traffic generated by events such as political party debates, MacWorld, South by Southwest, and the like.

Twitter has improved its system architecture and server performance, all in the midst of astounding growth; and Twitter also offers a status blog (http://status.twitter.com/) to keep its users in the loop on what is going on with its performance. Because of the improvements and the exponential interest in the service, Twitter has managed to remain stable and perform up to its potential, but this does not mean that the Fail Whale is extinct. An endangered species? Maybe, but it does occasionally pop up now and then. When it appears on your browser or if you find your client failing to make a connection, this might be a good time to take a break from tweeting. The crew at Twitter.com will get you up and running before you know it. It's only a temporary ghost in its networking machine.

A Little Birdie Told Me...

If you want to see a hilarious commentary on Twitter and its growing pains, take a look at this YouTube video (http://bit.ly/TwitterDown) entitled "No Twitter for Hitler." Taken from the film *Downfall*, the captions for this scene were rewritten in a parody that is "Not Safe for WorK" but still quite funny. Even if you are new to Twitter, a lot of the humor in this mash-up video rings true.

Something else to consider: We get this service *for free*. Twitter's "seven dark days" in 2008 is quite impressive considering it had no business model in place and does not charge anyone for this service. The critics who demand 100 percent uptime from Twitter seem out of bounds to me because no one can guarantee that kind of service, especially for a service that isn't charging you a dime.

Lost Tweets

You might find yourself in the middle of a conversation and then a reply comes across your stream that doesn't seem to make a lot of sense although you know it has something to do with your current topic. You might also receive an anxious *"Didn't you see my earlier tweet?"* direct message (DM) without warning. What gives?

Lost tweets can occur when a server is either experiencing a large amount of traffic or is close to Fail Whale territory. Sometimes, it can occur when your third-party client (Twhirl, TweetDeck, and such) isn't communicating effectively with Twitter.com. Granted, it is possible to miss a tweet if you multitask throughout the day. If a quick scroll through your client's @Replies reveals nothing new but a hop over to Twitter.com uncovers the missing tweet, then there's a problem

If the problem is the desktop client, a good idea is to decrease the amount of API requests, save the changes, and then reboot the application. If, however, a manual refresh on the website or a timed refresh on your desktop client of choice suddenly gives you several tweets out of chronological order, the problem may reside at Twitter.com. If this is the case you are left to the mercy of Twitter's servers to get caught up. This might mean a sudden fallout of @Replies and DMs on a manual refresh.

A Little Birdie Told Me...

When Twitter misbehaves, it might be a good idea to find out what is happening in the world. A friend of mine, on refreshing her page, was hit with a tsunami of tweets from me. (Apparently, I filled two pages worth of @Replies on her browser.) So what happened here?

That night, Barack Obama accepted his victory in the 2008 Election.

Traffic on Twitter was heavy that night, and unlike the past debates—both party and presidential—Twitter managed to stay online. This didn't mean the servers were not working hard. Whether you are on the receiving or sending side of a tweet fallout, try to be understanding. An email or a quick nudge on Skype asking "What happened?" might not be a bad thing to do.

In the occurrence of lost tweets, patience is a virtue. If you get a DM or a public tweet asking if you missed a tweet, and you cannot find the tweet on your desktop client, swing your browser by Twitter.com and take a look at your home page there. You might find what you're looking for there.

Followers Dropped Without Consent or Knowledge

It has happened to the best of us. To Chris Brogan. To Robert Scoble. To me. You log on to Twitter.com or pull up your statistics on DestroyTwitter or Twhirl, and notice that a large number of your Followers have suddenly disappeared. Especially if you work with a service called Qwitter (website referenced in Appendix A), you might get a large number of notices all telling you that certain people are no longer following you on Twitter. Just like that. and you scratching your head asking, "Was it something I tweeted?"

FIGURE 9.2

Twitter Support (http://help.twitter.com) provides online support for when Twitter begins to misbehave on its users.

Actually, no it wasn't. According to the Twitter crew manning the helm at Twitter Support (http://help.twitter.com), the problem is *"a result of cache and database inconsistencies"* on the Twitter servers.

Okay...so, less geek, more English. What does *that* mean?!

Your Twitter profile, which encompasses your Followers, who you follow, people you have removed from your network, accounts you have blocked, and so on, is kept up to date between the Twitter servers' *cache* (auxiliary memory for high-speed retrieval) and *database* (a more stable, structured set of details specific to your account). Sometimes, according to Twitter Support, these two elements get confused. The cache believes you're following a user when, in fact, the database confirms that user was dropped by you yesterday. This is a cache-database inconsistency.

Before emailing people and asking *"Are we cool, Marsalis?"* take some resolution that Twitter hasn't "lost" anything. Your requests and changes are still in the system. The database just needs to catch up. When it does, your account is restored to its up-to-date status.

So no need to panic—your followers are still there. Twitter is just catching up with how popular of a person you are.

Twitter Abuse

By design, Twitter can assume a variety of guises, and in the opening chapter, I cover some of its various applications. There really is a lot you can do with it. You can use Twitter as a microblog, just to get an idea of how the blogging process works. It can be a quick and simple exchange of ideas, or as I've heard it called "the coffeehouse that never closes" where all kinds of people from all walks of life come in to mingle. It can be all these things, but there are some things that it is most definitely not...

...and yet, people keep using (and abusing) it as such.

When Twitter Is Used as an IM

Twitter, as discussed in the opening chapter, is not an instant messenger, but this does not deter users from using it as an IM application regardless of the lag time in the reply.

It can easily be mistaken for a chat application with its interface at Twitter.com, on the various desktop clients, and even on various mobile phones; but between the delay, its 140-character limitation, and the open nature of Twitter's discussions, Twitter isn't an instant messenger. Still, some users get on a thought and go. They decide, instead of trying to condense their thought to one tweet (two at the most), they get out every detail they feel their network needs, filling desktop clients and Twitter home pages with their avatar and their manifesto.

TeeMonster

....I needed to do this for the book so I really appreciate everyone bearing with me through this painful experience. –end–

half a minute ago from TweetDeck

fashion and sometimes, yeah, I may spent two tweets to get a thought out but when you go as far as I'm going it is right annoying. Still....

1 minute ago from TweetDeck

....or ICQ. (Anyone remember ICQ? Wow, that seems so archaic now in comparison to Twitter.) But my point is that people use Twitter in this

2 minutes ago from TweetDeck

It's when people are wanting to make a point and they spend a series of tweets to do so, as if this is a chat application like Skype, AOL...

3 minutes ago from TweetDeck

ATTENTION, TWITTERS! For this All a Twitter chapter, I need to do something that I see often on Twitter but at present isn't happening.

3 minutes ago from TweetDeck

FIGURE 9.3

If your tweets exceed more than two tweets, then it might be a good idea to rethink what you want to say and where the best place is to say it.

The inner-now-outer monologues are also akin to @Mentions between two people on Twitter who attempt to keep their open conversation between themselves, even when others @Mention to them. If the nature of the conversation suddenly makes a turn to TMI-ville, and still no one is welcome to the conversation, this goes from awkward to just plain rude. Remember, it is only a private conversation you are having when you go to DMs. Depending on the tenor of the conversation and the subject matter, move your talk to Skype, iChat, Facebook Chat, or some other true IM.

As far as these online services and clients who have various "methods" in taking tweets longer than 140-characters, Jen Schaller (@JenSchaller) in my @TeeMonster network tweeted (following Figure 9.3's posting):

Twitter's greatest gift to the Internet: forced brevity. Strunk and White would approve.

William Strunk and E.B. White were the authors of *The Elements of Style*. Their advice in that title: *"Omit needless words."* Well said, you two.

Not only do I find clients' options like Tweetshrink and character-heavy entries automatically distributed across multiple tweets to be cheats, it completely dismisses and discredits the 140-characters limitation, Twitter's strongest attribute. Tangents, long-winded replies, and other tendencies inherent with other IM applications are no longer an obstacle. As stated in Chapter 1, "What Is Twitter (and What It Is Not)," Twitter was never designed to be a timesink.

When Things Get Too Personal

Suicide attempts.

Relationship breakups.

Births.

Porn stars on the set.

Let's face it—some things are better left *off* Twitter.

"What are you doing?" is taken quite literally by the Twitterverse, and for some in the community, it seems that Twitter is less of the coffeehouse that never closes and more like the psychotherapist's couch that is always available. I have no qualms about people sharing their thoughts and opinions, nor do I take offense on how personal they delve into their personal lives. (This is why I can unfollow someone or, if it gets really bad, block them from my feed.) I have seen people get personal on Twitter, but I know my own line for how personal I get on Twitter. That line for others, however, is set differently. Some keep things close to the vest. Others love to bear their soul so much that they're tearing the spine off that open book. Whatever you choose to share on the open network, consider the repercussions first—especially if you decide to use Twitter for commercial purposes. What you say and bear openly can backfire on you and cost you Followers. If you don't care, then feel free to tweet away; but remember that when you share with the group, you share with a globe-encompassing community of various cultures, backgrounds, and interests. Because the majority of people in your community probably share like interests, they won't agree with everything you have to say.

It's a good idea before pressing Update on your home page or client of choice that you think about what you're going to say. Will it contribute, enlighten, or alienate your community? No, you won't cost yourself Followers overnight (although the possibility is there), but a moment's consideration isn't a bad idea. Therapeutic as it might be, Twitter isn't group therapy.

Fail Whale says...

From Mashable (http://bit.ly/1322k) comes a story that only affirms my message on how to approach Twitter. @astrospace was the official Twitter account for Space Astronautics News (http://www.space.gs), a website dedicated to the latest news around space exploration. @astrospace did what one would expect and did just that: reported shuttle launches, gave reports on deep space probe data, and provided links to astronomy-related resources. The user also posted a variety of replies and nonastronomy postings. As a follower, I was impressed with its participation and dedication to building a community.

Then, on January 22, 2009, @astrospace went into orbit.

According to screen captures from the account (posted on TwitPic at http://bit.ly/SpaceRant), @astrospace's Followers were fluctuating by the thousands. Regardless that the account had a network numbering in the tens of thousands, this glitch instigated an explosion rivaling a Delta-II rocket experiencing an anomaly. The meteor shower of insults was first directed at Twitter, until @astrospace's 23,000+ followers suddenly became the gravity well to the criticisms. Ending with an enigmatic pro-Obama post, @astrospace logged off for the night.

Followers dropped from 23,000+ to 213 within days.

Twitter is not easy, and it's even harder when things aren't working the way they are promised and expected to. Rants and opinions like the one shared by @astrospace (which, shortly after this social networking SNAFU, came back online under @Astronautics, has a network of 90,000+ followers, and notably tweets news *only* related to aerospace and outer space news) should be reconsidered, even in the worst of situations. With Twitter or any Social Media initiative, success or failure comes down to the proper implementation of your initiatives. Provided you stick to what your goals are with Twitter, you should remain "All Systems Go!" even if there is a problem back at Houston Control.

Hi...My Name is Tee and I Have a Twitter Addiction

When you explain Twitter to those outside of the community, particularly to business representatives curious about what the mainstream media is talking about, you might get some strange looks in reaction. "People follow you on Twitter, and you follow them back?" It all sounds very odd, slightly narcissistic, and a bit like an encounter group for Stalkers Anonymous.

To add to this is the addictive nature of Twitter.

When I first joined Twitter in July 2007, I was also a bit skeptical about the service. When tweets started coming to me via Twitterfic, I started to see the appeal of Twitter and in connecting with friends both locally, across country, and around the world. The more I tweeted, the more I became connected with my network; and when I would disconnect during my day job, I felt the burning need to pull up the website and just give that one quick update that I was still around, still kicking, just—you know—not available. Or not as available as I liked to be. Not to worry because when I was available, I was going to be tweeting away.

When I was tweeting while driving (yes, I know what I said at the end of Chapter 8, "iPhone, Therefore iTweet") and struggling to drive a straight line on the interstate, I had to really ask myself, "Is this a problem?"

I hadn't wrecked the car, so no.

That was when I admitted that yes, I had a serious problem.

What is it about Twitter that is so addictive? I couldn't explain it until I was offered to write this title. To get a good head start on this book and test myself to see what I could do when really focused, I cut myself off from Twitter....

...for two weeks.

The addictive nature of Twitter comes from the connection with your network. If your network is particularly interactive, you are kept in the know with where your friends are, what they are up to, and what projects—be they creative endeavors or something for work—they have currently in the works. It's a bit like being James Bond (and I mean the Connery Bond as Craig's Bond is still learning the ropes of being a Double-O) in that you are in the know on everything. Admit it; there was something cool that Bond knew details about everything. Brandy. Guns. Women. How diamonds could power an orbital laser. Bond knew all this stuff because he was connected.

This is how you feel when you are on Twitter: connected.

I was speaking with a friend and colleague from Twitter, and told her about my two-week hiatus. She gasped and said, "I don't think I could do that." I challenged her then to step away from Twitter for a week.

She stammered, "Oh, wow...um, I don't know...."

Twitter is terrific, and I admit that I love that feeling of participating with • everyone in my respective networks. There is something exciting in staying in touch with people everywhere, inviting them into my life as they invite me into theirs, and even making them a part of writing this book.

This addiction, though, can be a bit challenging if not distracting when you are trying to interact with the real world.

A Little Birdie Told Me...

As a dedicated participant of the Twitterverse, even I am a little put off with people in the middle of conversations, producing iPhones, BlackBerries, and G1s when they're notified of a tweet. I look at it the same way as people who insist on having their mobile phone turned on at the movies and (even worse) at the theatre. If you are *that* busy, then stay at home for the call. Same thing with Twitter. Talk to me or tweet. Don't do both.

Sometimes, disconnecting from Twitter is the best thing you can do. As I mentioned before, I took a two week break from the network to give myself some time with this manuscript and also to see if I could go on and do it. Could I just walk away? No fanfare or production to it—just unplug and experience the outside world? I found out I could. I also found out that it made me appreciate the connections of Twitter all the more. I now had real-life experiences to share with people in my network, and this is essential: Twitter is a way of sharing things in your life, not a substitute for living it.

Social networking is a beautiful thing, but you will want to break away from it to make time for the real world. When you start to lose your manners, your etiquette, and your social skills on account of your need to tweet, a break is in order.

Remedying the Noise in Your Signal

Guy Kawasaki (http://www.guykawasaki.com) is one of the major players not only in Social Media, but also in technology. He has worked at the Mother Ship, Apple Computers, and was part of the marketing team behind Macintosh computers in 1984. He is an accomplished writer with many bylines under his belt including *Reality Check, The Art of the Start, How to Drive Your Competition Crazy,* and *The Macintosh Way,* and he is a columnist for *Entrepreneur* magazine. His blog "How to Change the World" is ranked in the Top 100 visited blogs in the world. He is also the cofounder of Alltop (http://alltop.com), the part search engine, part aggregator that delivers to subscribers various articles and topic to their desktops daily.

With so many credentials under his belt, it might seem arrogant of me to question someone of Guy Kawasaki's standing. (Oh, I forgot to mention his BA from Stanford, his MBA from UCLA, and his honorary doctorate from Babson College, so yes, he's smart.) But when it comes to Twitter, some of Kawasaki's advice is not only questionable, it's also just flat-out counter-productive.

From his November 2008, posting "Looking for Mr. Goodtweet: How to Pick Up Followers on Twitter" (http://bit.ly/FollowAll), Kawasaki give advice on how to build your network. Some of the tips (Create an effective avatar, Incorporate media, Use the right tools…) are rock solid, but one in particular shocked me. It was "Tip #4: Follow everyone who follows you."

To illustrate just how bad of an idea this is, try this exercise, preferably at home:

1. Set up your office, family room, decompression chamber, or wherever you like to unwind with a variety media resources: iPod, television, radio, and so on. If it plays media, have it at the ready. For myself I will have the following ready:

   - Television
   - iTunes on my laptop
   - iTunes on my desktop
   - iPod with external speakers
   - CD player

2. On one of you media players, find your favorite song. You know the song I mean. Your *favorite*. The one that makes you stop, smile, and remember something special. Play it for a few seconds. Make the volume high. Enjoy it for a moment, and be ready to play it again as you work this exercise.

3. While that song is playing, turn on the television. Find a favorite show of yours, or something that grabs your attention. (I'm a sucker for *The Deadliest Catch*!) Adjust the volume so it's about the same as your favorite song.

4. Start a movie on a DVD player. Preferably, your favorite action flick like *Die Hard* or *Quantum of Solace* (One of the best openings of a Bond flick ever!). Let that play as well.

5. Now, with all the other media players running something independent and at roughly the same volume, listen to your favorite song.

What you are experiencing is a real-world example of *Signal-to-Noise ratio* (SNR). There are many applications and definitions of it; but for our purposes, it is best-defined as the ratio of a signal power (your favorite song) to the noise power corrupting the signal (all the other media players). The higher the ratio, the less obtrusive background noise is to your intended signal.

Before you say, "But, Tee, that's audio. What does that have to do with Twitter?" Instead of regarding the previous exercise as using "audio," think of the various media resources as "data" both in aural and visual format. Had I asked you to add in another form of media (such as a book, newspaper, or graphic novel), it might have brought the point home even harder and pulled a muscle in your brain in the process. In this exercise you were bombarded with data, and when the additional sources of data (noise) became too much, it was difficult to focus on the favorite song (signal). You shut down.

This is what happens to you if you blindly follow everyone on Twitter. People you will want to stay in touch with are lost in tweets of famous quotes, musicians asking you to join them on Facebook, spammers selling you services you don't want, and bots that generate gibberish.

The quality of your Twitter experience goes back to the quality of your network. Are the people (if there are real people behind the spam accounts) you connect with people that you *want* to network with?

FIGURE 9.4

How does a Twitter telling people (with the same tweet) to join them on Facebook add to the value of your network?

And what about the rest of your network? By following everyone without looking to what they are all about, you are now connecting them with your network. This is particularly advantageous to the spammers on Twitter.

Check the first page of tweets and see what their content is. You can keep the level of participation and value of your signal in your account much higher by taking just a moment to review their recent tweets.

Fail Whale says...

Improving your signal within the noise is paramount in your success with Twitter, whether it is a personal or a professional success you strive to achieve. Sadly, as Twitter continues to rise in its popularity, the noise in the network grows. Daily. The debate of whether to "follow everyone" or not to is a heated one, and some on the side of "follow everyone" accuse those who do not follow back or (dare they?!) employ the block feature are labeled as "arrogant" or "rude."

I argue this is your choice to make, not theirs.

Remember that this is your network, and you have the final say in what is and is not acceptable. That is your right, and that is the final word concerning your Twitter account. Choosing not to follow back or block someone does not make you a bad person. It does make you cautious, and a little bit of caution on the Internet is a good thing.

In Chapter 12, I go deeper into abuses of Twitter and offer a perspective on what *isn't* working across timelines.

The Outsider's Perspective

Returning to what I mentioned earlier in this chapter about explaining Twitter to someone outside of the community, you remember those strange looks? Sometimes, you get those from people who try Twitter and just don't "get it." That doesn't mean they're missing out or not as sharp as you. It just means that...they don't get it.

If you try to make them get it, that makes a bad situation only worse.

Perhaps the best poke in the ribs from mainstream society comes from Jon Stewart of Comedy Central's *The Daily Show* (http://bit.ly/StewartTwitter). "This new technology sounds adorable," he stated with a seasoning of snark. (Come on, it's *The Daily Show*. What do you expect?) In his March 9, 2009, segment *"Old Man Stewart Shakes His Fist at...,"* he admitted not having a clue how it works, and then asked why members of Congress (caught on camera actively tweeting during the State of the Union Address) were not paying attention to President Obama. Stewart added, "There's a reason why they don't allow cell phones in seventh-grade class-rooms." He then invited Tech Correspondent Samantha Bee to explain the appeal of Twitter to him. "Because it's *awesome!*" she proclaimed. "It's no wonder young people love it, according to reports about young people by middle-aged people." The segment then illustratesd the addiction angle of Twitter as Bee tweets while Stewart is talking to her. Twitter has become a bit of a preoccupation (if not an obsession) with Stewart who has returned to it as a well of scorn and skepticism since this initial "Old Man Stewart" segment.

FIGURE 9.5

Jon Stewart struggled on March 9, 2009 to make sense of Twitter (on other Social Media initiatives) on Comedy Central's The Daily Show.

Comedy gold. And as *The Daily Show* tends to be, right on the mark.

NBC journalist Brian Williams dismissed Twitter (on *The Daily Show*, as a matter of fact) as only having sustenance at the moment, with no real-lasting impact. Williams, in the same interview, proclaimed he wouldn't tweet because "nothing he did at any given moment was interesting enough."

The narcissistic perception of Twitter tends to turn people off immediately, and the voyeuristic nature of being connected to so many people all the time. Not only are you sharing "what you're doing" with friends but with people you have never met but, according to Twitter, are your "Friends" in this network. Is it unsettling? Perhaps, yes, but then again if you look at Twitter as posting your current state of mind spontaneously and then replying to comments that others subscribed to your network's feed, this is nothing new.

I think we also call that blogging.

A Little Birdie Told Me...

Some of the funniest perceptions of what Twitter comes from people in its community. The previously mentioned animated short *"The Twouble with Twitter"* (http://bit.ly/TwoubleTwitter) from Current (http://current.com) is a sharp, witty punch-in-the-thigh at the Twittersphere (yet another name for the Twitterverse), complete with weblebrities, the delightful bliss of tweeting, and the summoning of the Fail Whale. Another hysterical take on Twitter, this time from the competitive nature of Social Media application developers, is SlateV.com's Flutter: The New Twitter (http://bit.ly/ITFlutter) where the Twitter concept is taken to the next level and Flutter condenses tweets to *26* characters.

For the obsessive nature of Twitter, video comedian Lisa Nova (Lisa_Nova) offers her two-part short aptly titled *Twitter Whore* (http://bit.ly/LisaTW).

Now before you think what you might be thinking—no, that's not what the video is about.

Nova, who has an impressive portfolio of spoofs on YouTube, looks at the life of the addicted Twitter. Whether it is walking the dog, enjoying cereal, or asking people to follow her, her embodiment of Twitters that refuse to unplug has her laptop and BlackBerry within reach to keep her army of Followers informed.

And yes, there is a scene where she is tweeting while driving. (I'm so ashamed....)

Twitter is experiencing a unique kind of growing pain in that half of mainstream society dismisses it simply by its "adorable" name and its slightly self-absorbed nature. The other half of society is tripping over themselves to use it, but don't quite understand how it works or how to implement it. It's both sides of the Social Media fence. The more mainstream Twitter becomes, the more Twitter will change; and for the community members that have been around the longest, this is a slightly mixed blessing.

Accept the fact that you will come across people who love Twitter, embrace it, and make the most of it. Also accept that there are going to be those who just won't want to share that much across a network. Relationship and business success can be influenced by Twitter, sure, but your success does not hinge on whether you implement Twitter.

If it does, you have far more important issues to grapple with.

10

Getting Personal

So where do we go from here? We covered the website, the variety of applications, the ways to tweet on a mobile phone, and we even took a serious look at when Twitter falls short of the great expectations that people put on it. Haven't I learned everything about Twitter yet?

Well, no, young Skywalker. You are not a Jedi yet, but you are very, very close.

This chapter and the next couple of chapters focus on how people use Twitter, how people take everything you've been thrown between the first page and here and actually make Twitter into something they truly enjoy.

Harkening back to the previous chapter where Jon Stewart shook his fist (If only Twitter had stayed off his lawn...), Twitter does appear to be "all about me" and somewhat lacking in depth and meaning. If you know how to approach Twitter, though, discovering the community in this social network is easy to do and even easier to enjoy. No; we're not going to don silk pajamas, sing "Kumbaya" or anything like that, or start up a commune (that's for the podcasters...), but we are going to look at what people are tweeting, and see how they turn what many view as an exercise of narcissism into personal relationships.

Staying in Touch with Friends

When starting out with Twitter, the numbers will not be there right away. Also, depending on your intentions, the numbers may never be there. It will be a modest start to the network, and chances are it will begin with people you know. It might feel a bit bizarre when you start tweeting with them when you could pick up the phone and just, you know, *talk* to them.

Let me give you some food for thought here....

Call Me When You Get Home

Remember back in the days of high school when you first got your driver's license, or how about when you first got into college. I know I wasn't the only one who heard the words *"Call me when you get back safely..."* or a similar request. To make sure the folks didn't fret too hard, you would make that all important phone call that assured them you made it home safe and sound. Maybe you would get home and check your computer for recent emails or the like, and it might slip your mind for a few hours. Eventually though, you would call, and it would put troubled minds at ease.

Twitter has become something like this: the quick assurance.

Several times, I have attended and hosted get-togethers where people were coming from all parts of Virginia and Maryland. Especially when the group meets up at a restaurant and disbands for respective homes, there is a slight trepidation concerning all my friends, particularly for ones coming from long distances.

Yeah, I blame my mom for that "Worry Wart" mentality.

This is where Twitter comes into play. On returning home, I tend to do a quick "tweet check" to see what the feed is doing. That is when I see in my Twitter feed messages from my friends all tweeting that they are home from events, still feeling the afterglow of the get-together.

Writer, artist, and podcaster Travis Nelson (@TD_Nelson) tells me he and his wife "...use Twitter to update status via DM when she is traveling cross-country," and while flying to different destinations, "We were DMing arrival time info as we went." Jullian Krute (@thesickchick) tends to get that motherly satisfaction I get. "My usual houseguests tweet me on their safe arrival home." And along the East Coast, @nuchtchas says, "I use Twitter to let people know where I am on all my business and road trips," keeping her friends, close and far, in the know on her whereabouts.

What Are You Doing This Weekend?

Beyond using it as the Internet's form of a phone tree, Twitter can also work as your instant "party network" in trying to organize special events. Instead of working down your list of contacts, Skyping and calling friends one at a time, a simple "Who's in town this weekend?" tweet can easily turn into an epic-sized social gathering.

Within the Twitter community, these kind of social events are referred to as either *Tribal Gatherings* or as the even more iconic term, *Tweetups*, as some Twitters in your local area might ask you to attend. This doesn't mean you have to turn your informal gathering into a networking opportunity, but you can broaden the scope of your get-together by inviting people outside your immediate circle to join you and your friends.

FIGURE 10.1

Tweetups are events organized on Twitter with the intent to gather with friends (old and new) from your network and put usernames with real faces.

When Shannon Farrell (@ShannonFarrell) found himself on the East Coast (far from his normal stomping grounds of the Midwest), he put out the call on his Twitter network for interest in a tweetup at a central location for Twitters in the Washington, DC area. "This was a chance to have a reunion with friends I had made at Dragon*Con," Shannon says. "As I was in the area, I used Twitter not only as a means of staying in touch with new friends, but also to bring everyone together for lunch."

Tweetups are quite common across Twitter, the motivations behind them all different but the same goal intended: to put faces and tangeable people with their Twitter names. "Using tweet-ups to meet with your core of friends works really well because you contact your friends but open the invitation to others." Shannon believes tweetups to be a valuable asset, no matter the size of the network. "Because my followers and my network was so intimate, I had a good idea who was going to be there. With larger networks, tweetups are great as this is an instant communication method with a variety of people."

Sharing with the Community

Twitter, as you have heard me comment throughout the book, is all about the network you create. This community can be brought together for a variety of reasons, and Twitter serves as a terrific way of sharing interests and opinions. It can also be a creative outlet for both professionals and amateurs, all wanting to share a moment's inspiration.

TwitFic

As Twitter offers only 140 characters, it is argued you really can't say a lot. However, authors of all genres and of all backgrounds (both professional to the aspiring) indulge in a writing exercise commonly known as *TwitFic*, or original fiction offered to their networks one tweet at a time.

No stranger to fiction (although some might argue he is stranger than fiction) is the creative mind that is Steve Eley (@sfeley), who is the creator and producer behind podcasting's first professional magazine, *Escape Pod* (http://www.escapepod.org). Steve indulges on occasion with a bit of 140-character long fiction but he admits, "I start each of mine with the word 'TWITFIC!' to tell people what I'm doing, so I really get 131." Some of his TwitFic went like this:

> "I'm from the future," she said.—"What's it like? Are we happy?" I asked.—"...I came _here_, didn't I?"

> I've always wanted to live in a haunted house. And if I just keep arranging enough accidents, sooner or later one'll stick around.

FIGURE 10.2

Writers like Steve Eley of Escape Pod *indulge in quick bouts of TwitFic, challenging how quickly and concise storytelling can be.*

And on the day I am writing this chapter:

> "TWITFIC! Uncontent with a mere 27 hours per day, J stole everyone else's time. Yes, we suffer in our hurry, but J...has had a very long day."

Some authors attempt to use Twitter as a means of promoting their current work in progress, using Twitter more as a notification system for the bog that is hosting the full novel. Writer Robert Zarywacz (@robznov) has been working on his own humorous English seaside novel, *Candyfloss and Pickles*, through Twitter and his blog. With two chapters completed, he is currently posting daily installments of the novel, and news and updates on his own career and life in Devon. "The initial idea came to me one day in a flash," he says. "Twitter offers a blog-style framework for writing and publishing with which I am experimenting. Writing a novel requires patience, commitment, self-discipline, and persistence, and finding time to write is always difficult. Twitter has me always writing, or at least thinking about writing." The big question is, though, is writing a novel 140-characters at a time actually practical or productive? "This approach has worked for me for almost eight months, although progress is slow. I hope to speed up in 2009."

Then there are authors who collaborate with one another to create a "collaborative cage match" of TwitFic. In response to his followers complaining that his tweets were too infrequent, writer and podcaster Matt Wallace (@MattFnWallace) turned to his background of professional wrestling and tweeted that he would fight "a creature of their choosing" to the death, live on Twitter. Thus, the epic TwitPic Death Tweet was conceived. "I meant it as a joke, but it spawned such a heated discussion and generated such a wide response that I decided to make an event out of it." Part of that event was inviting fellow authors Mur Lafferty (@mightymur) and J.C. Hutchins (@jchutchins) as ringside commentators. "I thought I would generate all the action, and they would just throw out some funny observations to add to the atmosphere. Instead we ended up on Skype while we were tweeting brainstorming on ideas back and forth."

FIGURE 10.3

Author Matt Wallace (center) invited fellow authors J.C. Hutchins (left) and Mur Lafferty (right) to a Twitfic event titled, Death Tweet, *a highly entertaining romp into a professional wrestling fantasy.*

Fail Whale Says...

Although *Death Tweet* was a riot to follow along with, Matt admits that not everyone enjoyed the creative exercise. "As much as people dug it, there was also a backlash. People dropped me from their networks on account of the constant tweets that particular day. I'm waiting to kind of gauge the mood of my followers."

Then there are collaborations that stretch across the entire community as podcaster and Podiobooks.com cofounder Chris Miller (@codeshaman) hosted Twitter Zombie Theatre (full unedited transcript available here—http://bit.ly/TwitZombie), a three-hour discussion across Twitter that started with a harmless enough tweet:

> codeshaman: Watching a guy who doesn't look too well shamble across the parking lot. Would think he was homeless except for the business suit.

Soon, though, corresponding tweets between Chris and others in his network evolved into something more sinister:

> codeshaman: Uh oh. Second ambulance has people in those hazmat type suits getting out. More cops are showing up. Can't see guy on the ground.

"I was playing with TwitFic, and then I realized I could pull an Orson Welles and turn it into something cool," Chris said. He then contacted John Cmar (@Cmaaarrr) to play along with the concept. As a doctor of infectious diseases, John was the perfect collaborator. Between the two of them, Twitters across the country told the story of zombie takeover. "I loved it. It was so neat. At the time, twitter conversations were sort of new. As people began to respond, it gave me ways to tune the story." Being so heavily involved in creating fiction, Chris recognizes Twitter's potential as a storytelling vehicle. "It's multifunctional and a good platform for that style of fiction."

Fail Whale Says...

Much like with comedy, timing is everything. If you do attempt real-time/real-setting story-telling via Twitter, consider when you're doing this. For Chris Miller's *Twitter Zombie Theatre*, this creative experiment could have lasted all day, but private messages and the date he happened to give this a try dictated otherwise. "If it hadn't been Sept. 11, I would have continued. People were starting to get freaked a bit. I got some DMs, asking me for details and that's when I stopped things."

Twitter does have the potential to be a fantastic stage for this kind of spontaneous creativity, but it can also backfire depending on current and (in the case of *Twitter Zombie Theatre*) past events. Consider the details and be ready to pull the plug, if necessary.

Tweet-by-Tweet Commentary and TwitReviews (No Spoilers Please!)

Chris Miller's Twitter Zombie Theatre is not a far cry from another communal activity on Twitter. Whether it is shuttle launches, Presidential inaugurations, or the latest episode of a popular television show, *tweet-by-tweet commentary* is quickly becoming the social networking approach to family gatherings around the television set. Some events I've enjoyed with my networks have included

- **President Barak Obama's acceptance speech**—This was a real delight to share with my network. Regardless of your political affiliation that night, the country (and even a few parts of the world) witnessed history as Barack Obama took the stage as the President-Elect. That night, *The New York Times* generated on its website active *tag clouds* (common keywords) that were appearing in various RSS feeds, including Twitter. Some of the reoccurring words appearing online that night included *hope, optimism,* and *belief.* Twitter Traffic was, as mentioned in Chapter 9, "The Trouble with Twitter," so heavy that some tweets were cached and delivered later than initially sent.

- **The Parsec Awards**—If you are unfamiliar with this honor, The Parsec Awards (http://parsecawards.com) are presented at Dragon*Con for outstanding achievement in Speculative Fiction podcasting. Since its inception in 2007, people attending have been tweeting the event; and with smartphones and mobile tweeting becoming more of the norm, this event is now brought to podcast fans everywhere as winners are announced as they happen. Award shows like The Parsecs are not the only kind of events that attract tweet-by-tweet coverage. Twitters have been spotted in classroom and special seminars, and even on the Congressional floor during the State of the Union address. Now, events you could not attend on account of distance are now brought to you 140-characters at a time through Twitter.

- **"24"**—Well, to be fair, I have delivered a tweet-by-tweet of "24," ""Castle, "Battlestar Galactica," and even "The Deadliest Catch." The hard part about delivering tweet-by-tweet of television shows is revealing *spoilers*, those surprises that you might see on the East Coast hours before your network out west sees the broadcast. If you do tweet-by-tweet of broadcast programming, consider that not everyone in your network is going to have access to the same signal you do. Some people might be recording the event with their DVR, some might be catching it in a different time zone, or at different times of the year if members of your network are international. Remember that whereas reactions are acceptable, giving away plot twists, surprises, and sudden reveals are not.

A Little Birdie Told Me...

In the case of "24," sometimes the spoilers comes from the characters you're watching. Every Monday night, during Season 7, a fan going under the moniker of @real_jackbauer tweets his own commentary on what is happening in that particular episode. There is just enough snark and sarcasm in his tweets to make you laugh.

This also makes "24" that much more fun to watch when you think that in the midst of gunfire, intrigue, and action, Jack Bauer is tweeting it all from his mobile phone.

Similar to tweet-by-tweet commentaries are *TwitReviews* that are exactly what they sound like. In quick bursts (usually opening with "TwitReviews:" and ending with a related hashtag), users post their thoughts and opinions on just about anything. Software, movies, books, music—if you have an opinion on it, it can become a TwitReview.

An example of a TwitReview can be

> TwitReview: After getting back from it, I'm just going to say: Alan Moore, get over yourself. WATCHMEN was a brilliant film. #watchmen

Although it is hardly a review along the lines of Leonard Maltin, it is a solid example of a TwitReview. There are no spoilers, a clear opinion given, an even a quick rant included.

TwitReviews should not necessarily be sensational, but what they should do is stimulate conversation. My earlier example (plucked from my own @TeeMonster feed, and cleaned up on account of—*ahem*—passionate opinions) sparked the following conversation in my network:

> pcharing: @TeeMonster SO SAY WE ALL! #watchmen

> TeeMonster: @pcharing Visually stunning, WONDERFUL performances, not too much blue *****, and KILLER fight sequences. Loved it! #watchmen

> pcharing: @TeeMonster NO question. I loved it. The Sound Track is no lightweight either. #watchmen

> docartemis: @TeeMonster Do you recommend reading Watchmen before seeing the movie?

> TeeMonster: @docartemis Only if you don't want to be surprised. I thought the changes worked, even the big ones. But I knew what was coming. #watchmen

docartemis: @TeeMonster Thanks!

sinspired: @TeeMonster The big change made more sense, neh? But to be fair, the original plan would make more sense to the perpetrator. #watchmen

TeeMonster: @sinspired The BIG change: considering how ((spoiler)) was portrayed, the change works. Moore's being a **** about it, methinks. #watchmen

sinspired: @TeeMonster Yeah. The other change I was a bit bothered by, but I understand why they did it that way. Not happy, but I get it. #watchmen

sinspired: @TeeMonster Moore will grumble, but he'll cash the damn check in the end. #watchmen

With TwitReviews, you can kick up conversation threads and trends. Also note that when I was closing in on a spoiler, I substituted the actual plot reveal with ((spoiler)). This is something that your network will appreciate and is just considerate of others.

Fail Whale says...

A common problem on Twitter are users who approach spoilers with an attitude of "If you haven't seen/read/listened to it by now, then too bad." For some things (movies, television shows) this might be passable (barely), but for some other forms of media (books, podcasts), it borderlines on the rude. One spoiler can seriously ruin someone's day.

Twitter is hardly a spoiler-free domain; but although some people slip with the details, there are some who just feel it is their duty to let the details fly free. Try to avoid being "that guy" or "that girl" and avoid spoilers when and where you can. Just a touch of consideration can go a long way on Twitter.

Trademark Tweets

Twitter is, as you have probably guessed, a fun place to make a name for yourself. Sure, you can be a professional and use Twitter as a place to make a name for yourself, but you also can enjoy your own claim on Twitter by creating a trademark tweet, a 140-character long signature that you come up with and people in your network (and elsewhere, if the signature goes viral) recognize as your moniker.

Solidarity (J.C. Hutchins)

If you listen to podcast fiction, there is a good possibility you know the name J.C. Hutchins (@jchutchins). This aspiring writer appeared in the podosphere with a story teeming with twists, turns, thrills, and shocking revelations. This three-part epic, *7th Son*, became one of the most popular podcasts available and then became part of the publishing schedule for St. Martin's Press.

The publisher, after signing Hutch on for its 2009 calendar, wanted to find out if he was up for another challenge. That challenge was to be a new novel of suspense with an interactive quality. Hutch couldn't resist, but then came the catch to this second publishing deal with St. Martin's: The manuscript had to be turned into the publisher for review within three months.

He agreed to the contract and turned to Twitter for inspiration.

Solidarity was J.C.Hutchins' battle cry and his invitation for other writers to join him in this push to write a novel in a matter of months. To participate in Solidarity was simple enough: Open your post with "Solidarity" and then announce your word count for the day and what you word count is applied to. (Now, with hashtags, it's customary to end a post with #solidarity.) This movement gained a lot of momentum, and soon Twitters around the world were producing blogposts, short stories, and novels of various genres. Amy Bowen (@amybowen) used Solidarity to motivate her through a NaNoWriMo (National Novel Writing Month) project titled *Bridging the Spheres* while J.T. Manis (@jtmanis) completed his epic novel, *The Rise and Fall of Leon House*. Canadian author and podcaster Drew Beatty (@drewbeatty) produced both short stories and his second novel, *Lost Gods*, with Solidarity as his motivator. As for myself, Solidarity became a matter of national pride as it was USA versus New Zealand with me matching (and topping) word counts against award-nominated author Philippa Ballantine (@PhilippaJane). Regardless of who beat whom (okay, yes, she beat me to the finish line!), the end results were her steampunk-fantasy, *Geist*, and my fantasy-mystery *The Case of the Pitcher's Pendant: A Billibub Baddings Mystery*.

For Solidarity's creator J.C. Hutchins, the movement produced St. Martin's Press' interactive thriller, *Personal Effect: Dark Art*.

11:11—Make a Wish (Heather Welliver)

If you ever need to set your watch, simply follow Heather Welliver (@HeatherWelliver). She, too, is also found on Twitter often; but in particular she can be found posting both in the morning and at night the following tweet:

> 11:11 Make a wish.

That's it. It seems a bit wide-eyed and a bit innocent for Twitter, but there is a reason behind this little trademark of Heather. In the earlier days of Twitter, a mutual friend of ours—Chris Lester (@etherius)—regularly posted at 4:20 p.m. what he called his "Moment of Zen," which was usually a thought-provoking quote. A change in vocations brought an end to Chris' Moment of Zen, something Heather found missing in her weekly Twitter regiment. So she began making wishes at 11:11. This became Heather's "Moment of Zen" or more like a moment where she encouraged her network to stop for a moment and think, to take a breather from what can be a relentless stream of data.

What is so interesting about Heather's 11:11 tweet are the lack of replies. Apparently, people are afraid if they tweet what they wish, it won't come true.

Set your watch and make a wish. Then, resume tweeting.

News from New Zealand (Philippa Ballantine)

In the past few years, the country of New Zealand has grown in popularity, becoming the "in place" to visit. The Kiwi Renaissance began with Peter Jackson who took his vision for J.R.R. Tolkein's *Lord of the Rings* and brought it to life in the land of Aotearoa. Then came the dry wit of Bret McKenzie and Jermaine Clemet in the HBO comedy *Flight of the Conchords*. On Twitter, it is podcaster and author Philippa Ballantine who tweets from Wellington, New Zealand. As she puts it, "I want to make sure people know that not everyone in New Zealand are hobbits, that there is more to the country than sheep, and that we are not a suburb of Australia." This is why she sends out her occasional News from New Zealand tweets. With headlines from Stuff.co.nz (http://www.stuff.co.nz) some of Philippa's recent headlines have included

- Wellington: The best little capital in the world
- Peter Jackson causes stir (at NZ air show)
- Avoid the travel faux pas
- You've been served (court papers)—on Facebook

All this is part of what Philippa calls her personal crusade to spread the goodwill of New Zealand. Although I have connections around the world (in two separate networks), I have noticed that only Philippa reports her country's perspectives of the world. Maybe an occasional headline from the BBC creeps into my feed, but you can always count on a completely different perspective from this unofficial ambassador of New Zealand. These tweets also tend to close the distance between her and the friendships she has established here in the United States. For Philippa, Twitter is a bit more than just goodwill from the edge of the map; it's a cultural link that other Twitters around the world can take a lesson from.

Follow Friday (All of Twitter)

Perhaps the most recognizable trend to dominate Twitter is *Follow Friday* where Twitters recommend across their network people in their network. Follow Friday started on January 16, 2009, with Lijit Networks VP Micah Baldwin (@micah) sending out on to his twitter feed:

> I am starting Follow Fridays. Every Friday, suggest a person to follow, and everyone follow him/her. Today it's @fancyjeffrey & @w1redone.

Web designer, blogger, and Social Media junkie Mykl Roventine (@myklroventine) pinged back moments later:

> @micah Great idea! You need a hashtag for that - #followfridays

When Chris Brogan (@chrisbrogan), Erin Kotecki Vest (@queenofspain), Aaron Brazell (@technosailor), and Jim Kukral (@jimkukral) tweeted on Micah's request the message "Follow Fridays - suggest someone to follow / everyone follow / use the hashtag #followfriday," the concept of Follow Friday was born. Throughout the day, the concept grew. By the end of the first Follow Friday, a tweet tagged with *#followfriday* hit Twitter's main timeline every half second.

That was the *first* Follow Friday.

Follow Friday has now become something of an end of the week tradition, actually starting on Thursday with a few endorsements coming from those on the other side of the world (and time zones) and continuing well into the evening with some Saturday stragglers on the following day. Across the board, Twitters that find themselves mentioned in a Follow Friday tweet pick up Followers; and this "networking in action" exercise is a testament of how active and how involved you are in the community on a whole.

Fail Whale says...

Micah's appeal to retweet his first Follow Friday was met with skepticism by one person, Techstar.org's Community Director Andrew Hyde (@andrewhyde) His take on Follow Friday was it could be a "spammer lovefest" in the making.

It could be argued this is beginning to happen.

Follow Friday was extremely humbling for me, considering the amount of people recommending me in their own feeds, but equally startling were the people who they themselves were not following me but recommending others to follow me.

Come again?

Perhaps I was getting caught up in the undertow of retweets but on looking at the profiles of others, I was noticing that some of these Twitters were, in fact, filling their feeds with retweets on retweets of various Follow Fridays. Whatever the intention, be it a way of thanking the instigator for the Follow Friday or a veiled attempt at participation in the community, it did make me wonder why people who weren't even in my network were encouraging others to follow me; and it made me wonder if the intent of Follow Friday was still there.

I still believe in the community vibe of Follow Friday, but I remain wary of people retweeting the goodwill when they have no idea who I am or what I stand for. As much as I want to know you, I also want you to know me.

Perhaps the real appeal of Follow Friday, as Micah puts it, is its inherent karmic nature. It feels good, both in giving and receiving. It feels good to let a friend know how you feel, and it's a good feeling to think that people from your network hold you in high enough regard to share you with their network.

Rick Rolling

If you are reading this book and if you are unfamiliar with certain trends of the Internet, I need to first bring you up to speed on exactly what "Rick Rolling" is. It involves a seemingly harmless tweet; an active, valid hyperlink; and 80s singing sensation Rick Astley.

Still with me? Okay, great. So let's say you're on Twitter one day, and you're enjoying the network's banter when someone tweets:

Instead of a cup of coffee from Starbuck's, do something different today. http://bit.ly/BeakerRickRoll $5 can have an impact. Make it happen.

Curious, you click on the link (and a particularly clever prankster will not be so blatant as I am in this example) and are routed to a YouTube video. In my hypothetical tweet, you land at a Muppet Show clip that you assume by its label is some unearthed outtake. Suddenly, Beaker is singing Rich Astley's "Never Gonna Give You Up" with Dr. Teeth and the Electric Mayhem providing accompaniment.

Congratulations. You've just been Rick Rolled.

Rick Rolling is very much a part of geek culture, starting with YouTube, moved into automated services that Rick Roll you over the phone (and if it can happen to me, it can happen to you), to podcasters performing "drive-by Rock Rolling" on their listeners. Rick Rolling can happen any-where, and it can happen when you least expect it on Twitter.

If it does happen to you, remember—it's all in fun.

Twitter is a great place to build networks, exchange ideas, and make con-nections. Twitter is also a great place to have a bit of fun, and Rick Rolling *in moderation* can serve as a fantastic means to make your net-work smile.

I emphasize *in moderation* because if all you're doing is Rick Rolling, you become "that guy" or "that girl" on Twitter you just can't trust. (Take a look at an earlier "Fail Whale Says…" in this chapter for more on being "that guy/girl" on Twitter.) The same joke over and over again will get old, and Rick Rolling is like any kind of comedy. It's all about the timing.

A Little Birdie Told Me…

If you want to build a sound, reliable network, you want to avoid becoming "that guy" or "that girl" on Twitter. The question is how do you do that?

The answer might be a little easier to discover: Be yourself and be courteous.

Think about how you would like to interact with others on Twitter and consider what you are about to do or say before doing it. You can make a first impression only once, and provided you take a second (maybe two) to consider your tweet, you might find that will make a world of different.

Don't be afraid to be yourself. That is part of what makes Twitter so cool.

Becoming Part of the Community

This chapter represents what I have seen over two years of tweets. Under the @TeeMonster moniker, I have connected with more than 2,000 people from around the world. I have built a virtual community and do what I can to connect with them through @Mentions, an occasional retweet, and sharing of links. I participate in the conversations and enjoy many a quick exchange between Twitters everywhere.

A quick exchange? *With 2,000 people?* How do you pull that feat?

I do exchange barbs, jests, links, pictures, opinions, and rants (within two tweets, of course); but I am usually doing this with the members of my network who choose to participate in my network. Not everyone in my @TeeMonster is tweeting, and fewer actually tweet back to me, but I look for the posts in my feed that engage me, and I try to make sure I reply (if they are looking for a reply) to people who address me directly. Participation is key in becoming part of any community, be it online or in the real world.

What do I define as participation? I go into more detail on exactly where I draw the lines for participation in Chapter 12, "ANTI-Social Media," but in a nutshell I define participation in a community by:

- Asking questions that provoke thought, be they reflective or trivial (but not rhetorical), and *responding* to them
- Asking directly of me an opinion on something
- Making a statement or observation that is uniquely your own

This kind of participation is what I define as a fearless approach to Twitter. Why fearless? Because this kind of communication, regardless if it is on Twitter, Facebook, or even in real life, can open you up for a lot of opinion and criticism. You might say something that won't agree with everyone in your network. You might do something that rankles the feathers of a few. You might risk new relationships that you have worked hard to cultivate. Twitter will challenge you in ways you might not expect, and being fearless in how you participate on Twitter can only make you a stronger member of this online community. Sure, you still need to be careful. Sure, you still need to consider others. But Twitter offers you an opportunity: Take a chance and express yourself. This is part of the Twitter experience, and this is part of participating in your network.

Be fearless. Speak your mind. Find out just how far 140-characters can take you.

11

Taking Care of Business

So, this is Chapter 11...and I'm going to talk about using Twitter for running and promoting your business. (No, this was completely unintentional, I swear!)

Like anything on the Internet, people want to know how to make money at Twitter. In fact, a vast majority of Twitter books on the market are all written by marketing experts (making this title unique as I am approaching Twitter from a *practical user's* point-of-view) who want to help you make a fast buck here.

I'm not saying Twitter can't do that. I'm not saying I don't do that. What I am saying is you need to know what you are getting yourself into.

I run workshops on Social Media, host seminars on Twitter and other Social Media outlets, and use social networking as a way to promote myself and my works. I am the first to say that as a marketing and promotions tool, Twitter has changed how business is conducted and has covertly rewritten the rules on how professional relationships are forged, nurtured, and cultivated. It has truly been awe-inspiring to watch.

Still, there are those who completely muck it up; and while I am reserving much of that ire for Chapter 12, "ANTI-Social Media: The Dark Side of Twitter," I am going to give you here some straight talk about making money with Twitter.

Yes, it can be done, but there is a method to the madness.

Identity Crisis

I have been asked several times why I have *two* Twitter accounts. Yes, I host two Twitter accounts on my feed, and I do so specifically for professional reasons. This is not—I repeat, not—some sign of a Twitter addiction or what I have heard referred to as a *Twitaddiction.* That just isn't the case with me. Yes, I love this social network, but I can stop Twitter. Anytime. Anytime I really wanted to. Just...not...today. I mean, I have a deadline to meet. I'm under contract for the book. I bought this third monitor specifically for Twitter....

Look, we're getting off the point....

When I joined Twitter in July 2007, I came in under the "TeeMonster" moniker as my friends were all telling me that I just had to give this thing a whirl. Within a month, I was well addic—*invested* into my community, making snarky remarks and responding to feedback on whatever podcasts I was producing. It was a comfortable, online kaffeeklatsch, so yeah, I got behind Twitter, sure.

It wasn't until I noted other bloggers and podcasters using Twitter as a notification device that I took a more serious look at it. The ability to "touch base" with a network that actively follows you? Promotional ideas came to mind. Networking possibilities opened up. Twitter as a cost-effective marketing tool made perfect sense to me.

Then I paused again and considered how people knew me in this network. As this was still within Twitter's first year, there was less professional traffic in the timeline. I watched the community's reaction to members turning their feeds into 24-7 promotional opportunities, their reaction usually negative. Twitter's line between promotion and participation is deceptively (if not dangerously) thin. Could I walk it without alienating my established audience? That's when I considered a second Twitter account: @ITSTudios for Imagine That! Studios. Why not? It's free and a business account could focus entirely on promotional and professional aims. Sounds simple enough.

"Why do I want to follow ITStudios?" asked my new and established Followers. "Why not stick with TeeMonster? I mean, they're both *you,* right?"

Both @TeeMonster and @ITStudios are me, but each account represents two different personas.

FIGURE 11.1

When Tee decided to establish a professional presence on Twitter, he chose a different avatar (left) to represent himself there as opposed to his favorite avatar on TeeMonster (right).

- **TeeMonster**—This is me kicking back in cargo pants, an All Blacks practice jersey, and a Dogfish 90 within reach. My network is composed of fellow authors, to podcast listeners, to old friends, to other Social Media enthusiasts and evangelists. My avatar fits my mood, but lately it's floating between a J.R. Blackwell (@jrblackwell) original of Rafe Rafton, and the right half of Figure 11.1 image of me. My tweets in this feed are seasoned with snark, LOLCat speak, and (in some cases) utter inappropriateness. I still tend to promote blogposts and podcasts, answer questions ranging from iPhone apps to podcasting, and even cross-promote the ITStudios account via retweets; but that is becoming less and less as I build, refine, and encourage followers to join me at @ITStudios.

- **ITStudios**—Here, I am wearing khakis and an upscale shirt. The Dogfish is traded in for a glass of ice tea or a cup of coffee. My avatar features the Double Koru, my branding on Twitter. This is the professional side of Tee Morris. All business, all the time. (Okay, 90 percent business—ten percent of humor can go a long way!) My tweets focus on the status of my projects (podcasts, latest AppleiPhoneApp.com postings, writing deadlines, and such), give updates on where I will be, offer TwitReviews and TwitTips on software and hardware, and share technology and Social Media links. Under the Double Koru, this feed remains free of sarcasm and silliness. (Sometimes, yes, LOLCat speak does creep in. Call it the mischievous streak in me.)

Maybe it does appear on the outside as a split personality, and it could be argued that by managing multiple accounts, I'm diluting my potential network impact. I am finding just the opposite: Both accounts have a clear direction and actually improve my signal-to-noise ratio. When I am in the Social Media zone, I believe in implementing solutions, getting the job done, and always providing results with a positive attitude. Off the clock, I'm unwinding with a scotch and stogie, inviting a good rant if the passion grabs me, and allowing myself a pat on the back for my time in the pool. So how do you like your Tee Morris? Professional or personal? It is really up to you.

A Little Birdie Told Me...

One of the toughest lines to draw with Social Media (be it Twitter, Facebook, or any outlet) is defining the line between professional and personal. If you are all business on Twitter, you might find yourself tweeting in a vacuum. There needs to be a personal approach to business when working in Social Media, but you also need to curtail many of your opinions, personal rants, and personal insecurities. With this interactive approach to the Web, the line between life in the office and life at home is blurred, and you have to decide where those parameters are drawn.

So what is the magic formula in balancing between the professional and the personal on Twitter? There isn't. It will be different from person to person, but I would recommend asking yourself, "Would I make a statement like this in a professional setting?" If I were having lunch with a client, how personal would I get? Would I be focused more on what we need to do to accomplish goals, or on how my day is going and my plans for tomorrow? Consider what you are saying or asking before your tweet, and ask yourself how appropriate it is for the mutual goals of you, your client, and both your businesses.

Of course, like any approach to Social Media, there will probably be some overlap. I still answer questions concerning media production on my TeeMonster account, and I have been known to share my excitement on the return of *Deadliest Catch* on ITStudios. You can, however, expect a definite platform and identity on visiting both accounts. Yes, they are both Tee Morris, but they are different aspects of the same person. It all depends on what you are looking for. Either way, you'll know what to expect after a few tweets.

And if you're following both, all I can say is this: Thank you for being a fan.

Using Twitter to Market Your Business

Establishing your identity on Twitter is merely the start for promoting your business on Twitter. After you have your profile up and running, consider that Twitter is really an even playing field. Your business could be Dunkin' Donuts, Whole Foods, Air New Zealand, or Filthy Farmgirl Soaps. You could employ several thousand across the country, or hundreds of thousands around the world, or employ yourself and your two housecats for morale. You could be a company that has been in business for decades, or a business that has just launched from the basement of your house. On Twitter, everyone is coming in the same way.

So, where do you begin?

Build Your Network

Time to get cracking on finding people to talk to. There are a number of ways you can do this, many of which you can find more details about how the services work and what they offer you in the ways of finding Followers. There are also some uncommon practices you can employ to lay down the foundation of your network.

Establish a personal account first. This is a great way to give Twitter a test drive to see exactly how you can effectively use it in your business. By setting up a personal account first, you can offer to friends, close clientele, and new associates the option of following you or not. Then, on deciding how often you tweet and the amount of response you get from your Twitter account, you can make the choice to either maintain the personal account for your own means or simply shut it down, and then launch an officially endorsed Twitter presence for your business.

Use Mr. Tweet. Described in more detail on Chapter 5, "Terrific Twitter Tools," Mr. Tweet (http://mrtweet.net) works as your Personal Networking Assistant for you, your business, and Twitter. Search out people either seeking services similar to your own, or connect with Twitters that offer resources important to your business. Mr. Tweet can recommend other people for you to follow based on those initial tweets of yours. Although there are many other services that do what Mr. Tweet does, Mr. Tweet remains the best of Twitter assistants, and when starting out it is a good tool to have working for you.

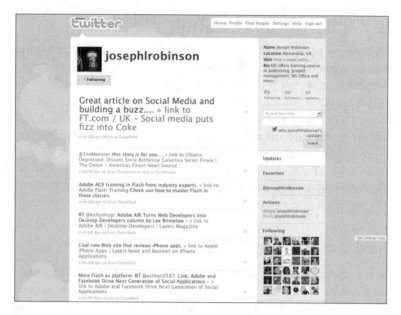

FIGURE 11.2

Joe Robinson of EEI Communications in Alexandria, VA, established a personal account in Twitter, to gauge interest for EEI and find out how Twitter could be applied as a promotional tool.

A Little Birdie Told Me...

On building Followers, make sure what kind of a network you are building. If your intent it to market and promote, you do not want to fill your network with other people in the same business as you. You want to bring in customers and clientele interested in what you do and how you do it. If your intent is to network with others in your profession, network with others in your industry with less emphasis on what you sell. Selling what your network is selling is preaching to the choir, after all.

Use Twitter. From way back in Chapter 2, "Setting Up Twitter," Twitter helps you build your network based on your own search parameters and your bio details—its suggestions coming from the active Twitter accounts online. Head to your Twitter home page and look at the top-right corner of it. Click on Find People, and Twitter presents you with four options: Find on Twitter, Find on Other Networks, Invite by Email, and Suggested Users. This feature is offered at the beginning of your account registration and can be accessed at any time from your home page.

FIGURE 11.3
Under Suggested Users, Twitter looks at your traffic and bio details and suggests Twitter accounts that would be a good match for you.

Use Twitter Search and TweetScan. Chapter 6, "Tracking Twitter," covers Twitter Search (http://search.twitter.com) and TweetScan (http://tweetscan.com), two Google-style search engines that search throughout all Public Timeline tweets for keywords, names, and places you set up. Based on the results of your searches, you can then tweet a complete stranger. You can also use RSS to subscribe to a search, receiving Twitter-versions of a Google Alert to find out who is tweeting about you, keep up to date on topics of interest to you, and meet people that might be interested in working or networking with you.

A Little Birdie Told Me...

When contacting people not in your network, you can send them only a public tweet. They should receive it as an @Reply, and they can either reply back to you or add them to your network. Sending DMs to someone you find in a search like the one mentioned above will not work. Remember: You can send DMs only to people who are following you and vice versa.

Use Traditional Media. You might hear some in Social Media circles argue, "Old Media is dead! This is our time!" But have you ever noticed that the same people who boast that traditional media no longer matters, they are busy securing book deals, writing columns for magazines and newspapers, appearing on broadcast television shows when invited, and handing you business cards after their talks?

Traditional media, dead? Hardly. In trouble, maybe, but not dead.

Although the role of traditional media has changed (dramatically), it does not mean that Social Media cannot succeed without working with it. By utilizing print ads, radio spots, and even news media and television ads to get the word out that you and your business are on Twitter will only help you in building your network and your online presence. We must work with traditional media as mainstream society, although connected to the Internet, is still learning the basics and Social Media. The concept might not be as easily grasped or understood, so it is traditional media that we rely on to help us reach out to the mainstream.

Make no mistake though. As much as we need traditional media, traditional media needs us. To stay current. To stay relevant. To keep up.

But yes, traditional media remains a viable option in building your network.

Now that you are on your way to build your network, what is the next step in promoting your business? Well, let people know what you do, right? Start pushing websites and point people to what you sell? Right?

Wrong.

That was the old approach to promotion and marketing on the Internet, and perhaps there are still a few things you can apply from that approach, but with Twitter, marketing and promoting your business works differently.

Observe

With this network and if you use a service such as TweetDeck or Twhirl to fetch your tweets for you, you should sit back and gauge what people talk about in your network. Note I didn't say what people are talking about in the *Public* Timeline but what people are talking about in *your* Timeline. In mobile and desktop Twitter clients, *Trending Topics* or *Trends* appear in the right column. Trending Topics are hashtags and reoccurring keywords that appear throughout the Public Timeline, but these are popular topics throughout Twitter, not in your network.

Instead of talking about what is trendy on Twitter, watch the discussion among members of your own network. Watch what it is they talk about and see what is on your network, be it open questions, requests, or simply topics that might be striking interest among a smaller group of your Followers.

FIGURE 11.4

Trends are easily accessed in mobile Twitter clients, like Twittelator Pro (left) and TwitterFon (right).

Engage

You can observe for as long as you like but sooner or later, you *need* to comment on what is talked about. The conversation is not going to go anywhere without some input from you, and neither is your network going to establish a personal relationship with you outside of anything other than just another Follower in your network. This is the "get to know me" phase for people in your network where they assess your value to your network, and for you to find out your network's needs. This only happens when you engage your network in conversation.

Here are just a few easy ways to get a conversation started on Twitter. Some of these tips *might* strike you as common sense, but some might spark some inspiration in how to conduct business on Twitter.

Answer a question. It could be in answer to a question about the product you represent. It could be some trivia you are curious on. Whatever the question, be ready with a quick answer and—if called upon—an extended follow-up. An example of this happened for me on November 13, 2008, when a TV spot came on for the F-150. I stopped what I was doing and caught a familiar voice telling me about the truck. I tweeted, "Is it just me, or does that guy doing the VO for Ford sound like Denis Leary?" Within minutes, I received this reply from @FordTrucks:

> That was definitely Denis Leary.

The tweet came with a YouTube link to the commercial I had just seen. I immediately replied with how incredibly cool I thought it was that Ford Motors was using Denis Leary and his trademark snark in their ads. Ford Trucks immediately replied with

> We think so, too. Plus, having a damn good product helps too. :)

This quick exchange with Ford Trucks (or at least a representative of Ford Trucks) impressed me as this was Ford Motors making the effort to reach out to say "Hi." Not something you would expect from a company as huge as Ford, but nevertheless I am tweeting trivia with them.

These efforts do make lasting impressions, and this is a good way of getting your Twitter presence known.

Offer a solution. In this hypothetical, let's say your business is workforce recruiting. Your job is to make sure that when businesses need specialists, you make people appear the next day. You have decided to give Twitter a go, and in watching your feed, your Twitters pose a variety of situations on your feed such as...

- I'm not getting peak performance out of my computer today.
- I could really go for some Thai food.
- Going on a long flight. Any good books you would recommend?

Why not weigh in with viable options? The difference between answering a question (as seen earlier with @FordTrucks) and what we're discussing now is that the tweets you're responding to really have no common thread or might have nothing to do with your profession. On seeing tweets like these (and trust me, it's Twitter—you will), making the sale doesn't matter. What matters here are your interests. Some replies to these tweets could be

- What kind of computer are you running? Mac or PC?
- Are you in the Alexandria area? If so, try Royal Thai on Royal Street.
- If you're crossing the Atlantic, read Tee Morris' *Case of the Singing Sword*. If you're crossing the Pacific, read Morevi.

Exactly what are you selling here? Nothing? Actually, you are. You are marketing and promoting an image. You are establishing yourself as a voice in the Twitter community that pays attention to the people in your network. You can also establish roots for mutually profitable relationships and reliable resource exchanges.

Greeting and Salutations. You get situated at your desk, you fire up your desktop client of choice, and your network appears. What is your first tweet of the day? Is it a sales pitch, a plug of a website, or your agenda? I've been guilty of the last one, I admit. Lately I've taken a different approach on Imagine That's Twitter:

- Awake, finally. Still a bit groggy.
- Good morning, Twitter. It's a Monday (in this hemisphere), and I wish you all well!
- Looking forward to today. I teach, for the first time today, my Social Media class. This is going to be a lot of fun!

Perhaps that last tweet does announce my agenda for the day, but the agenda was also given an opinion of my high expectations for the class I was preparing to teach. The tweet you begin your day with can say a lot about your state of mind. Are you all business today? Then people might be giving you a wide berth. If you are more on a personal level, you might have some busy traffic on your Twitter feed that day. Consider what that opening tweet is telling your network, and if you happen to open with a salutation such as "How is everyone?" or "How is the day beginning for you?", consider a sincere reply to that. It will speak volumes for you as a member of the community.

What you might notice in the tips I'm giving here is that I've not mentioned product placement or promotion once. How, then, am I promoting my business when I've not mentioned my website or product yet? How is this working for me?

Although you might not realize it, you are promoting your business by your *participation*. People see in your greetings, in your replies, and in your exchanges that yes, there really is a person on the other side of that avatar. By making an effort to become part of the community, of getting to know those in your network, you take on a very personable, very human approach to business. Twitter, which was built on the basis of community and communication, is a device for making connections. Make sure you keep that in mind when setting up shop.

Fail Whale says

Participation on Twitter seems to have a broad definition; but if you want a good, solid parameter for what quality participation is, regard the conversations you have on Twitter the same way you would have conversations in the real world. Similar to the signal-to-noise ratio discussed in Chapter 9, "The Trouble with Twitter," try going into a social setting and hold a conversation with someone using only quotes from famous people, from repeating what someone else standing next to you just said, or including your website in every reply. You might find the conversation will not go very far, and the individual you're trying to "participate" with will not want to have anything to do with you. I cover common mistakes like this (and how to avoid them) in Chapter 12.

Approach Twitter as you would a true social gathering, and this kind of faux pas can be avoided.

Twitter for Nonprofits

What if your corporation or business isn't a money-making venture but more about raising awareness or working to better the community out in the real world? What if, instead of making cold, hard cash, you want to make a difference? Organizations that are dedicated to educate, to assist, and to enrich the world are usually funded by donations—donations of a generous community. When it comes to technology, though, there is a divide that is difficult to cross because of financial commitments, learning curves with software and hardware, and the time and resources allocated to properly apply it to an organization's mission statements and goals.

Twitter, like many Social Media initiatives, is free. Twitter is easy to learn. Twitter can be easy to manage and apply to building a strong and supportive online community.

By design, Twitter's application to the nonprofit sector is limitless.

Some of the nonprofits currently on Twitter include

- Amnesty International (@amnesty and @amnestynews)
- The Brooklyn Museum (@brooklynmuseum)
- The Juvenile Diabetes Research Foundation (@sugarcube)
- The National Wildlife Federation (@nwf)

With the rise of Social Media and the popularity of Twitter, Chris Brogan (as in the same Chris Brogan behind the Foreword of this book) established *Twitter Packs, a wiki* of various people and organizations who use Twitter to help further their goals and missions.

But exactly how can organizations, or one individual, use Twitter for the good of the community?

Fund-raising. Promoting services and products on Twitter should be approached with caution, just as raising money for a cause. It can be done, and has been done quite successfully, but what made the fund-raisers on Twitter a success can be traced back to individuals and their involvement in their own community.

Beth Kanter (@kanter), a Social Media consultant for nonprofits, has been online and building her community for years, building a reputation as an advocate of Social Media for nonprofits. At the Seattle Gnomedex 8.0 Conference in August 2008, Beth challenged her network to *"Send Leng Sopharath, a young Cambodian woman, off to her junior year of college in good health."* Within 90 minutes $2,500 was raised; and by the end of the conference, nearly $4,000 was collected for this student.

On a more personal level, Diana Schubert (@VividMuse) participates in the Susan G Komen Race for the Cure (http://ww5.komen.org) to raise money and awareness for breast cancer research. The walk is done in the memory of her mother, Linda Stockman, who passed away from breast cancer in 2006, and in 2008, she turned to Twitter to ask her community to reach her goal of $500. Quite unexpectedly, her community rallied on her behalf and asked that everyone in their respective networks donate what they could. Tweets like *"Skip that $5 Starbucks for one day, and donate to @VividMuse's Walk for the Cure."* And *"If you donate $1 or $10, you will have made a difference...."* were being retweeted by her Followers. Within several hours her goal of $500 was met, but the donations kept coming in. Before the actual race, Viv raised more than $1,000 (double her original goal) with the majority of her donations coming from people she had never met.

Fail Whale Says...

I won't give out the Twitter's true ID, so let's just call this individual Clueless Entrepreneur Online (CEO). This CEO did something similar to both Beth Kanter and Viv: CEO, to raise awareness for a cause and to illustrate the impact of Twitter, turned to (at that time) a network of 7,000 Followers and told them to all donate $1. CEO was determined to raise awareness for this cause and tweeted for three days asking for donations. After three days, few people in CEO's network paid it forward and his goal fell short. That might have been the worst of it...

...until CEO went on a blog, berated the network for being lazy, greedy, blue meanies, and then tweeted the blogpost's link.

continues

continued

If you want to raise awareness for a cause, turning to your network for support might seem like a simple and logical thing to do, but you should not expect your network to perform. Twitter isn't there to serve at your pleasure but to work with you and others to build strong communities of strong relationships, no expectations included. Another thing you should not do to your network is alienate them if something falls short of your expectations. Simply put, the Followers in your network have chosen, for whatever reason, to follow you. That alone should be enough to respect their decisions in supporting you in raising awareness, concern, or (in this case) money. If you alienate them, you only undermine yourself and the reputation that you have built online.

FIGURE 11.5

Diana Schubert (pictured here with her mother, Linda Stockman) turned to her Twitter network for support and underestimated her network, who rallied on her behalf to raise funds and awareness for breast cancer research.

Build awareness and promote events. For nonprofits, attention to a cause is their business. With the ability to swap links and retweet people in your network, Twitter is one of the most powerful tools in making a movement viral.

The 1010 Project (@the1010project), as stated in its mission statement, is "…a nonprofit organization that provides income-generating grants to indigenous development partners in Kenya and raises awareness in the United States on behalf of the global poor." Its tweets range from personal messages between its Followers to links promoting its Power of $10 campaign to Poverty Facts:

> Poverty Fact #14—In the U.S., low-income working families grew 350,000 between 2002 and 2006. http://bitly.com/1010p

Issues can also cover Social Media. With The Lamp (@thelampnyc), demystifying technology and bringing it closer to inner-city communities of New York City is its cause. LAMP (Learning About Multimedia Project) hosts workshops concerning media creation, information exchange, and technology skills for current and future generations. Its feed primarily focuses on link exchanges ranging from tech news headlines to case studies to recent blogposts:

> What's your take on #amazonfail? Programming glitch or malicious censorship? http://tinyurl.com/dmo2wo *(April 14)*
>
> Our latest post! Twitter in the classroom http://tinyurl.com/cjsvn4 *(April 10)*
>
> Students retain more when listening to lectures on podcast vs. in person. http://tinyurl.com/c67lvv *(Feb 21)*

LAMP's feed also includes snarky notices to its interns (who do not follow its Twitter feeds close enough apparently) to Follow Fridays. Although focused more on the link exchange, there is still the effort to capitalize on the personal nature of Twitter.

As discussed in Chapter 6, #hashtags were an invention that came from a crisis. Twitter has already become such a device to give people up-to-date bytes of information and relevant links, time delays taken into consideration. No stranger to the importance of communications during a crisis, the American Red Cross (@RedCross) utilizes Twitter's inherent capability to report to many people simultaneously what is happening:

> We're responding to #wildfires in north central Texas. Follow @ChisholmTrailRC for local updates.
>
> Is your local Red Cross Chapter on Twitter? We mapped them here: http://tinyurl.com/d593ec
>
> If you are in need of #tornado disaster assistance, you can call 1-800-RED-CROSS (1-800-733-2767). #okstorms

Being instrumental in a worldwide movement offering neutral humanitarian care to victims of natural and man-made disasters, the American Red Cross continues its mission with Twitter providing a powerful, worldwide network to people everywhere.

Achievements and Personal Inspiration. Twitter can be applied to promote a product, an idea, or a cause, but Twitter can also promote success stories that can rally the troops and bring people hope.

Along with the earlier success story of Viv Schubert, there are the celebrations and tributes shared on the Lance Armstrong Foundation's feed (@livestrong). At @livestrong, its mission is to "...inspire and empower people affected by cancer. We believe that unity is strength, knowledge is power, and attitude is everything."

RT @KarenGary: Celebrating my 5 year Cancerversary! I LIVESTRONG for my son! WOOOOOOOOOOOT! Congrats @karengary!

39 minutes ago from TweetDeck

LIVESTRONG

FIGURE 11.6

Lance Armstrong's "Live Strong" movement now rallies support and inspires others through tweets of encouragement and hope.

What began with awareness through rubber bracelets, the Lance Armstrong Foundation now has a full presence in Social Media with blogging, RSS-related services, and Twitter. @LiveStrong, with the inspiring stories and tweets as shown in Figure 11.6, also uses Twitter to circulate information on research, promote events and fund-raisers, and encourage and educate cancer survivors with ways to "live strong."

A Little Birdie Told Me...

Mashable.com's Lon S. Cohen features at http://bit.ly/NPT "26 Charities and Non-Profits on Twitter" that invites you to leave links pointing to other nonprofits in the network. If you are looking for inspirational stories, assistance in establishing Twitter for you not-for-profit, or wanting to see who is out there using Twitter for the greater good, pay Mashable a visit.

From larger organizations such as Amnesty International to the individual looking to make a difference, Twitter taps into the power of global networking, an advantage that should be utilized by nonprofits. Twitter can provide your nonprofit a cost-effective communications center; and with the right plan in place, you can also build your network into a support team for your organization. From here, you can (and will) accomplish anything.

Using Twitter to Market Yourself

After looking at Twitter for the larger companies or for nonprofits, we return to Twitter for who it was built for: you. When it comes to a business or a passion you want to share with the world, no one can promote it for you better than you. Whether you start up a business in your garage, you have a book coming out from a major publishing house, or if you launch a podcast and want to spread the world about where you are on iTunes, you want to let people know what you're up to and where to find you.

Using Twitter Tools to Promote Your Blog or Podcast

As mentioned in Chapter 5, WordPress is the world's largest self-hosted blogging tool, and very Twitter-friendly thanks to the Twitter Tools plug-in, created by developer Alex King. Twitter Tools, in a nutshell, is full integration of Twitter into your WordPress blog. If you run your blog on WordPress, follow the steps in Chapter 5 to install Twitter Tools. After that, come back here to set up your blog to turn Twitter into a notification device.

After the plug-in is installed, you can configure Twitter Tools by reaching Twitter Tools Options by going to either

- Plugins > Twitter Tools Options link
- Settings > Twitter Tools
- Post > Tweet > Twitter Tools Options

These options are covered in Chapter 5, but here we focus on what we need.

1. Under Username and Password, enter in the account you want Twitter Tools to work with. Single-click Test Login Info to verify that the Username and Password are verified.

2. Enable Option to Create a Tweet When You Post in Your Blog?, on a blog post being published, composes a tweet that says:

   New blog post: (Title of the Entry) (condensed URL)

   Select Yes from its menu and the Set This on by Default? option.

Two sets, and you're done. Now, WordPress automatically generates a simple tweet, or you can go to Write > Tweet in your WordPress Dashboard to compose a tweet in the provided field.

FIGURE 11.7

With Twitter Tools activated, WordPress can generate a tweet with the subject header of your new post and a direct link to it (seen here using PowerTwitter).

Now whenever you post a new blogpost or a podcast, Twitter helps spread the word. This is a fantastic way to expose your podcast to new Followers who might not be aware of your podcast or blog. Others in your network who are familiar with your work might turn the Twitter Tools-rendered tweet viral and retweet it along their individual networks.

A Little Birdie Told Me

After you see your tweet appear, keep a sharp eye on your Twitter feed. A trend with Twitter users is to not leave comments but start up discussions about your post on Twitter, either with you directly or within their networks. It might not be the same as getting a shower of comments on your blog, but feedback is feedback. Make sure to reply and let people know how much you appreciate hearing from them.

Using Twitter to Market a Product or Event

When you have a network in place, you can now effectively promote your business. Before bombarding your network with links and tweets, consider how you want to promote your work using Twitter. Along with tweets (which I discuss in more details in a moment), consider some of the other ways Twitter can work for you.

Promotional avatars. Particularly popular with authors and filmmakers, avatars promote release dates, cover art, and featured characters from their works. Avatars, as discussed in Chapter 2 are easy to create and even easier to distribute. Create a variety of avatars (and keep them a consistent size and layout) and then offer them from one location on your website. Release a few tweets (no more than three a day, I would recommend) encouraging people to come and download an avatar for themselves. Your network then swaps out for a time their own avatars for your promotional one.

FIGURE 11.8

Custom avatars can serve as passive promotions for your business or event, allowing those in your network to promote for you.

Authors such as Scott Sigler, Mur Lafferty, Philippa Ballantine and myself have invited readers into our stories and podcasts via Twitter. Taking the idea of a promotional avatar one step further, we created custom avatars for our listeners. For Hutchins, he invited members of his network to join him "at the Brink" or the fictional asylum of Brinkvale as depicted in his novel, *Personal Effects: Dark Art.* Those who followed his link on Twitter and filled out the paperwork received a special "Brinkvale Psychiatric Hospital: COMMITTED" avatar that users could proudly display. My own invitation to invite people into the story was to create custom avatars designating them as either Askana's Royal Guard, Rafton's Crew, or (for the more daring) Rafton's Wenches. Popular as they were, the avatars themselves were easy to create.

What makes custom avatars so popular on Twitter can be traced back to that sense of community, that connection with a group or an idea. Custom avatars, as shown in Figure 11.8, are just one way of promoting your work.

Bring your network into your business. Part of Twitter's appeal is bringing people directly into the action of whatever it is you are doing at the moment. You can now offer unique perspectives on your company or your product simply by inviting your followers to take a role in your business' creative process. As Hutchins and I discovered with the exclusive avatars, your Followers will want to become involved in what you do. Why not allow your network behind the scenes?

How do you do that? Ask S.A.R.A.H. (@_S_A_R_A_H_), one of the characters from the SciFi Channel's popular television shows, *EUReKA*. The show is set in a small, mid-western town that is actually a think tank of supergeniuses. S.A.R.A.H. (short for Self Actuated Residential Automated Habitat) is one of the show's more unique characters because she is an artificially intelligent house. As I am a fan of the show, it was brought to my attention that @_S_A_R_A_H_ was, in fact, on Twitter. At this time, spambots had already started to appear on the network (something discussed in the final chapter), but I thought I would make an exception as this was *EUReKA* and I am a fan. On following the account, I posted the tweet "If you are going to follow any bot, follow @_S_A_R_A_H_. I friggin' love EUReKA!" It would show the SciFi Channel, I figured, just how adored that unassuming little show is.

Imagine the surprise I got when I received this moments later:

> @TeeMonster It's safe to say that Eureka loves you too, but I am more than a "bot". I am a Self Actuated Residential Automated Habitat.

Yes. I got a personalized tweet from S.A.R.A.H.

Along with communicating with fans, @_S_A_R_A_H_ also drops hints about upcoming shows, news on where EUReKA actors, producers, and writers will be appearing, and (still) defends her authenticity on Twitter:

> @ScottMahan I have no idea why they would call me a "counterfeit twitterer". After all, I am self-actuated.

S.A.R.A.H. even makes a few wisecracks, on occasion:

> The citizens of Eureka are prohibited from participating in social media for obvious reasons, but Global Dynamics trusts me.

Do I dare call that authen-Twit-ity? Yeah, I dare.

FIGURE 11.9

The SciFi Channel's EUReKA continues innovative promotion through Social Media by inviting fans to chat with S.A.R.A.H. on Twitter.

This Twitter initiative proved so successful that the SciFi Channel now has an account for the network. Craig Engler (@Craigatscifi), the senior vice president and general manager of SciFi Digital, has joined the Twtterverse. "I first started using Twitter in January 2009 as a great place to listen to what people were saying about *Battlestar Galactica*," Craig says. "Then I started answering questions about the network and throwing out some behind-the-scenes details about working here, along with sending out news tidbits." The response has been so positive that SciFi is, in Craig's words, "...going to keep the experiment going and see where it takes us."

What makes this a bold move from a business perspective is that SciFi now has an open channel between its network and its viewers, opening the floodgates for instant feedback.

Customer service. Another way to promote your business is to not necessarily promote your service or business but provide support and assistance for it. Over the years, businesses have been making a lot of cuts in customer service, becoming more and more reliant on automated services and websites to carry the burden. Twitter is now offering an alternative to calling your local customer service number and waiting on hold for an hour (or three) and giving you access to a real person representing customer service. Here are just a few of the success stories on Twitter where businesses have made an effort to reach out to their clientele:

- **Comcast**—Comcast was an early adopter of Twitter and met with early skepticism. It usually involved someone on Twitter complaining about his Comcast service, and then—seemingly from out of nowhere—a tweet would arrive from either a representative of Comcast (For me, it was @ComcastBill who has successfully helped me both times I needed help on Twitter.) or from @ComcastCares, a Twitter account staffed by Frank Eliason and several other Comcast employees. At first, Twitters weren't sure if these Twitters were legitimate Comcast representatives or someone pulling their leg; but with confirmation from the mother ship, Comcast representatives were, in fact, monitoring Twitter in hopes to improve customer relations by attempting to diagnose failure in service and act on it in a prompt and speedy manner. This approach to customer service now sets the bar for other companies to deliver fast-and-effective service such as Comcast does.

- **The airline industry**—With its constant bailouts from the government and notoriously bad reputation for customer service, airlines, such as jetBlue (@JetBlue), Southwest (@SouthwestAir), and Air New Zealand (@FlyAirNZ), are now turning to Twitter for ways to keep their passengers informed and (above all) happy. Sometimes, this form of customer service also manifests itself as special deals offered only through their respective websites (a nice perk for following airlines on Twitter), but in many cases these feeds also include weather reports, flight statuses, travel tips, and even sights to see when you visit from out of town or out of country. (Thanks, Air New Zealand!) If you do have a question, simply query your airline on Twitter. There might be a lag in response time, but many of the airlines are quick to respond because Twitter is proving to be an effective (and successful) tool to improve customer relations for an industry that has come under fire for not caring about its passengers.

A Little Birdie Told Me...

Along with making airlines more personable and more effective in customer relations, Twitter is also making airlines more competitive for your business.

From New Media Chatter (http://newmediachatter.com), Dave Peck (@davepeck) tells of his journey home (http://bit.ly/112Qk6) from South by Southwest (http://sxsw.com). His JetBlue flight heading home was delayed. No reason given. Peck posted a quick grump on Twitter that was immediately responded to on Twitter by JetBlue, asking him to follow them and DM flight information. Peck attempted to do this, but was blocked by Jet Blue. Anxious to get home, Peck threw out his flight information in a public tweet and waited for a response. On his follow-up query about finding a flight to San Francisco, Peck did receive a follow-up…

…from Southwest Airlines, opening a dialog with Peck and offering an alternate way to get home.

The moral of this tale is that if you implement Twitter as part of your customer relations, make sure you are not unintentionally making things tougher for your clients. Also, make sure that you touch base with them periodically to assure them you are on top of the situation and taking care of the problem at hand.

Remember. Not only are customers following you but so is the competition.

FIGURE 11.10
Creatures 'n' Crooks Bookshoppe in Richmond, VA, offers a different kind of customer service with personal picks from the store's shelves.

- **Creatures 'n' Crooks Bookshop**—Customer service takes on many guises. Perhaps some of the best customer service you can receive is in independently owned establishments, small businesses that intimately know what they deal in and what their specialties are. From my own hometown of Richmond, VA, the indie bookstore Creatures 'n' Crooks (@cncbooks) offers this kind of customer service on its

Twitter feed. Along upcoming events at the store, happenings both literary and artistic in Richmond, and answering feedback to customers, Creatures 'n' Crooks also offers "Today's Favorite Book" tweets. These are not necessarily *The New York Times'* bestsellers nor are they always the top-selling titles in the store, but they are books that are personal favorites for science fiction, fantasy, horror, and mystery. The tweets are informal, sincere recommendations, offering a good read that you might not have been looking for but you can find at Creatures 'n' Crooks.

Promotion. Now we reach the most obvious application of Twitter: Promotion. Blatant, shameless, "click on this link to visit my site" promotion. Yes, this is an application of Twitter, but there is a good reason why I put this approach at the very end, and this is where many businesses, big and small, fail on Twitter. When corporations or individual practices launch a Twitter account, there is a tendency to begin the promotion and hype machine, but this is why you should follow my advice here and save blatant promotion for last. Simply telling people where to find your stuff and constantly repeating your own home page over and over *and over* again is the *last* thing you should do.

Samson Technologies' Zoom Handy Recorders (@zoomfx) just released, for example, the H4n. If you subscribe to their feed, you'll hear about it. You will also get links referring back to websites with more detail, sure. But promotion isn't the only thing that you'll find on Zoom's feed. You will also find links to firmware updates, technical support, news and reviews on audio gear (and some of these links do not pertain to either Zoom or Samson), and banter back and forth with customers on other Zoom products. Although there is promotion for the H4n, the Samson/Zoom crew also applies the other tips featured here: customer support, asking questions and providing options, and engaging their audience. Although they have something to promote, they also acknowledge and respect the community they are building.

This new approach to promotion can also work for the individual. On the Day of Double Trouble, a promotion that New Zealand author Pip Ballantine and I hosted, we did not promote the links to our books until the very day of the event. If asked, we did point people into the direction of those Amazon links; but before the day of our Amazon push, we offered promotional avatars, invited people to listen to our interviews across the podosphere, and also read our thoughts on the upcoming day we would take Amazon by storm. Not once did we *tweet bomb* (a link that appears repetitively throughout a Twitter stream) our followers with the Amazon link. Instead, we waited for the day of the event; and on 08.08.08, we dropped in our Amazon-ready tweet once at the top of the hour, every hour.

For ourselves, for our publisher, for our readers, the Day of Double Trouble was a huge success.

Promoting our books, though, came last, as with Zoom. Endless, constant promotion can easily cross the line with Twitter communities who feel they are subject to spamming. There is a time and a place to blatantly promote your work, but it is a good idea to try to keep your hard sells at a minimum. Sure, the in-your-face-approach might work for BILLY MAYS AND HIS OXY-CLEAN PRODUCTS, but that tends to crash and burn on Twitter.

Becoming Part of the Community: Revisited

Another reason both Zoom and Double Trouble score success on Twitter is in how we engage our Followers, offering additional media (links to free PDFs of our books, promotional avatars, interviews seen in Double Trouble), going beyond the promotion (customer support, news and related articles to audio, seen in Zoom), and replying directly to our respective networks. We were (and still are) active participants in our communities, and we strive to connect with our Followers.

It all comes back to participation and becoming part of the community.

As I mentioned Chapter 10, "Getting Personal," with my @TeeMonster feed, not everyone is in my @ITStudios tweets, and although there is plenty of crossover in this network, this is a different network from my original @TeeMonster network. Very different dynamic. Very different atti-tude. Still very much me. It is a very different network, but still very much me in the amount of participation I aim to achieve in Twitter.

Along with some of the success stories I cover here, participation can also happen if you

- Ask and reply to questions that spark an opinion or an idea.
- Ask directly from your Followers feedback on your performance or your company's performance (and don't always expect that feedback to be good feedback).
- State opinions and observations *within your company's mission state-ments.* (This can be tricky to follow.)

This kind of participation is what I defined in the previous chapter as a fearless approach to Twitter. Why fearless? Because this is not public relations, promotions, and marketing as it was previously regarded. Once upon a time, business was all about making the sale and never about blurring the lines between the professional and the personal. Twitter challenges this axiom by turning your business—whatever size it might be—and makes it the "Floyd's Barber Shop of Mayberry" where people walk away with a smart haircut and a few new perspectives on what is happening in town. Now, in the Twitterverse, the clientele and the corporation are on an even playing field, and how you succeed is based on how fearless you participate in Twitter. Avoiding the old rules of promotion and giving some of the angles I offer here a try might not equate into big money—at least not right away—but they will assist you in building a community, a community that will support you in your endeavors. You still need to be careful, stay within guidelines that you and your company both agree are necessary, and remain considerate to others. You also need to be prepared to get personal. This is, as I have said before, part of the Twitter experience and part of the participation crucial for success.

Be fearless.

12

ANTI-Social Media: The Dark Side of Twitter

You've heard me reference this chapter throughout the book, and here it has looming like the great monolith of knowledge from *2001: A Space Odyssey*. This chapter is a topic I am asked to talk about in various parts of the country and even around the world. It is a topic I am near and dear to, especially because I have been using Twitter for as long as I have (and still there are people who have been using it longer than me). Although I do understand that change and evolution is inevitable, I also argue that there is a way to use Twitter and not have it misrepresented. Featured in this chapter is an accumulation of experiences on Twitter that lead people to believe, "Oh, this *must* be what Twitter is all about..." when it is the farthest thing from it. These are the mistakes and mishaps that we can learn from and become a stronger community by growing from their lessons.

There are a lot of things out in the Twitterverse you have to keep an eye out for, and there are a lot of people that you might want to consider before clicking on the Follow button. Although Twitter is all about community, there are a few troublemakers out to break the rules and ruin the party for the rest of us.

To Follow, or Not to Follow?

Still a great debate in the Twitterverse is whether you should follow everyone who follows you, or not. Back in Chapter 9, "The Trouble with Twitter," I introduced you to Guy Kawasaki (http://www.guykawasaki.com), one of the major players of Social Media. Let me just run down a quick review of this guy's background:

- BA from Stanford
- MBA from UCLA
- Honorary doctorate from Babson College
- Part of the marketing team behind Apple Macintosh computers in 1984
- Accomplished writer and columnist
- Hosts "How to Change the World," ranked in the Top 100 visited blogs in the world
- Cofounder of Alltop

So it's safe to say that Guy Kawasaki's got game. Absolutely.

But when it comes to Twitter, I find his strategy one that only General Custer could get behind.

Many "Social Media Gurus" use Kawasaki's November 2008, posting "Looking for Mr. Goodtweet: How to Pick Up Followers on Twitter" as the cornerstone on which to build successful networks on Twitter. It was "Tip #4: Follow everyone who follows you." that makes me stop and ask "Are you serious?"

In his own words, Kawasaki explains why Tip #4 is a good idea:

> *When I first started on Twitter, Robert Scoble told me to follow everyone who followed me. 'But why, Robert, would I follow everyone like that?' The answer is that it's courteous to do so and because when you do, some people will respond to you and everyone who follows them will see this—which is more exposure for you.*

A Little Birdie Told Me...

In Kawasaki's defense, the advice in the article is about earning followers on Twitter. It is not about building a network of people you connect with or secrets of a successful network on Twitter, but on how many followers you can gain. For some people on Twitter, it truly is all about the numbers; and if that is what your aim is, then following everyone who follows you could work for you.

You also heard me talk in Chapter 9 about Signal-to-Noise ratio (SNR). If your mission is to accumulate numbers, then following people without question might work for you, but those monster numbers do not come without a cost. You now have to contend with some extra setup on

TweetDeck or your Twittelator Pro if there are tweets from *specific* people you don't want to miss. Yes, if you follow everyone, it will guarantee you exposure; but is that the kind of exposure you want?

For additional perspective, here are just a few examples of people I choose not to follow on Twitter:

- Spammers and phishers (both real and bots)
- Headlines from local news affiliates in states other than my own
- Professional unions with professions I am not involved with
- Small businesses looking to sell me stuff
- Accounts without updates
- Accounts telling me to follow them on Facebook or MySpace
- Accounts that are only retweets, famous quotes, and random links elsewhere

FIGURE 12.1

Just because someone is following you does not mean you should follow them back. It's always a good idea to know something about the people behind the username.

There is no Prime Directive of Twitter that insists you must follow everyone who follows you back. In some cases it is better not to follow back some users because they tend to be either bogus accounts (that Twitter will eventually shut down) or users that tend to stretch the definition of participation. Do you *want* to network with these content-light users? And do you want to expose your network to these users? Without taking a moment to find out something about the person who wants to follow you, you are now connecting them with your network.

Before employing the third-party service that automatically follows back all requests, consider the request and the people (if applicable) behind it. Check the first page of tweets to see what their content is. You can keep the level of participation and value of your signal in your account much higher by taking just a moment to review their recent tweets. Strive to keep the quality of your feed high.

Why Would I Want to Block Someone?

The Block feature is a more extreme version of not following (or even unfollowing someone) as you are automatically removed from their list as well. Once you single-click the "Block" option, the offending user cannot follow you or even reach you with an @Mention. They are *removed* from any and all access to you on Twitter.

This is another opinion shared by Kawasaki and others drinking his Twitter-flavored fruit punch: "It is arrogant to think you are worth follow-ing, but the person following you is not worth following." If that is the case, then this piece of advice might throw him into apoplectic fits: *It's okay to block people following you.* After all, that is why you have a "Block" feature on the Twitter user's homepage.

What?! If not following someone who follows is considered "arrogant," then blocking someone requesting to follow is downright dastardly. Totalitarian, even!

There are times when not following someone just isn't enough. Although I gave examples of people who follow me and I refuse to follow back, here are instances where I simply clicked on the "Block" feature:

- Tweets using lewd, crude, or offensive language repeatedly
- Tweets promoting hate agendas
- Tweets that constantly talk about "ways of building your numbers" and "how many people are following me today"
- Users that auto-DM me with links to their sites, Facebook accounts, or "must-use" services for Twitter

- Users that are abusive, annoying, or "nest kickers" (they specifically look for a fight)
- Dominatrixes and porn stars

These are all real-life accounts from both @TeeMonster and @ITStudios. And no, I didn't follow back the dominatrix. (Her posts made me hide under my desk.)

FIGURE 12.2

Blocking someone on Twitter is not only an option, but encouraged if you have people on Twitter that you really want to keep at a distance.

Blocking someone might sound extreme; but as seen in the preceding examples (and in a few that are to come), blocking might be your only option. Just because you choose not to follow someone does not mean they cannot reply to you. Additionally, while you do not follow them, they are still following you and can either react to your tweets or to the people in your network. Blocking prevents all that.

Where things get bizarre, blocking is how people react to it. I have seen people get abrasive (and abusive) with others on finding out they have been blocked by someone on Twitter. Although it might seem a bit jarring (especially if the user in question asks you to follow them and you can't because—well—you're *blocked*), this is no different than not being followed. The last person to have a say in your account is you, and if you do not care to have someone monitor your feed, block them. It's your right.

Guaranteed Drops and Blocks

As Twitter grows in popularity, so does the amount of unwanted traffic. The beautiful thing about Twitter is that data control rests with the user. You have the ability to follow, to unfollow, or to completely block the amount of content coming from a single user. As Twitter is, while during the writing of this book, exploding on the scene in 2009 as a well-oiled Social Media machine, you want to make sure that your signal is more powerful than the outside noise.

To keep your signal clear, this means making the tough choices on who stays and who goes, and some Twitters make it extremely easy to say no to.

Spammers and Twitterbots

Spammers appear on Twitter as thoughtless, soulless, and pointless tweets usually promising free laptops, ways of making money on Google, and "fun webcams" all in a single click. If you are fortunate, Twitter will have already shut down the account; but it is inevitable you will be found by these online pariah. Some programmers will also design automated Twitters or *Twitterbots* that generate everything from ads to random sayings to random words strung together to resemble a sentence. The second question to ask here is "What's the point in following?" with the first one being "Who the heck are these people following me?" (You'll find out. Keep reading.)

Tweeting in L33t

Wat iz L33t? 4 real, yo? Y U hav 2 ask? R U sum kind of n00b r sumthin?

Imagine a page of tweets like this. Yes, I hate this. *With a passion.* The writer in me screams in pain and agony.

L33t (also read as "Elite") is the language of the Internet. Sometimes, it is abbreviations that are familiar ("LOL" for "Laughing Out Loud" or "FWIW" meaning "For What It's Worth") and other times it is truly a language all its own ("hax0r" for "hacker", "n00b" for "newbie" or novice, and "pwn3d" for "owned" or falling prey to a joke or con). It is part street slang, part LOLcat, part "Let me get this out quickly as I'm being charged for this SMS by the character…" and this is what happens to your tweet when you apply *Tweetshrink* to it. So if you were to tweet something along these lines:

To get to my current location, set aside money for the subway. Within two stops, you'll want to get ready to transfer from the Red Line to the Green Line.

Tweetshrink will turn it into this:

2 get 2 my current location, set aside $$ 4 the subway. w/in 2 stops, U'll wnt 2 get ready 2 trnsfr from the Red Line 2 the Green Line.

This may be an accepted method in preserving precious characters, but to me this smacks of laziness and poor grammar. I've been called a "Grammar Nazi" and "Typo Nazi" because of this opinion....

I'm a writer. What do you expect?!

Some claim that L33t is the "Language of the Internet"; but to me, L33t is the dumbing of the Internet and the dumbing of Twitter. Now, done as a laugh or for a humorous end, I have no problem. When I first saw the "Rock" symbol (the "goat horns" seen at rock concerts which translates at \m/ in L33t) in Twitter, that made me smile. It's when people try to be "hip" or "efficient" that I take exception. I cringe at people that I know are articulate, brilliant people swapping out words for numbers and tacky abbreviations, and they adopt this method as Standard Operational Procedure. That is unacceptable, particularly when it appears in the automated DMs from public speakers and published authors on "Improving Networking Skills."

And speaking of automation in Twitter....

Automated Direct Messaging

Services such as Tweet Later and Twitter DMer might have been a good idea with good intentions, but if you do a search on "Automated DMs in Twitter," you see exactly how much venom has been spewed over this topic. (On my Google Search "Hot To Stop Receiving Auto DMs" and "HOWTO: Deal with Spammers, Trolls & Automated Direct Messages…" were hit *before* "Promote My Site: Auto DMs on Twitter are Just Fine" and "How to Create an Automated DM on Twitter," just as a benchmark for you.) From Social Media authority Chris Brogan to ReadWriteWeb.com, the backlash against automated Direct Messaging reached such a pitch that SocialToo (http://socialtoo.com), an organizer for your various social networks, proclaimed "Time to Take a Stand - Yes, We're Ending the DMs" (http://bit.ly/SocTooDM) and eliminated automatic Direct Messaging from its options. Perhaps it is the impersonal nature of the tweet ("I'm far too busy to welcome you, so I'll have this bot do it for you, and while I'm at it go on and visit my Facebook and subscribe to my blog.") or perhaps it suddenly being told, "You have a DM!" which usually means "Priority: For Your Eyes Only!" and you find the message "Got a question on how to increase traffic to your website? I'll show you how!", but Auto DMs are so detested that people are unfollowing and blocking people they just met.

Incomplete Profiles

The reason you complete a profile on Twitter is in order to make a solid first impression. This means I'm already on the defensive if you have Twitter's default avatar (o_O) staring back at me. If I have no location, bio, or other information to go on, your chances of me returning the follow are slim. It takes only a few minutes to fill out a Twitter profile (even fewer if this book is your guide) to let people know who you are. It might take a few extra minutes to find an appropriate avatar, but it does say a lot about who you are.

It also says a lot about you when you leave your profile blank. If you don't have the time to complete your Twitter profile, where will the time come to connect with me (and others) on Twitter?

Few To No Updates

Now before you say "Come on, Tee, no one tweets as much as you!" I'm not saying that is the standard I hold for others. (Only for a few in my network.) What I mean is people who have hundreds (and in some cases, thousands) of people following them and their tweets number less than ten over a long period of time. "But what if they are just starting at Twitter?" Again, that's not what I mean. I mean if the user have five tweets over a period of three months (or longer) and their last tweet was made in the previous week, interaction with this user is close to impossible because of their infrequency on Twitter.

And if you follow hundreds or thousands of people and have no updates, what's the point?

Selling Your Twitter Self

Wouldn't it be great to tweet for cash? Have a job where someone actually *paid* you to tweet? That is what Magpie, Adjix, and TwittAd promise: You sit back, tweet the day away and make cold, hard cash while doing so. These services puts ads into your Twitter stream at a frequency (that is, for every twenty tweets, one ad appears either in your tweet or independently as its own tweet) you set up. Payment back to you is based on the reaction to the ad and how often ads enter your Twitter stream.

According to Magpie, I could have made around $7,000 a month with @TeeMonster.

Easy money, right? That was my knee jerk reaction until I considered my own Social Media mantra: Be part of the community, and actively contribute to it. How then would it look if every twentieth or, if I was feeling particularly aggressive, *tenth* tweet an ad related on something I was tweeting about suddenly popped up. How does that reflect back on me? After all, these would be ads (with no say whatsoever from me who I'm supposedly backing) with my handle, my face.

These services rely on the network and reputation *you* have fostered to help promote *their* sponsors.

Apart from the mystery meat of sponsors that latch onto Twitter streams like remoras to Great Whites, consider how the community you have worked to build would regard a sudden flow of random ads. In the middle of your exchanges, an ad appears pointing to somewhere completely unrelated and totally innocuous to the subject of what I was talking about.

And if you're a professional on Twitter, what would it say about you and your service if your Twitter feed is sending out auto DMs or random tweets pointing to sites that tweet your favorite songs, offer a free blogging service, or the best prices on running shoes?

No matter how you approach Twitter, from a personal or professional manner, you work to earn the respect of your network. My networks respect me. In turn, I respect them. Is that respect worth more noise, less signal? Is the reputation you foster worth that? My own Twitter personas can be described as many, many things, but "spam" has never been associated with any of my tweets.

"What's in a name?" William Shakespeare once asked. Quite a lot, it turns out. What's a name worth to you?

FIGURE 12.3

Services now exist online that will do all your tweeting for you, removing the human element from social networking. (Think about that for a moment.)

Automated Twittering

Yes, it was bound to happen. Between TweetGetter promising you thousands of followers within a month to the geniuses (one looking fresh from a frat party with his fashionable lei) behind the Twitter Traffic Machine, developers and programmers have now removed the human element from Twitter and completely automated this social networking service.

Let me back up and say that again: They have *removed* the *human* element and completely *automated* this *social networking* service.

No longer do you have to worry about monitoring Twitter, checking on who is joining your network, or even what people say in response to you. Now with automated tweets, you simply write up a few solid, juicy tweets, maybe even go out on a limb and put a question together that might get people talking, and then you set your Twitter on auto pilot. Watch your numbers climb! Watch your Twitter credibility (that's right, Tweet Cred) elevate as you reach the same ranks as the Twitter elite! And prop your feet on your desk because the amount of traffic you, as a professional, are driving to your website will equate itself to the fancy sports car you will drive one day!

Try again. When any of these shortcuts are activated, they can be spotted for what they are: glorified bots. One of the first giveaways is the lack of response if anyone replies to your tweets. Silence can be loud. Anytime a service tweets for you, it becomes apparent that although you want to stay current, you are too busy to work with Twitter so employ a bot to do the work for you.

This is a poor choice to make concerning *social networking* and a worse one to attempt building a network with.

A Broad Definition of Participation

Perhaps you run down that list of guaranteed drops and you think, "Well, that's not me. I do my own tweets! I participate."

But exactly *how* are you participating with your network?

The more Twitter matures, the more traffic it receives; and the more requests I receive, the more critical I get with whom I do and don't follow back. That might sound, according to Kawasaki's perspective, arrogant; but I go back to that "P" word: *participation.*

"Sharing with others or to take a part" and "the state of being related to a larger whole" is the *Merriam-Webster's* definition of "participation" but there is more to it. Participation also includes a sense of engagement, involvement, and interaction.

There is also another sense involved: *common* sense.

When you are followed by someone, take a moment to review someone's feed. I usually review the first page, but if you are in a particularly curious mood, go another page in by clicking the More button at the bottom of the home page. Look at how these potential followers are participating with their own networks.

Many times, what people are defining as "participation" is the farthest thing from it.

Retweeting Isn't Participation

Yes, I retweet. People in my network retweet. Retweets aren't the problem, but they are a problem when your opening page is nothing but retweets. It's a cry for help when two to three pages of your Twitter feed are composed only of retweets.

"But I'm participating! I'm giving to my network what gems I find elsewhere!" If you really think this is active participation and effective networking, try this when you're out with a group of people: Hold a conversation with someone *using only what you hear others around you say* at that moment. If you know the people who are helping you with the conversation, add in their names. "Tee says...." or "Michelle says...." followed by what they said. If someone asks you a question, don't answer but throw out something else you've overheard. Watch the reaction of the person you're talking to, and the people around you.

This is how consistent retweeting comes across.

Tweeting Famous Quotes Isn't Participation

"I tweet these pearls of wisdom to inspire and motivate the people in my network," I heard someone say in my @ITStudios Twitter feed. Yeah, that's terrific; but if they follow you, doesn't it stand to reason they would rather hear *your* pearls of wisdom versus those of Anthony Robbins, Stephen King, or Serena Williams? When your Twitter feed is nothing more than thoughts of other people, be they philosophers, movie stars, political figures, or historical icons, what do I learn about you in following you? (So far, it's that you don't have an original idea in your head; and because your bio reads "Social Media Innovator and Problem Solver," you have bigger problems to contend with, my friend.)

FIGURE 12.4

A Twitter feed composed of nothing but quotes from other people could send out the wrong impression to a potential Follower.

Again, try this in a social setting (provided you still have friends after the first experiment): Attempt to hold a conversation with people *using only famous quotes*. If someone asks you a question, reply with the words of

Albert Einstein or Walt Disney. If you want to make your quotes all the same theme; go ahead but even with the extra work and thought you have put into your quotes, I guarantee you will be met with the same reaction. People talk to you because they want to know what's on your mind, not hear the past brilliance of others. If all your tweets are the words of other people, what does that say about you and how you value your own words, opinions, and beliefs? Yet there are Twitters that seem to believe quoting others is participation.

Not only is tweeting exclusively in quotes pointless, it also turns you into the equivalent of an RSS-driven fortune cookie; and your quotations, no matter the intentions, can come across condescending. Never be afraid to be original. Feel free to use quotations now and then, sure; but consider that people are following you for your words, not the words of someone else. Remember the words of Ralph Waldo Emerson: *"I hate quotation. Tell me what you know."*

Hey. Wait a minute...

Circulating Links (Especially if the Only One You're Circulating Is Your Own) Isn't Participation

Again, from his often-referenced blogpost, Guy Kawasaki states

> The fact that your cat rolled over or your flight is delayed isn't interesting, so get outside of your mundanity and link to interesting stories and pictures—you should think of yourself as a one-person StumbleUpon. The Twitter pickup artist's mantra is ABL ("Always Be Linking").

When I got the notification that "Guy Kawasaki was following me on Twitter," I was flattered. I thought "That's awfully kind of him to seek me out." (This was before I discovered he has a staff that works his account for him. More on weblebrities later...) I didn't follow Kawasaki for long because I burned out on all the endless links back to AllTop (his website), many of his links are simply random headlines ranging from celebrity gossip to sports scores to tech news to news of the weird. So although Kawasaki (or one of his staff) did "reach out" to me on Twitter, I cannot tell you a thing about him other than what I've learned about him from his online biography.

Do I consider him a connection? No. Not at all. I do think he is a wellspring for random trivia though. Not what I expected when following one of the major players of technology.

Guy Kawasaki isn't the only Twitter (weblebrity or otherwise) guilty of this. Although I find Twitter a fantastic resource for sharing links with one another, it is a little annoying when all one does with his feed is circulate links. It's simply obnoxious if it is his link exclusively, and flat-out spam if it is his link in every single tweet. I understand that by providing a variety of resources, it does make you a reliable resource others will want to follow.

What I mean by "common sense" when it comes to participation in your community is to return to the analogy of the coffee shop that never closes; and when you are circulating links, it should be used as a means of getting conversation started. One of the most creative people I know, writer, podcaster, puppeteer, and gifted Renaissance Man, Jared Axelrod (@planetx), distributes in his feed an eclectic mix of links, ranging from steampunk to off-beat news stories to provocative photo shoots. What makes Jared's feed one I hang on every tweet is that this isn't the *only* thing he does. Many times, the links he circulates sparks traffic across many feeds, and Jared—in most cases—replies. Jared participates wholly with the community, speaks his mind, and replies in earnest.

What kind of a conversationalist are you? I do all these things: Retweet, quote people (usually movies), and circulate links, but that is not solely what I do. Moderation with these tactics is key. If you want a community that knows you, interacts with you, and works with you, participate. Invest more of yourself into Twitter than just cool links, an extremely funny tweet, or snappy quotes from someone else.

Concerning Weblebrities, Celebrities, and Gurus

I tend to enjoy that idea of Twitter being my own personal coffee shop (Oh heck, why not—it's my own "Café Diem," right @craigatscifi?) where my friends hang out and swap stories or the ups and downs of their day. It is not out of the ordinary, though, to look up from the cappuccino maker and through a wisp of steam catch glimpses of Nathan Fillion (*Firefly, Serenity, Castle*), Eddie Izzard (comedian, *Shadow of the Vampire, Oceans 13*), or Stephen Fry (podcaster, *Peter's Friends*, the *Black Adder* Series). On a particularly good day, LeVar Burton (*Roots, Reading Rainbow, Star Trek: The Next Generation*) and Robert Llewelyn (*Red Dwarf, Junkyard Wars, Carpool*) will pop in and ask for a Café Mocha to go. Then I catch shout-outs from the regulars, CC Chapman, Felicia Day, and Joel Comm.

Yeah, my Twitter feed is a busy place, and the stars always seem to come out.

Weblebrities: Life on the A-Listserve

I think William Shakespeare would have loved the Internet. At the time he was writing his plays, the English language was exploding, and the Bard had all these wonderful new words to play with. The Internet has become something of a Digital Renaissance, inventing words that we snicker at on first hearing them and then slowly these words become ingrained with society. Blog. Podcast. eCommerce. eTrading. Twitter. Twittersphere. Twitterverse. Some words I love. (Podiobook.) Others I roll my eyes at. (Tweeple.)

But the one that makes me grin the widest: *Weblebrity.*

What makes a weblebrity? First off, what exactly *is* a weblebrity? People like Robert Scoble, iJustine, Cali Lewis, and Twitter creators Jack Dorsey, Evan Williams, Biz Stone would be considered weblebrities. Some people like Leo LaPorte and Felicia Day would be considered "crossover weblebrities" because they have appeared on television or worked with A-List producers, directors, and actors. They might not be household names to you, but to various bloggers, podcasters, and consumers of the Interwebs and its vacuum tubes, these people are the stars of the Internet.

What makes a weblebrity is that following, that fan base this individual commands. He or she gives you a tap on the shoulder and suddenly visits to your blog spike, your Facebook requests multiply, and your Twitter numbers start to climb. Some are famous, others are infamous. Weblebrities are, however, people that manage accounts well into the tens of thousands, if not hundreds of thousands.

When following weblebrities, you need to keep in mind that your tweet cred does not rest on whether these people @Mention you, DM you (provided they are following you back), or retweet you. Weblebrities do have influence, sure, but this is not some Megabyte Mafia we're talking about here. They are people with blogs, podcasts, Facebook, and Twitter accounts, just like you. Perhaps the biggest difference between them and you is they were "breakthroughs" in Social Media. Their livelihood that comes from their Internet endeavors, and it is that attention that gives them this status.

FIGURE 12.5

Ghost Twitters attempt to keep weblebrities' respective networks happy when they are far too busy to tweet.

This means they might reply to you, but they might not; and when they do reply to you (as was recently discovered when Kawasaki, during his Search Engine Strategies: New York conference talk), there's no guarantee you're actually talking to *that* weblebrity. You might be talking to *ghost tweeters*, people hired to write under another's Twitter account. (Kawasaki employs three for his account.) So if you follow them for entertainment purposes, enjoy the witticism that might come through their feeds. If you search for legitimacy in your online existence (whether it's a retweet or the "LOL" @Mention), you might want to reconsider the reasoning why you are following. Are you truly connecting with them? Can you really connect with someone who has nearly half a million followers but only follows back a fraction of those numbers?

Which begs another question of weblebrities: Does their online success entitle them to certain "passes" that you wouldn't tolerate from other Twitter users?

I find myself holding weblebrities on a higher level of expectation than celebrities because, based on the word alone, weblebrities know better. Their fame and fortune is coming from the Internet, and in many instances these individuals have earned their fame and even set standards based on their *webetiquitte*. (As we are talking about Twitter though, it's *Twittiquite*.) With that understanding, weblebrities should be held accountable for what they tweet and how they tweet. And if you choose not to follow a weblebrity or drop her from your feed, you will not be shunned or branded with a scarlet "UFM" (Guy Kawasaki's "UnFollow Me" response). The world will continue to spin. The sun will rise and set.

Oh you might get some rude responses from people on your blog or Twitter, but that is why we have the power of moderating comments.

Celebrities: A Peek at the Life of a Hollywood Star

The first *celebrity* I ever followed on Twitter was Wil Wheaton (@wilw), writer, blogger, and actor, best known for his roles in *Stand by Me* and *Star Trek: The Next Generation*. If Ashton Kutcher is the "King of Twitter," Wil Wheaton would be the woaded-up William Wallace who is flashing the opposition at the Battle of Stirling, raising his bloody sword aloft after a victory, and rallying his armies with the battle-cry "They may take our bandwidth, but they'll never take away *OUR TWITTER!!!*"

Wil Wheaton has never DMed me nor sent me an @Mention. He follows just over 100 people (while nearly *half a million* follow him). His posts go from family-friendly and extremely funny to edgy, raw, and not safe to share with mom and the kids.

So why do I follow him? He participates by using Twitter as a microblog, and although I have never met or know Wil Wheaton, I can tell you this much about him from following him on Twitter:

- Wil loves hockey. I mean, this man lives for keeping the stick on the ice.
- As much as he is associated with a geek icon, he himself is a die-hard geek.
- He believes that if you don't tell it like it is, pack it up and go home.
- Wil Wheaton's cat has taken out a contract on his life.
- When facing the BLACK (explicative) DRAGON, Wil needs to roll double digits. At least.

There's something else I know about Wil Wheaton: He gets it.

I don't follow a lot of celebrities nor do I intend to wow you with the variety of celebrities that I follow or make you gasp in awe at those who have actually replied to me, both on Twitter and in direct messages. *(Ooooohhh!)* I'm not going to do any of that because it really doesn't matter. I follow the celebrities I follow simply because I'm curious what they are doing when the cameras are off and they're in between gigs.

When I follow a celebrity, I accept two things right off the tweet:

- If I send @Mentions to celebrities, they will not reply.

- If a celebrity does @Mention to me, this does not make us buddies, pals, mates, or any other connotation of "friend" because they don't know me.

It's easy to get swept up and star-struck, but the reality of Twitter is if I walk up to LeVar Burton at a Science Fiction convention and say, "Remember me? I'm TeeMonster. You retweeted me on Twitter!" he will not remember who in the blue blazes I am. It might have something to do with the 350,000 (and change) people already following him. I'm asking him to remember me. You know? *That* guy?!

A Little Birdie Told Me...

Just for the record, LeVar Burton did DM and retweet me. What grabbed his attention on January 23, 2009? A comment I made on how good it was to work with teachers. I won't lie to you, it made this Trekkie's day...but I doubt if he remembers the exchange. That doesn't take away the little kick it gave to my day!

Following celebrities is Twitter's "commentary track" where celebrities (who *get it*, mind you) riff on just about anything. Sure, some of the tweets seem trivial, but this is when you find out that yes, sometimes, even the people you see on television and at the movies suffer failed hard drives, bad habits needing to be broken, and missed appointments because the alarm clock wasn't set to Daylight Savings. I have a blast following celebrities, and I also have a realistic understanding about following them.

But are there celebrities you shouldn't follow?

Some famous people or television shows hop on Twitter and turn it into their own private press center. The tweets are less about what they are doing and when their next guest appearance will be, retweets on who is talking about them, where to click to get tickets for the next showing of their current movie, and so on. This is usually not the celebrity themselves but their press agent or personal assistant throwing out juicy tidbits about their client. Although there is a slightly narcissistic nature to Twitter, turning your Twitter feed into an "All About Me News Feed" outlet with no personal interaction or touch of any kind gets old after a while, particularly if the feed in question is retweeting other sites ad nauseam. What separates @S_A_R_A_H_ from these other entertainers is the personal touch and interaction, a gap that some studios would prefer not to close.

And then there's The Ellen Show (@TheEllenShow).

Ellen DeGeneres, comedienne and talk show host, discovered Twitter and decided to talk about it on her show. To me, this is a wonderful thing because now Twitter is reaching into the mainstream. What a breakthrough! Finally, Social Media is growing up a bit, taking a step into a larger world and getting beyond snap misconceptions that people make about it. I was excited to hear that Ellen was giving it the attention it deserved.

Using her show as a platform to gain followers didn't really shock me. After all, it stands to reason that you are going to use your available resources to promote your Twitter account but what was more offensive was the scorekeeping on her feed:

> We just passed LeVar Burton—thanks for your support! (March 13)

> Only 64,00 more followers to catch up to MC Hammer... (March 14)

Then came the cheese for the mice in Ellen's maze...

> If I hit 500,000 followers in the next hour, I'll show an exclusive clip of Hallie Berry dancing in Twitter. Pass it on. (March 30)

This begs the question: Why, Ellen? Are you using Twitter to connect with your fan base or to feel better about yourself? And do you really need to ask people to follow you considering your celebrity status? I thought this was a real step backward for the Social Media movement.

But that was before Thursday, April 16, 2009, when Ellen was given a pass.

In fact, you could say it was a hall pass.

Fast Times at Twitter High: How CNN, Ashton Kutcher, and Oprah Completely Missed the Point

Actor and Blahgirls.com producer Ashton Kutcher and his wife, actress Demi Moore, were just another pair of celebrities on Twitter until, on April 3, 2009, Moore received a tweet from a woman preparing to commit suicide. Thinking quickly, Moore reached out to her vast Twitter network and within moments, word reached the police who reached the distraught woman before she could hurt herself. Kutcher tweeted later:

> "Wifey reported a suicide attempt based on a at reply tweet she got and saved someones life. The woman is in the hospital now."

This event would have been a real testament for Twitter and its potential, but as irony would have it, Kutcher would totally overshadow and undermine this wonderful impact of Social Media two weeks later.

Kutcher took it upon himself to challenge CNN to "a race" to see who would first reach 1,000,000 followers. CNN agreed, and the race was on. What followed was continuous coverage from CNN, reporting the neck-and-neck competition. Spammers took it upon themselves to perform Twitter Searches for anyone talking about Kutcher, and then asking for Follows. Kutcher upped the stakes by promising a donation of malaria nets to charity if he reached this milestone before CNN. Lamar, the third-largest billboard company in the United States, carried ads asking people to follow Kutcher on Twitter (which had http://bit.ly/TwitterPunkd asking questions on Kutcher's sincerity). Then there was Twitter itself who had placed "safeguards" on both CNN and Kutcher's account so that you could not unfollow them after you followed. When the dust finally settled in the Twitterdome, it was Ashton Kutcher who "won" the race. CNN ran his victory as a breaking news headline.

The following day, Kutcher went on *The Oprah Winfrey Show* where he and the creators of Twitter all worked with the daytime talk show diva in setting up her account and getting her first tweet online. Before the show's conclusion, Oprah proclaimed Ashton Kutcher—based on the performance of the previous day—the King of Twitter.

In the Twitter community, the blogosphere, and the Internet, opinion was polarized, pros calling it "Twitters Turning Point" whereas cons voiced dissent (inspiring some to run with the hashtags #backlashton and #washerebeforeoprah). Speaking as someone with deep roots in the Social Media community, not all of what happened was bad. The positive was that Twitter received a lot of attention; and now with Oprah and her people talking Twitter (for the moment), it will only go up from here. Earlier mentioned naysayers who were all calling it a deep-sea dive in "Lake Me" and those who looked at it askance as Jon Stewart did on *The Daily Show* stepped up to show their support for Kutcher and the charity he would donate to by joining Twitter. Suddenly what the news media and mainstream regarded as an afterthought was now a lead story. Because of Kutcher, people paid *close* attention to Twitter. And now with the media powerhouse that is Oprah Winfrey on board, investors might also start paying attention.

That said, I was disappointed in Kutcher's mistreatment of Twitter. Yes, mistreatment. When he speaks on the Internet community, it is impressive and downright inspiring how well he understands the audience:

> "The web is not a passive playground. It's an environment that is a tool for connectivity and social engagement so every piece of content that we have will have some type of engagement because that engagement is what creates retention...."

That was Kutcher at the TechCrunch 50 in San Francisco, CA, during the unveiling of The Blah Girls. Amazing! But with his own words describing the Internet so aptly, this is coming from the Twitter user who, in his acceptance speech, proclaimed

> "One man can have a voice that's as loud as an entire media company. And you can have that voice as well. And we can all have that voice together. And we can change media forever."

We can have that voice *together*? With the guy who now has 1.2 million Followers, and he himself follows just over 80? With the same guy who has media connections that only A-list Hollywood stars can tap, if needed? With that guy who can get one of the nation's largest billboard producers to donate space? Exactly how is Kutcher connecting with us to do this *together*? Or did Kutcher mean he could tell 1.2M people to do something, and if we do it, he will make a donation to charity?

This was another foul I called on Kutcher: using charity as incentive. If you want to make a donation to a worthy cause, don't slap a condition on that—just make the donation. Using it as leverage to gain Followers felt very wrong to me.

Still, the ire I felt toward Kutcher paled to what I felt toward CNN.

In a seminar I host concerning success stories in Social Media, I pointed out how bold and fearless CNN had been in not just talking about Twitter but actually incorporating it into its news programming. It was refreshing to see: Instead of a brush-off of Social Media, journalists embraced it and used it to take news reporting to the next level.

This is why I was so disgusted when they participated in this silly race.

When this challenge was issued, CNN should have smiled, patted Kutcher on his head, and said "That's okay, you reach for 1 million followers. We'll be over here reporting the news because, you see, we're the Cable *News* Network. We're journalists and we've got a lot of work to do." Instead, CNN decided to become Fox News for a day and accept this ridiculous wager. That was a real tragedy.

As for Oprah proclaiming Kutcher the "King of Twitter," I find it sad that one of the most influential people in modern media so desperately wants to be one of the cool kids at the school cafeteria table. Opera should have, instead of giving out titles (and how about some titles for the creators of Twitter, seeing as they were on your show?), gotten to know this networking tool just a bit more intimately before anointing Kutcher. She might have seen through the veneer of his "Golly, lookitwhatIdid!" smile, and get to know the network that she is now beginning to build from the ground up. She might find that under the "King" are many lords, ladies, knights, and yeoman who know the land better.

Gurus: Snake Oil Salesmen 2.0

The third tier of famous people on Twitter go by a variety of names, under a wide variety of specialties with many of the popular topics being Social Media, SEO (Search Engine Optimization), Internet Marketing, Personal Life Matters, dating, and (of course) making money. This might come from Kawasaki's sixth tip from that blogpost I've been talking a lot about:

Tip 6: Establish yourself as a subject expert. One thing is for sure about Twitter: there are some people interested in every subject and every side of every subject. By establishing yourself as a subject expert, you will make yourself interesting to some subset of people.

The catch-all to use for these experts, these mavens, these all-powerful online oracles, is *guru*. These are people who weave on their Facebooks or website impressive credentials, but no real credentials to back them up with. Some of these gurus sport everything from certifications in Personal Life Success programs to convicted felonies for Fraud. You will meet best-selling authors that can show you how to use Social Media to make your new book a bestseller! How do you do that? Look these authors up on Amazon, and you'll find their complete bibliography there: books on how to make your book a bestseller. Then there are the 20-something Internet entrepreneurs who want to help you make money online and keep it! You quickly discover on accessing their links that one way they keep their money is in designing their home page themselves, in a free copy of FrontPage. Their lesson plans usually mean offering up your credit card. (And now you see how they are making money online...and keeping it!) Then you have the Social Media moguls, who are also SEO moguls, who are also Internet Marketing moguls, who are also self-employed because they were far too forward-thinking for mainstream corporate America, and they will help you (for the right price) help you monetize your online persona and make you a millionaire-in-a-month.

So, yeah, you get the picture.

These gurus promise you the answer to life, the universe, and everything; and they have found a new home with an endless field of potential marks. That home is Twitter.

I know I'm painting with a brush of the broadest make, and through Twitter I have met some amazing people who are Social Media authorities, personal life coaches, and financial and nutritional experts. They, like me, feel as if they are the salmon swimming upstream against the rushing current of gurus. If you are new to Twitter, it can be easy to accept an invitation from a guru with the best of intentions, and then notice your feed is junked up with a lot of rhetoric you would be happier without. The good news is that gurus make themselves easy to find and either not follow or flat-out block.

FIGURE 12.6

Gurus on Twitter claim to have the secret to wealth, health, and happiness and will be happy to share that with you…for the right price.

Before you worry about whether the gurus will pick up my book, read their giveaways, and then change their modis operandi, have no fear. We're talking about gurus. They already know everything and are enlightened. (Any more enlightened and they would be blinded by their own brilliance.)

When reviewing gurus feeds, look at

- **Their profiles**—Do they make promises of instant cash? Do they use the words maven, expert, or guru? Are the URLs reading like make-moneynow.com, beyourownboss.net, mylifeismineon.tv, or the like? If you visit their site, does it reroute you to another site? Is the profile even completed? And, more important, where are they located? These are details you should know.

- **Followers and who they follow**—As people have grown less and less tolerant of auto DMs (something gurus love because they are *so* convenient!), some Twitters automatically drop them. If there is a "gap" between how many the guru follows and how many follow back, there's a good chance an auto DM will be arriving. It says a lot about someone "dedicated to the betterment of his/her fellow man" when they send you an auto DM.

- **Their feed**—What are they tweeting? How are they tweeting? If they are tweeting to tens of thousands of followers, how interactive are they? Go to the earlier sections of this chapter to get a checklist to look for. (HINT: Gurus love quotations and links, especially to their own sites.)

- **Their questions**—Sometimes gurus love to ask the rhetorical questions with no real intention of answering. They just "want to get you thinking," which is fine; but unlike the few who actually can ask these thought-provokers and then engage their followers, gurus never reply to you with additional insight or input. (That's gonna cost you extra.)

- **Their conversations**—If you do start following a guru (who got past your first screening), you might get into a conversation with one of them. If you suddenly find yourself at the end of a quotation machine, you might want to consider unfollowing them.

The incredible thing about Twitter is that there are some incredibly insightful, incredibly talented, and incredible kind people out there in the Twitterverse. Sure, you have your scam artists, but you also have Personal Life Coaches who have been there and back again. You have bodybuilders that do have workout plans that actually *work*. You also have Social Media specialists that can answer your questions online and give you some sage advice concerning Twitter, iPhone applications, and really cool games for the Windows platform.

There's nothing wrong with being careful, but there's also nothing wrong with reaching out to the community you're creating. There are some really neat people just waiting to talk to you.

You might be a little wary and wondering why I chose to wait, after such a positive ride through this incredible Social Networking tool, to blindside you with this hard, tough-love look at what is happening across the network.

Hold on. I'm not *quite* done yet.

13

Why I Am on Twitter

After hearing me talk about the frustrations, the automations, and the tribulations of Twitter, you are probably wondering "If Twitter has become such a pain for you, Tee, why do you still do it? Why do you deal with the ups and downs of people in and out of your community, the days when everything feels like noise, the times when nothing you tweet comes out right? Why, with all the hype that happened just within the writing of this book, do you remain connected with the network?"

That's what's behind this chapter—a sum-up of the enthusiasm, the optimism, and the overall good vibrations I get from Twitter. You can call this the "Feel Good" chapter, the "Warm Fuzzy" chapter, or the "Tee Morris Wears His Heart as a Three-Piece Armani" chapter; but this is where I give you a final word on why, in light of those who are making Twitter a challenge, I return to the network, sift through the Follow requests (sans automation), and tweet incessantly.

Professional and Personal Connections

Twitter, from your first tweet to your most recent one, will always be about the people sitting at their computers and the folks working their thumbs quickly against smartphone keypads. Many people have been following me because they heard through a podcast I was on Twitter. One tweet at a time, they discovered that there was a method to my own personal mayhem, and a personality that welcomed both sides of feedback. Twitters have seen me on my best and my worst days, and they also have reached out to me to show support at both times. Some tweet more than others, and those new to my network ask me "But you're Tee Morris. Why do you want to talk to me?"

My response is usually "Because you asked me a question."

At tweetups is where the real influence of Twitter is made evident. When I attended in 2008 the Science Fiction-Fantasy Convention, Balticon 42 (the con itself found on Twitter at @Balticon), its New Media Track was a checklist of people from my TeeMonster network. Now, instead of a User Interface, it was face-to-face contact. The tweets came with local dialects. It was communication in real time, and everyone took a lot of delight in speaking beyond Twitter's limitations. While I was always aware of the human element with Twitter, this weekend made Twitter far more personal. I accepted for myself a deeper responsibility and accountability for the people I connected with, both in real time and on the network, throughout the year.

From the professional perspective, I have enjoyed talking about various strategies in Social Media. I have been humbled by the number of podcasters out there thanking me for my previous work in the field, and it's been a delight continuing to help audio engineers with their various projects. I have also improved my own blogging techniques and even expanded a bit my reach on Facebook, all with the help of my @ITStudios network. I have made valuable connections locally and around the world, all of them working with me to bring Social Media to a more mainstream level while still remaining personal. Not an easy feat but a touch easier with a network striving for the same goals. I have also benefited by those that pass along valuable resources, TwitReviews, and blogposts, many of which made their way into this book.

A Deeper Appreciation for the Real World

Connected as you are on Twitter, you are open to a lot of tweets coming in from a lot of people around the world, provided you are paying attention. There are some days that you can pay closer attention; and if (or when) you reach that weblebrity status of tens of thousands or hundreds of thousands, it is harder to become personally invested into your network. Still, when you really pay attention you get a gauge of what is happening outside your own world. I still remember one week where three Twitters, two of them close friends, lost their jobs. What can you really articulate about something that shattering in 140-characters?

I've said it before—quite a bit actually.

Good and bad times shared with the community have helped me appreciate and cherish the friends and relationships I have in the real world. As seen in Figure 13.1, I am a dad. I have received tweets that have made me stop, consider, and then type out "Away from keyboard. Need a hug from Sonic Boom." It is the connections that I have made virtually that remind me to also maintain the ones in the real world, because those are people, relationships, and memories that I will not get a second chance at.

FIGURE 13.1

Being connected through Twitter can also help you appreciate your connections for the real world, as well.

Twitter has also helped me appreciate the times when I feel as if I'm doing something wrong as a dad. My network affirms that what I'm feeling is 100% normal, and I am far from alone.

A Little Birdie Told Me...

For me and my network (primarily Science Fiction and Fantasy authors), we dubbed our kids with superhero names, a trend that is a lot of fun and says a lot about our offspring. "Sonic Boom" is the moniker I have given my daughter. It not only provides me a way of referencing her in conversations, but also protects her identity on Twitter. Yes, Twitter is all about the community, but it is still the Internet. Until you establish a sense of tangible trust and a face-to-face contact with people you're connecting with, exercising caution is a good idea, particularly when it comes to talking about your kids.

Sure, Twitter is extremely cool but it is not a substitute for enjoying your life. While I truly dig the people in my network and the fun that happens there, I don't want to miss the world around me.

That is another strength of Twitter—now, particularly through the mobile clients available—life can be shared instantly, globally, and can inspire others to step away from the computer and indulge in an inspiration. I have taken those intermittent moments to throw out a tweet and share experiences with a network that, through Twitter, is closer to the Global Village that the Internet was envisioned to be. Don't discount the truth of it: Tweets can inspire. They can turn a day around, provide support, and bestow hope.

Yes, some moments I have kept to myself. Others I have openly invited my network to enjoy with me. If it's a movie, a symphony, or a tea party with my daughter, I appreciate it all the more as Twitter reminds me of the many different personalities, cultures, and happenings around the world. I am reminded that beyond my computer, amazing things are happening. I should not only "go out and play" but also cherish those memories.

When I get back from tripping the lights fantastic, *then* I'll tweet about it.

I Believe in Twitter

Everyone has their own reasons for being on Twitter. It might be their own personal microblog. It might be to try and reach beyond their own solitude. And it might be to just sell something. As you have seen in this book I have pretty strong convictions in my application of Twitter; and as seen in Chapter 12, "ANTI-Social Media: The Dark Side of Twitter," there are shady, nefarious, and just plain obnoxious types online that are tainting the experience for me and (Yeah, I'll go on and say it!) everyone else who "gets it." So as I asked at the beginning of this chapter, why am I always returning to Twitter? With celebrities competing for numbers, self-proclaimed experts and gurus who define success by popularity, and jerks bent on spoiling the fun through spam, automated services, and Mikeyy worms (http://bit.ly/TwitVirus), why do I take a seat on the morning commuter train, fire up Twittelator Pro, and begin the trip into Washington D.C. with a tweet?

Because I still believe in Twitter.

When I first came on to Twitter, I was surrounded by a lot of familiar faces and friends of my podcasts; and although my humble numbers climbed, I met new and interesting people, people I would have probably never connected with if it wasn't for this incredible tool that connected me with the larger world. I then found myself becoming a better communicator, thanks to the many different points of view around me. I learned how the simplest of statements such as, "*In Your Eyes* might not have been the song it is, if it hadn't been for the movie *Say Anything*," could spark a conversation of many opinions and emotions. I have been taken back to early memories of childhood, rediscovered a few old passions that I had let slide for too long in my life, and I have—most importantly—forged some truly unique friendships in this area, across the country, and in the farthest points of the world. Behind every account, even the Self Actuated Residential Automated Habitats and Martian probes (pictured behind me in Figure 13.2), there's a personality I have grown to know.

I have done all this 140 characters at a time.

If I am lucky, perhaps at a tweetup, a science fiction convention, or an expo dedicated to Social Media initiatives, I will physically meet these people I have grown to know on Twitter. This is what Twitter is all about. Not the number of followers you have, or how many people you yourself are following. Twitter is not about changing media as we know it. Twitter is not about redefining the boundaries between who we are at the office and who we are at the end of the day. Twitter is about the connections we make. Twitter is about the communities we build. Twitter is, and always will be, about the people. Without it, you have nothing to say, nowhere to go, and nothing to do. In everything we have talked about in *All a Twitter*, that is something I hope you have taken to heart and remember: You can't have the Social Media without the *social* aspect of it.

I believe in Twitter. How about you?

FIGURE 13.2

Tee, in his keynote talk at CREATE South 2009, addressed the incredible impact NASA-JPL's Mars Phoenix probe (@MarsPhoenix) made on Twitter. (Photo by Kreg Steppe (@steppek) of spyndle.com)

Tools for Twitter

When I first started working on *All a Twitter*, the two biggest wise-cracks I heard were

- Are you going to use more than 140-characters?
- Can you really write an entire book on Twitter?

Although you already have an idea of my feelings on the first wise-crack, the second one I answer here in this appendix. Here I list the services that I just did not have the time or the room in this book to write about in *All a Twitter*. I consider my networks a wellspring of information as, nearly everyday, someone circulated a link to me with an accompanying tweet, "Maybe this would be good for AAT?" (AAT is the abbreviation for *All a Twitter* in my networks.) It was truly humbling and slightly overwhelming, the outpouring of support I received from my friends and followers.

It also reaffirmed my initial thought: If I had the time and the interest from Que, I could easily write *two* books on Twitter. (Que, you know where to find me!) There are a lot of tools out there for Twitter, expanding in a variety of ways the applications and capabilities of Twitter.

In this appendix I break down into groups extensions to Twitter that did not make it into this book but should be pointed out for what they offer. As mentioned in Chapter 5, "Terrific Twitter Tools," and Chapter 6, "Tracking Twitter," there is a lot more to Twitter than just the website and its desktop clients. Although I cannot vouch for the services here and encourage caution because some of these services ask for your passwords, I can say without question that they are out there and can offer you even more options for your online Twitter experience. So if you want to get an idea of what's out there beyond those tools featured in *All a Twitter*, here is a sampling of the many services developers are offering.

Adding Media to Your Tweets

12seconds (http://12seconds.tv)—A website that offers video sharing in twelve-second clips; 12seconds offers Twitter integration so that when enabled, your Twitter network receives tweets concerning your latest video uploads.

Blip.FM (http://www.blip.fm)—A website that turns your corner of the Internet into a DJ booth where you feature either approved music or music you have created. Twitter integration gives your network a chance to share what you're playing and where to listen.

Last.FM (http://www.last.fm)—Similar to Blip.fm, this is a social network for musicians and fans of musicians. Through Hype Machine (http://hypem.com), Last.fm fully integrates with Twitter and shares with your networks what you listen to.

Mobypicture (http://mobypicture.com)—Now integrated with Twittelator Pro, offers its own app at the iPhone App Store and offers additional integration with WordPress, Flickr, Facebook, and others. Mobypicture gives you the ability to share a variety of media in the same way as TwitPic. You can upload to Mobypicture and share your media instantly.

Qik (http://qik.com)—Another video sharing site, this one specifically targeting videographers using mobile phones. Qik generates tweets that let people know your video is streaming live on the main website.

Seesmic (http://seesmic.com)—Similar to 12seconds, this a video sharing site that is fully integrated with Twhirl. You can use Twhirl to manage in a separate window your Seesmic and easily tweet notifications of new videos to your network.

TweeTube (http://tweetube.com)—Whether it is 25-second videos from a webcam, YouTube videos, or other online media, TweeTube makes sharing media on Twitter an easy and painless process.

Twisten.fm (http://twisten.fm)—Twisten.fm is part Twitter Search, part jukebox. Twisten.fm searches for tweets referencing music or musicians and adds to the tweets of its registered users' links to the song so that they can be played.

Twittershare (http://www.phoreo.com/twittershare)—Enables you to share audio, video, and other media 10MB or smaller through Twitter. You download its widget, register with your Twitter account, and start sharing.

Adding Organization to Your Tweets

Remember the Milk (http://www.rememberthemilk.com/services/twitter/)—With this online service, you can receive To-Do list reminders as DMs, sent according to your Reminder Preferences set at rememberthemilk.com.

Timer (http://twitter.com/timer)—A clever Twitter account that gives directions for use via the background art (so make sure you see it!), Timer reminds you the time you set to do something by sending you a DM.

Twellow (http://www.twellow.com)—Grabs your open tweets (that is, no DMs) and categorizes both you and the Twitters involved in the conversation into various groups. You can also create your own account and add members of your network to specific categories, serving as an online organizer of your contacts.

Twitter Snooze (http://twittersnooze.com/)—This website, after you log into it with your username and password, allows you to temporarily ignore someone on Twitter without unfollowing or blocking them. Simply set in a user who is acting a bit verbose and put him or her in "Mute" for a set period of time, clearing out the noise from your signal. For a moment, anyway.

Twittercal (http://twittercal.com)—A free service connecting your Twitter account to your Google Calendar. (So to really take advantage of this, you need to have both Twitter and Google Calendar.) Follow the setup and then add events, To Do items, and important dates with a tweet.

Tracking Your Tweets

Tweetmarks (http://tweetmarks.com)—Helps you bookmark and organizes all your Twitter-shared links. Along with integration with Twitter, Tweetmarks works with del.icio.us.

Twitscoop (http://twitscoop.com)—Tracks the hottest, most current topics tweeted. Twitscoop's search engine can also look for usernames and keywords. A tweet cloud is featured on the main site and refreshes automatically every 20 seconds. Twitscoop is also integrated directly with TweetDeck.

Twitt(url)y (http://twitturly.com)—Best described as Digg for Twitter, Twitturly tracks URLs and trends in the Twitterverse and provides a real-time ranking of what people are talking about. Twitturly takes a tweet featuring a tracked URL and uses that as a "vote" for that URL. The more votes a URL receives, the higher it ranks on Twitturly's Top 100.

Network Maintenance

Nearby Tweets (http://nearbytweets.com)—Extends Twitter's capabilities in helping people within close proximity of one another networking to build customer relationships, while monitoring real-time trends centric to your locations.

Qwitter (http://useqwitter.com)—Not for the faint of heart or for anyone who has a delicate ego. When people drop you from their feed, Qwitter emails you a notification. On some days, you can receive a Qwitter bomb of several people dropping you simultaneously.

SocialToo (http://socialtoo.com)—Works with many social networks, including Twitter, in syncing your follower lists, generating updates, and reporting people who have followed or unfollowed you.

Tweepler (http://www.tweepler.com)—An online application that assists you in managing Follow requests. The interface enables you to process potential followers by sorting them either in a Follow or Ignore column.

Simply for the Fun of It

Post Like a Pirate (http://postlikeapirate.com/twitter.php)—Serves no other purpose other than to turn your Twitter into a Sparrow and convert your tweets into "pirate-speak" before posting it for you on Twitter.

Tweet What You Eat (http://www.tweetwhatyoueat.com)—The site for Twitters that are either health conscious or working on trimming the waistline with a little help from the community. You set up your own food diary on the website, and then Twitter helps you track what you eat. Tweets concerning your caloric intake come at you now through your phone, IM, or the web. If you find yourself staring down at a dinner and you aren't certain how healthy it is, Tweet What You Eat assists you with its own database search. This is your own health consultant on call, at 140-characters.

Twictionary (http://twictionary.pbwiki.com)—Exactly what it sounds like; it is a dictionary for Twitter, by Twitter users, full of all those silly words you hear people use when tweeting. Some are fun. Some are idiotic. Many are clever.

Twittascope (http://twittascope.com)—Your horoscope for the day, complete with an interface that sends it out to your network as a tweet. You can also opt to have Twittascope tweet your horoscope for a subscription fee.

Twitterholic (http://twitterholic.com)—a Hall of Shame for people who have worked to the top of a Top 100 Twitterholics, based on number of Followers. You can also look up people based on numbers they follow and updates, and you can also turn the spotlight on yourself and see where you rank. (At the time of writing this, I hold the #1 Twitterholic position for Manassas, VA. Testify!)

Twittervision (http://twittervision.com)—Your moment in the spotlight of the global stage. Log into Twittervision; then log into Twitter and tweet. You, along with others logged into Twittervision, appear via real-time geographic locations across a world map.

These sites are merely a cross-section of what is out there. You can find even more add-ons to Twitter suiting your individual needs by visiting blogs like:

smartech—69 Twitter Web Services You Should Know
http://smartech.blogetery.com/2008/05/16/69-twitter-web-services-you-should-know/

Helmiasyraf.com—The Best Twitter Applications. You will definitely be amazed! http://www.helmiasyraf.com/2008/11/17/the-best-twitter-applications-you-will-definitely-amaze/

Online Best Colleges.com—100 Twitter Tools to Help You Achieve All Your Goals http://www.onlinebestcolleges.com/blog/2009/100-twitter-tools-to-help-you-achieve-all-your-goals/

Woork.com—30+ Interesting Twitter Services and Applications— http://woork.blogspot.com/2009/01/30-interesting-twitter-services-and.html

And while this account may not be the most interactive with its followers, Twitter.Alltop.com does provide solid resources for new tools, latest news, and fun facts concerning Twitter. Follow them here:

http://twitter.com/Twitter_Tips

Have these folks in your Twitter network and keep your finger on the pulse of what is happening in the Twitterverse.

Take a look at what's out there, and keep a sharp eye on your Twitter feed as some in your network might retweet or suggest another new wellspring of resources to take your Twitter experience to a new level.

B

Twitterspeak

Throughout this book, I have been pressing upon you all the importance of Twitter's language. Before opening this book, you probably didn't know what social networking was, would not understand why watching your API Usage was so important, or why you needed to always keep an eye out for @Mentions and DMs. This is part of the Twitter culture.

Here's a word, though, you *didn't* hear me drop in this book: *Tweeple.*

I refer to my networks as Twitters, as my network, or as Friends. I will *not*, however, refer to those in my network as my Tweeple or my Peeps. Why? Because I find both terms slightly condescending and a wee-bit silly. However, others in my network—many of them close friends—use *Twitterspeak* as Mashable.com refers to it. At first I thought I was just being the Old Man shouting from the porch, "Speak English, and get off my lawn!" but in their November 15, 2008 blogpost "Twitterspeak: 66 Twitter Terms You Don't Need to Know" (http://mashable.com/2008/11/15/twitterspeak/), I enjoyed a good laugh at what Pete Cashmore called an "unforgivable abuse of the English language."

With that article and the Twictionary (http://twictionary. pbwiki.com/) and Twittonary (http://twittonary.com) as my guide, here are a few words that I like, that grate, and that will—so long as I am of sound mind—never appear in any of my tweets in earnest.

Twitterspeak That's Just Plain Fun...

Twittersphere and *Twitterverse:* These are words created in the same vein as *Blogosphere* and *Podosphere* as names for the Twitter Community at large. During the chapters concerning smartphones, I came up with a more aggressive alternative: *Twitterdome.* I found the image of Mad Max Beyond Thunderdome finding a place within the Twitter canon really satisfying.

Tweetaholic—Someone addicted to Twitter, so much so that it might develop into a real problem. (Guilty as charged.) I have also seen **Twitteraddict** used as well.

Tweeter—A user of Twitter. I prefer the term *Twitter* because it's simple. My geek flag flies proud, though, as creative advocate Rob Suarez (@rob-suarez) refers to his network as *Twitterakians.* Straight out of my favorite Scott Sigler (@scottsigler) offering, *The Rookie.* I love it!

Tweet(ing) —The act of posting to Twitter; used throughout the book, along with *Tweets* (posts or updates). It does push the "cute" factor of Twitter, but when I heard Stephen Colbert proudly say on *2008 Indecision* "I'm tweeting, Stewart. What are you doing?!" it did give the term a hint of legitimacy.

Tweetup—A Twitter meet up when members of a network meet in person.

Drive-by-Tweet(ing) —When a Twitter, in between tasks at home or at work, makes a quick post, just to touch base with his or her network.

Twetiquette—Proper behavior on the public stream. I've also seen this as *Twitteretiquette* and *Twittiquette.*

Tweet Cred—One's reputation on Twitter. Simply put, if you represent yourself as someone who understands Twitter, you better make sure you have the credibility to back up the swagger.

TwitFic—Mentioned in the book, this is original fiction composed on Twitter.

TwitReviews —These are critical looks at films, computer gear, television, or any critique on just about anything composed in 140 characters or less.

Twitterspeak That's Just Plain Annoying...

Tweeple, Tweople, or Peeps—Members of your community. I find these terms along the lines of calling listeners of podcasts Pod People. If you're doing it as a joke, maybe; but it really grates on me when I hear people refer to their Followers and friends as any of these terms....

...and close on its heels...

Twibes—Another name for the network and the circles you travel in. Wow. I cannot tell you how much that one grates on me.

Twewbie—Someone brand new to Twitter. I have a tough enough time with terms like "newbie" or "n00b" but this one just makes me shudder.

Twiplomacy—Practicing good manners and keeping the peace on Twitter by being a neutral party in the midst of a feud. Trying to practice twiplomacy is about as effective as the word itself.

Twilighter—Apparently, this is someone who tweets only at night. (Their tweets are easy to spot. They sparkle.)

Twitterspeak That I Hope Never to Hear Uttered Again...

Tweekend—Spending your weekend on Twitter. This one just makes me feel all nerdy.

Twatters—Defined by Twittonary as "two tweeple *(Grrr!)* who have extended tweet sessions with each other," with the amendment "With apologies to Brittweeps." Well, it means the same thing in the United States, so please...no.

Twesbian—An openly lesbian Twitter user, also referred to as a **Twesbo**. No, I am not making this up. That one's straight from the Twictionary wiki.

Twitgasm—Do I really need to explain this one? Well okay, if I have to... It's when someone says or does something *really, really exciting* on Twitter. (Blushing yet? There are some others that I could share with you that follow this theme, but I don't think my editors are that open-minded...and even if they were, I don't think I am!)

Tweetheart—This is that special tweeter who makes your heart skip a beat. I think if I were to call anyone my "tweetheart" I would get punched. Repeatedly.

Twitterati—This is the label given to the order of A-list Twitters (composed mainly of weblebrities) also referred to as the Twitter Elite. Nothing says "community" quite like this and is a word I pray I never hear in the Twitterverse again.

...and finally...

Any word with TWI-/TWE-/TW- slapped on as a prefix—There's being clever and then there are words like *twadd* (adding followers), *twaffic* (the current traffic on Twitter), *twalking* (walking while twittering), and (no, I'm not kidding) *twapplications* (Twitter applications) that make you sound like Elmer Fudd. Although the English language was made to grow and evolve, this kind of creative etymology is really unnecessary. Stop the madness!

Maybe you think I'm making some of these words up to end *All a Twitter* on a big laugh, but see for yourself:

Mashable.com— Twitterspeak: 66 Twitter Terms You Don't Need to Know

http://mashable.com/2008/11/15/twitterspeak/

Twitcionary

http://twictionary.pbwiki.com/

Twittonary.com

http://twittonary.com

There are some words you can find in Twitterspeak that make you shake your head and say, "They just didn't say that!"

Walk away from this appendix with one thing learned—make sure that whether you embrace this terminology with zeal or find Twitterspeak a bit too Orwellian for your liking, remember that in the end it is all about communication. Twitter is about making the connection and conveying your thoughts clearly. When there are only 140 characters on call, you have to be concise and straight-forward. Make the most of your characters; and talking the talk on Twitter, you will find, is best kept to the basics and what works.

Got it? Great! As they say in New Zealand, "Tweet as, bro!"

Index

SYMBOLS

@Mentions option, 54-56
@Replies option, 54

NUMBERS

11:11 Make a Wish tweets, 196
12seconds website, 260
140-character limitations (tweets), 19, 77
1010 Project website, 214

A

accounts
  avatars
    animation, 41
    caricatures, 39
    hobbies/interests, 38
    logos, 36-37
    personal photos, 34-35
    selecting, 32-33
    switching, 39-40
  passwords, changing, 43
  preferences
    (DestroyTwitter), 71
  registration, 26-28
    password creation, 27
    username creation, 27, 30
  security, protecting
    updates, 41
  Twitter notices,
    receiving, 44
  updates, protecting, 41
addictive nature of Twitter, 177-179

airline industry, promoting customer service via Twitter, 222-223
alerts
  TweetDeck, 89
  Tweetie, 155
  Twhirl, 82
  TwitterFon, 165-167
Amnesty International, 216
Android G1
  Twidroid, 141
    benefits of, 143-144
    drawbacks of, 145
    installing, 143
  TwitterRide, 145
    benefits of, 147
    drawbacks of, 148
    installing, 147
animated avatars, 41
answering
  DM (direct messages), 57
  tweets, 55-57
API (Application Programming Interfaces)
  Blackbird, 129-130
  DestroyTwitter, 69
    Account preferences, 71
    Application preferences, 71
    benefits of, 74
    Canvas preferences, 71
    Debug preferences, 71
    drawbacks of, 74-75
    Enter and Shorten URL option, 73
    Home column, 71
    installing, 70
    Messages column, 71
    Notifications preferences, 71
    Replies column, 71
    Rules preferences, 71
    setting up, 70-72

Setup API usage
preferences, 70
Single Column view,
74-75
Themes preferences,
71
Tweet/Message
preferences, 71
Tweetshrink option,
73
TwitPic option, 73
viewing threads, 71
Workspace
preferences, 71
Tiny Twitter, 132-134
TweetDeck, 83
alerts, 89
benefits of, 88-89
drawbacks of,
90-91
hashtags and, 89
installing, 84
setting up, 84-85
setting up groups,
85-88
spell-check feature,
89
updates, 89
Tweetie
alerts, 155
benefits of, 153
drawbacks of,
154-155
refreshes, 155
setting up, 151-152
updates, 154
viral tweeting, 153
Twhirl, 76
alerts, 82
API Usage meter, 80
benefits of, 80-81
drawbacks of, 82
installing, 77
notification
pop-ups, 80
searches, 82
setting up, 77-79
spell-check feature,
81
tweet character
limitations, 77
updates, 82

Twibble, 130-132
Twidroid, 141
benefits of, 143-144
drawbacks of, 145
installing, 143
TwitFic, 188-191
Twittelator, 155
auto-refresh
feature, 160
benefits of,
160-161
drawbacks of, 161
landscape
keyboard, 160
notifications, 161
reading tweets, 157
Twitterlator Pro
setup, 157-159
writing tweets, 156
TwitterBerry
benefits of, 138
drawbacks of, 140
installing, 136
TwitterFon
alerts, 165-167
auto-refresh
feature, 166
benefits of, 165-166
color-coded
tweets, 165
drawbacks of, 166
searches, 166
setting up,
163-164
Twitterific
benefits of, 67
drawbacks of,
67-68
installing, 64
registration fees, 67
setting up, 66
TwitterRide, 145
benefits of, 147
drawbacks of, 148
installing, 147

API Usage meter
(Twhirl), 80

Application preferences
(DestroyTwitter), 71

applications, finding,
263-264

Archives, 59
Armstrong, Lance, 216
audio, adding to tweets,
260-261
Auto Nudge feature, 44
auto-refresh feature
Twittelator, 160
TwitterFon, 166
automated DM
(direct messaging), 233
automated tweets, 236
avatars
creating, 32-33
animation, 41
caricatures, 39
hobbies/interests, 38
logos, 36-37
personal photos,
34-35
profiles, selecting for,
32-33
promotional avatars,
219
switching, 39-40

B

backgrounds, profile
customization, 44
Balticon 42 Science
Fiction-Fantasy
Convention
2008, 254
Bit.ly URL-shortening
service, 115-116
BlackBerry, 128-129
Blackbird, 129-130
Tiny Twitter, 132-134
Twibble, 130, 132
TwitterBerry
benefits of, 138
drawbacks of, 140
installing, 136
Blackbird, 129-130
Blip.FM website, 260
blocking followers,
230-231
automated DM, 233

automated tweets, 236

incomplete profiles, 234

L33t (Elite) Internet language, 232

promotional/marketing tweets, 235

rare/no updates, 234

spammers, 232

Twitterbots, 232

blogs

history of social media, 10

microblogging, 17

nanoblogging, 17

promoting, 217

Twitter and, 20-21

Twitter Tools

configuring, 103-106

installing, 102-103

book stores, promoting customer service via Twitter, 223-224

branding, logos as avatars, 36-37

Burton, LeVar, 244

business applications, Twitter and

personal information, 204

promotional opportunities, 202-204, 225-226, 235

blogs, 217

building networks, 205-208

events, 219-224

interacting with followers, 209-211

nonprofit organizations, 212-216

observing reactions to networks, 208

podcasts, 217

products, 219-224

reasons for joining Twitter, 253-254

C

Calendar (Google), connecting Twitter accounts to, 261

Candyfloss and Pickles, 189

Canvas preferences (DestroyTwitter), 71

caricatures as avatars, 39

celebrities, following, 243-245

cell phones

BlackBerry, 128-129

Blackbird, 129-130

Tiny Twitter, 132-134

Twibble, 130-132

TwitterBerry, 136-140

G1

Twidroid, 141-145

TwitterRide, 145-148

iPhone, 149

Tweetie, 151-155

Twittelator, 155-161

TwitterFon, 163-166

tweets, receiving, 43

Twitter and, 127

character limitations (tweets), 19, 77

chat applications, Twitter and, 19

CNN, attracting followers, 246-248

colleges, finding, 264

color-coded tweets, TwitterFon, 165

Comcast, promoting customer service via Twitter, 222

commentaries (tweet-by-tweet), 191-192, 244

communities, becoming part of, 200

customer service, promoting businesses via Twitter, 221

airline industry, 222-223

Comcast, 222

Creatures and Crooks Bookshop, 223-224

customizing profiles, 30-32, 44

D

Daily Show, outsider's perspective on Twitter, *The,* 182

Day of Double Trouble, 224

Death Tweet, 190

Debug preferences (DestroyTwitter), 71

DeGeneres, Ellen, 245

DestroyTwitter, 69

Account preferences, 71

Application preferences, 71

benefits of, 74

Canvas preferences, 71

Debug preferences, 71

drawbacks of, 74-75

Enter and Shorten URL option, 73

Home column, 71

installing, 70

Messages column, 71

Notifications preferences, 71

Replies column, 71

Rules preferences, 71

setting up, 70-72

Setup API usage preferences, 70

Single Column view, 74-75

Themes preferences, 71

threads, viewing, 71
Tweet/Message preferences, 71
Tweetshrink option, 73
TwitPic option, 73
Workspace preferences, 71

dictionary applications, 263, 268

Digg social networking website, 15

DM (direct messages)
automated DM, 233
replying to, 57

dropping followers, 173-174
automated DM, 233
automated tweets, 236
incomplete profiles, 234
L33t (Elite) Internet language, 232
promotional/marketing tweets, 235
rare/no updates, 234
spammers, 232
Twitterbots, 232

E - F

editing tweets, 50-51

Eley, Steve, TwitFic, 188

email, network development via Invite by Email option, 46

Enter and Shorten URL option (DestroyTwitter), 73

EUReKA, promoting television programming, 220

events, promoting, 219-224

Facebook social networking website, 15

Fail Whale, 170-172

famous quotes, 238-239

Favorites (tweets), 59-61

fiction, writing via tweet
Solidarity, 195
TwitFic, 188-191

Find on Other Networks option, network development via, 46

Find on Twitter option, network development via, 46

finding
applications, 263-264
colleges, 264

Flickr social networking website, 14

Flutter: The New Twitter, 184

Follow Friday tweets, 197-198

followers
attracting, 179-181
CNN, 246-248
Kutcher, Ashton, 246-248
Looking for Mr. Goodtweet: How to Pick Up Followers, 180
Moore, Demi, 246
Winfrey, Oprah, 247-248
blocking, 230-231
automated DM, 233
automated tweets, 236
incomplete profiles, 234
L33t (Elite) Internet language, 232
promotional/marketing tweets, 235
rare/no updates, 234
spammers, 232
Twitterbots, 232

celebrities, 243-245
communities, becoming part of, 200
dropping followers, 173-174
automated DM, 233
automated tweets, 236
incomplete profiles, 234
L33t (Elite) Internet language, 232
promotional/marketing tweets, 235
rare/no updates, 234
spammers, 232
Twitterbots, 232
following, 53-55, 227-228
Following Followers mode, 53-55
friends, staying in touch with
status updates, 186
tribal gatherings, 187
tweet checks, 186
tweetups, 187
gurus, 248-251
L33t (elite) Internet language, 232
marketing applications, 209-211
networks, building, 227-228
not following, examples of, 229
options for, 22
SNR, 228
spammers, 232
Twitterbots, 232
updates, rare/no updates, 234
weblebrities, 241-243

food-related applications, 263

forums, history of social media, 9

friends, staying in touch in
status updates, 186
tribal gatherings, 187
tweet checks, 186
tweetups, 187

Friendster social networking website, 13

fundraising organizations, promoting via Twitter, 212-216

G - H

G1
Twidroid, 141
benefits of, 143-144
drawbacks of, 145
installing, 143
TwitterRide, 145
benefits of, 147
drawbacks of, 148
installing, 147

Google Calendar, connecting Twitter accounts to, 261

groups, setting up in TweetDeck, 85-88

gurus, attracting followers, 248-251

hashtags (#), 52, 89, 123-125

Helmiasyraf.com website, 264

hobbies/interests as avatars, 38

Home column (DestroyTwitter), 71

horoscope applications, 263

HTC Dream. *See* G1

Hutchins, J.C., *Solidarity*, 195

hyperlinks, circulating, 239-240

I

IM (instant messenger), Twitter as, 174-175

images
avatar creation, 32-33
caricatures, 39
hobbies/interests, 38
logos, 36-37
personal photos, 34-35
Mobypicture website, 260
tweets, adding to, 260-261
TwitPic, 73, 107
uploading images on, 108
using with Twitter clients, 108-109

incomplete profiles, 234

interests/hobbies as avatars, 38

Invite by Email option, network development via, 46

iPhone, 149
Tweetie
alerts, 155
benefits of, 153
drawbacks of, 154-155
refreshes, 155
setting up, 151-152
updates, 154
viral tweeting, 153
Twittelator, 155
auto-refresh feature, 160
benefits of, 160-161
drawbacks of, 161
landscape keyboard, 160
notifications, 161
reading tweets, 157
Twitterlator Pro setup, 157-159
writing tweets, 156

TwitterFon
alerts, 165-167
auto-refresh feature, 166
benefits of, 165-166
color-coded tweets, 165
drawbacks of, 166
searches, 166
setting up, 163-164

Is.gd URL-shortening service, 98-99

J - K - L

Kanter, Beth, promoting nonprofit organizations, 213

Kawasaki, Guy
followers, following, 228
Looking for Mr. Goodtweet: How to Pick Up Followers, 180

keyboards (landscape), Twitterlator, 160

Kutcher, Ashton, 243, 246-248

L33t (Elite) Internet language, Twitter and, 232

LAMP (Learning About Multimedia Project), 215

landscape keyboards, Twittelator, 160

Last.FM website, 260

LinkedIn social networking website, 14

links, circulating, 239-240

Linux
DestroyTwitter and, 74
TweetDeck and, 89

logos, avatar creation, 36-37

Looking for Mr. Goodtweet: How to Pick Up Followers, 180

lost tweets, 172-173

M

Macs
DestroyTwitter and, 74
TweetDeck and, 89
Twitterific and, 68

marketing applications, Twitter and, 202-204, 225-226, 235
blogs, 217
building networks, 205-208
events, 219-224
followers, interacting with, 209-211
nonprofit organizations, 212-216
observing reactions to networks, 208
podcasts, 217
products, 219-224

media, adding to tweets, 260

messages (direct), replying to, 57

Messages column (DestroyTwitter), 71

microblogging, 17

Miller, Chris, *Twitter Zombie Theatre*, 191

mobile phones
BlackBerry, 128-129
Blackbird, 129-130
Tiny Twitter, 132-134
Twibble, 130-132
TwitterBerry, 136-140
G1
Twidroid, 141-145
TwitterRide, 145-148

iPhone, 149
Tweetie, 151-155
Twittelator, 155-161
TwitterFon, 163-166
tweets, receiving, 43
Twitter and, 127

Mobypicture website, 260

Moore, Demi, attracting followers, 246

Mr. Tweet website, 47, 93-96

multiple accounts, promotional opportunities and, 202-208

music, adding to tweets, 260-261

MySpace social networking website, 15

N

nanoblogging, 17

Nearby Tweets website, 262

networking (social), 262
Digg website, 15
Facebook website, 15
Flickr website, 14
Friendster website, 13
LinkedIn website, 14
MySpace website, 15

networks
building, 227
CNN, 246-248
Find on Other Networks option, 46
Find on Twitter option, 46
following people at random, 47
following people who are following you, 48
following people you know, 47

Invite by Email option, 46
Kawasaki, Guy, 228
Kutcher, Ashton, 246-248
Moore, Demi, 246
Mr. Tweet website, 47
SNR, 228
Suggested Users option, 46
Winfrey, Oprah, 247-248
followers
blocking, 230-236
not following, 229
SNR, 228

News from New Zealand tweets, 196-197

nonprofit organizations, promoting via Twitter, 212-216

notifications
preferences (DestroyTwitter), 71
Twhirl, 80
Twittelator, 161

Nova, Lisa, an outsider's perspective on Twitter, 184

O - P

Obama, Barak, tweet-by-tweet commentaries on acceptance speech, 192

Online Best Colleges.com website, 264

opinions/rants, sharing, 176-177

organizing tweets, 261

Parsec Awards, The, 192

participation, defining
famous quotes, 238-239
link circulation, 239-240
retweets, 237

passwords
  changing, 43
  strong passwords, 27
personal information
  business accounts,
    204
  profiles, customizing
    in, 30-32
  sharing, 176
phones (cell)
  BlackBerry, 128-129
  Blackbird, 129-130
  Tiny Twitter,
    132-134
  Twibble, 130-132
  TwitterBerry,
    136-140
  G1
    Twidroid, 141-145
    TwitterRide,
      145-148
  iPhone, 149
    Tweetie, 151-155
    Twittelator,
      155-161
    TwitterFon,
      163-166
  tweets, receiving, 43
  Twitter and, 127
pictures
  avatar creation,
    32-33
    caricatures, 39
    hobbies/interests,
      38
    logos, 36-37
    personal photos,
      34-35
  Mobypicture website,
    260
  tweets, adding to,
    260-261
  TwitPic, 73, 107
    uploading pictures
      on, 108
    using with Twitter
      clients, 108-109
podcasting
  history of social
    media, 12

promoting, 217
  webisodes, 12
pop-ups, Twhirl notifica-
  tions, 80
Post Like a Pirate web-
  site, 263
posting tweets, 51-53
pound signs (#) as hash-
  tags, 52, 123-125
products, promoting,
  219-224
professional applica-
  tions, Twitter and
  personal information,
    204
  promotional opportu-
    nities, 202-204, 225-
    226, 235
    blogs, 217
    building networks,
      205-208
    events, 219-224
    interacting with fol-
      lowers, 209-211
    nonprofit organiza-
      tions, 212-216
    observing reactions
      to networks, 208
    podcasts, 217
    products, 219-224
  reasons for joining
    Twitter, 253-254
profiles
  avatars
    animation, 41
    caricatures as, 39
    hobbies/interests as,
      38
    logos as, 36-37
    personal photos as,
      34-35
    selecting, 32-33
    switching, 39-40
  customizing, 30-32,
    44
  incomplete profiles,
    234
  personal information,
    30-32

usernames, creating,
  30
promotional applica-
  tions, Twitter and,
  202-204, 225-226, 235
  blogs, 217
  building networks,
    205-208
  events, 219-224
  followers, interacting
    with, 209-211
  nonprofit organiza-
    tions, 212-216
  observing reactions to
    networks, 208
  podcasts, 217
  products, 219-224
protecting updates, 41

Q - R

Qik website, 260
quotes (famous),
  238-239
Qwitter website, 262
rants/opinions, sharing,
  176-177
RE-Tweets, 57
real world relationships,
  reasons for joining
  Twitter, 254-256
refreshes
  Tweetie, 155
  Twittelator, 160
  TwitterFon, 166
registration (accounts),
  26-28
  passwords, 27
  usernames, 27, 30
Remember the Milk
  website, 261
Replies column
  (DestroyTwitter), 71
replying to
  DM (direct messages),
    57
  tweets, 55-57

retweets, 237

reviews (media), writing via TwitReviews, 193-194

Rick Rolling, 198-199

RSS (Really Simple Syndication), history of social media, 10-11

Rules preferences (DestroyTwitter), 71

S

S.A.R.A.H., promoting EUReKA television program, 220

Schubert, Diana, promoting nonprofit organizations, 213

searches
Twhirl, 82
Twitter Search, 112-113
TwitterFon, 166

security, accounts
changing passwords, 43
protecting updates, 41

Seesmic website, 260

Setup API usage preferences (DestroyTwitter), 70

sharing
personal information, 176
rants/opinions, 176-177

shorten URL services
Bit.ly, 115-116
Is.gd, 98-99
SnipURL, 100-102

Single Column view (DestroyTwitter), 74-75

Slate.com website, Flutter: The New Twitter, 184

smartech - 69 Twitter Web Services You Should Know website, 263

SnipURL URL shortening service, 100-102

SNR (Signal-to-Noise) ratio, 179-181, 228

social media, history of, 9
blogs, 10
forums, 9
podcasting, 12
RSS, 10-11
social networking, 13-15
threads, 9
Twitter's role in, 16

social networking
Digg website, 15
Facebook website, 15
Flickr website, 14
Friendster website, 13
LinkedIn website, 14
MySpace website, 15

SocialToo website, 262

Solidarity, 195

spambots, 22

spammers, 232

spell-checking
TweetDeck and, 89
Twhirl and, 81

"spoilers"
movies, 194
television programming, 192

statistics (usage), TweetStats website, 116-119

status updates, 186

Stewart, Jon, an outsider's perspective on Twitter, 182

strong passwords, 27

Suggested Users option, network development via, 46

support, Twitter Support website, 173

Susan G. Komen Race for the Cure website, 213

T

T-Mobile G1
Twidroid, 141
benefits of, 143-144
drawbacks of, 145
installing, 143
TwitterRide, 145
benefits of, 147
drawbacks of, 148
installing, 147

television programming, tweet-by-tweet commentaries, 192

text, spell-checking
TweetDeck, 89
Twhirl and, 81

Themes preferences (DestroyTwitter), 71

third-party applications
Blackbird, 129-130
DestroyTwitter, 69
Account preferences, 71
Application preferences, 71
benefits of, 74
Canvas preferences, 71
Debug preferences, 71
drawbacks of, 74-75
Enter and Shorten URL option, 73
Home column, 71
installing, 70
Messages column, 71
Notifications preferences, 71
Replies column, 71
Rules preferences, 71

setting up, 70-72
Setup API usage
    preferences, 70
Single Column view,
    74-75
Themes prefer-
    ences, 71
Tweet/Message
    preferences, 71
Tweetshrink option,
    73
TwitPic option, 73
viewing threads, 71
Workspace prefer-
    ences, 71
Tiny Twitter, 132-134
TweetDeck, 83
    alerts, 89
    benefits of, 88-89
    drawbacks of,
        90-91
    hashtags and, 89
    installing, 84
    setting up, 84-85
    setting up groups,
        85-88
    spell-check feature,
        89
    updates, 89
Tweetie
    alerts, 155
    benefits of, 153
    drawbacks of,
        154-155
    refreshes, 155
    setting up, 151-152
    updates, 154
    viral tweeting, 153
Twhirl, 76
    alerts, 82
    API Usage meter, 80
    benefits of, 80-81
    drawbacks of, 82
    installing, 77
    notification pop-
        ups, 80
    searches, 82
    setting up, 77-79
    spell-check feature,
        81

tweet character
    limitations, 77
    updates, 82
Twibble, 130-132
Twidroid, 141
    benefits of, 143-144
    drawbacks of, 145
    installing, 143
TwitFic, 188-191
Twittelator, 155
    auto-refresh feature,
        160
    benefits of, 160-161
    drawbacks of, 161
    landscape keyboard,
        160
    notifications, 161
    reading tweets, 157
    Twitterlator Pro
        setup, 157-159
    writing tweets, 156
TwitterBerry
    benefits of, 138
    drawbacks of, 140
    installing, 136
TwitterFon
    alerts, 165-167
    auto-refresh feature,
        166
    benefits of, 165-166
    color-coded tweets,
        165
    drawbacks of, 166
    searches, 166
    setting up, 163-164
Twitterific
    benefits of, 67
    drawbacks of, 67-68
    installing, 64
    registration fees, 67
    setting up, 66
TwitterRide, 145
    benefits of, 147
    drawbacks of, 148
    installing, 147
threads (forums)
    DestroyTwitter, view-
        ing in, 71
    history of social
        media, 9

Timer website, 261
Tiny Twitter, 132-134
tracking tweets, 52-54,
    123-125, 261-262
    Bit.ly USR-shortening
        service, 115-116
    TweetStats website,
        116-119
    Twitalyzer website,
        120-123
    Twitter Search,
        112-113
trademark tweets
    11:11 Make a Wish
        tweets, 196
    Follow Friday,
        197-198
    News from New
        Zealand, 196-197
    Solidarity, 195
tribal gatherings, 187
Tweepler website, 262
Tweet What You Eat
    website, 263
Tweet/Message prefer-
    ences (DestroyTwitter),
    71
TweetDeck, 83
    alerts, 89
    benefits of, 88-89
    drawbacks of, 90-91
    groups, setting up,
        85-88
    hashtags and, 89
    installing, 84
    setting up, 84-85
    spell-check feature, 89
    updates, 89
Tweetie
    alerts, 155
    benefits of, 153
    drawbacks of,
        154-155
    setting up, 151-152
    updates, 154-155
    viral tweeting, 153
Tweetmarks website, 261

tweets
@Mentions option, 54-56
Archives, 59
audio, adding, 260-261
automated DM, 233
automated tweets, 236
character limitations, 50, 77
color-coded tweets, TwitterFon, 165
commentaries, 191-192
editing, 50-51
Favorites, 59-61
Following Followers mode, 53-55
friends, staying in touch with
status updates, 186
tribal gatherings, 187
tweet checks, 186
tweetups, 187
hashtags (#), 52, 123-125
images, adding, 260-261
L33t (elite) Internet language, 232
lost tweets, 172-173
media, adding, 260-261
mobile phones, receiving on, 43
Mr. Tweet website, 93-96
music, adding, 260-261
networking resources, 262
organizing, 261
personal information, sharing, 176
photos, adding, 260
posting, 51-53
rants/opinions, sharing, 176-177

Re-Tweets, 57
replying to, 55-57
retweets, 237
Rick Rolling, 198-199
searches, Twhirl, 82
shorten URL services
Bit.ly, 115-116
Is.gd, 98-99
SnipURL, 100-102
status updates, 186
threads, viewing in DestroyTwitter, 71
tracking, 52-54, 123-125, 261-262
Bit.ly URL-shortening service, 115-116
TweetStats website, 116-119
Twitalyzer website, 120-123
Twitter Search, 112-113
trademark tweets
11:11 Make a Wish tweets, 196
Follow Friday, 197-198
News from New Zealand, 196-197
Solidarity, 195
tribal gatherings, 187
tweet checks, 186
Tweetshrink option (DestroyTwitter), 73
tweetups, 187
TwitReviews, 193-194
Twittelator, 156-157
Twitterspeak terminology guide, 266-268
video, adding, 260-261
viral tweeting, 153
writing fiction via
Solidarity, 195
TwitFic, 188-191
TweetScan website, 207
TweetStats website, 116-119

TweeTube website, 260
tweetups, 187
Twellow website, 261
Twhirl, 76
alerts, 82
API Usage meter, 80
benefits of, 80-81
drawbacks of, 82
installing, 77
notification pop-ups, 80
searches, 82
setting up, 77-79
spell-check feature, 81
tweets, character limitations, 77
updates, 82
Twibble, 130-132
Twictionary website, 263, 268
Twidroid, 141
benefits of, 143-144
drawbacks of, 145
installing, 143
Twisten.fm website, 260
Twitalyzer website, 120-123
TwitFic, 188-191
TwitPic, 73, 107
Twitter clients, using with, 108-109
uploading pictures on, 108
TwitReviews, 193-194
Twitscoop website. 261
Twittascope website, 263
Twittelator, 155
auto-refresh feature, 160
benefits of, 160-161
drawbacks of, 161
landscape keyboard, 160
notifications, 161
tweets
reading, 157
writing, 156

Twitterlator Pro
setup, 157-159
Twitter
accounts
avatar selection,
32-41
changing pass-
words, 43
password creation,
27
protecting updates,
41
receiving Twitter
notices, 44
registration,
26-28
switching avatars,
39-40
username creation,
27, 30
Archives, 59
blogs and, 20-21
Calendar (Google),
connecting to
character limita-
tions, 19
chat applications
and, 19
commentary tracks,
244
followers
blocking, 230-236
options for, 22
microblogs, Twitter
as, 17
multiple accounts,
promotional oppor-
tunities and,
202-208
network develop-
ment
Find on Other
Networks option,
46
Find on Twitter
option, 46
following people at
random, 47
following people

who are following
you, 48
following people you
know, 47
Invite by Email
option, 46
Mr. Tweet website, 47
Suggested Users
option, 46
networking resources,
262
outsider's perspective
on, 182-184
problems with
addictive nature of
Twitter, 177-179
attracting followers,
179-181
dropped followers,
173-174
Fail Whale, 170-172
lost tweets, 172-173
sharing personal
information, 176
sharing rants/opin-
ions, 176-177
SNR, 179-181
Twitter as IM,
174-175
profiles
avatar selection,
32-41
customizing, 44
customizing per-
sonal information,
30-32
switching avatars,
39-40
username creation,
30
reasons for joining,
256-257
personal connec-
tions, 253-254
professional connec-
tions, 253-254
real world relation-
ships, 254-256
social media, Twitter's
role in, 16

third-party applica-
tions and, 18
Twitterspeak termi-
nology guide, 266-
268
Twitter Search, 112-113,
207
Twitter Snooze website,
261
Twitter Support website,
173
Twitter Tools, WordPress
configuring in,
103-106
installing in, 102-103
Twitter Whore, 184
Twitter Zombie Theatre,
191
TwitterBerry
benefits of, 138
drawbacks of, 139-
140
installing, 136
Twitterbots, 232
Twittercal website, 261
TwitterFon, 163
alerts, 165-167
auto-refresh feature,
166
benefits of, 165-166
color-coded tweets,
165
drawbacks of, 166
searches, 166
setting up, 163-164
Twitterholic website, 263
Twitterific
benefits of, 67
drawbacks of, 67-68
installing, 64
registration fees, 67
setting up, 66
TwitterRide, 145
benefits of, 147
drawbacks of, 148
installing, 147

Twittershare website, 261

Twitterspeak terminology guide, 266-268

Twittervision website, 263

Twitt(url)y website, 262

Twouble with Twitter, The, 184

U

updates
accounts, protecting, 41
follower updates, 234
status updates, 186
TweetDeck, 89
Tweetie, 154
Twhirl, 82

URL (uniform resource locators)
Enter and Shorten URL option (DestroyTwitter), 73
shorten URL services
Bit.ly, 115-116
Is.gd, 98-99
SnipURL, 100-102

usage statistics, TweetStats website, 116-119

usernames, creating, 27, 30

V - W

video, adding to tweets, 260-261

viral tweeting, 153

webisodes (podcasting), 12

weblebrities, following, 241-243

weblogs. *See* blogs

Welliver, Heather, 11:11 Make a Wish tweets, 196

Wheaton, Wil, 243-245

Williams, Brian, an outsider's perspective on Twitter, 183

Windows
DestroyTwitter and, 74
TweetDeck and, 89

Winfrey, Oprah, attracting followers, 247-248

Woork.com - 30 + Interesting Twitter Services and Applications website, 264

WordPress Twitter Tools
configuring, 103-106
installing, 102-103

Workspace preferences (DestroyTwitter), 71

writing
commentaries, 191-192
fiction via tweets
Solidarity, *195*
TwitFic, 188-191
reviews, 193-194
tweets via Twittelator, 156

X - Y - Z

YouTube, adding video to tweets, 260

Zarywacz, Robert, *Candyfloss and Pickles,* 189

Zoom Handy Recorders, 224

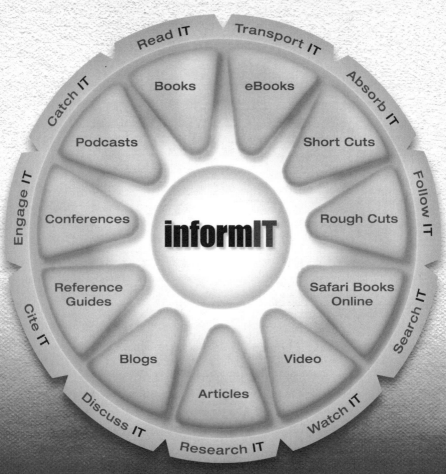

FREE Online Edition

Your purchase of **All a Twitter** includes access to a free online edition for 45 days through the Safari Books Online subscription service. Nearly every Que book is available online through Safari Books Online, along with more than 5,000 other technical books and videos from publishers such as Addison-Wesley Professional, Cisco Press, Exam Cram, IBM Press, O'Reilly, Prentice Hall, and Sams.

SAFARI BOOKS ONLINE allows you to search for a specific answer, cut and paste code, download chapters, and stay current with emerging technologies.

Activate your FREE Online Edition at www.informit.com/safarifree

> **STEP 1:** Enter the coupon code: IHHVNCB.

> **STEP 2:** New Safari users, complete the brief registration form. Safari subscribers, just log in.

If you have difficulty registering on Safari or accessing the online edition, please e-mail customer-service@safaribooksonline.com